Getting Started in
Investment Clubs

Marsha Bertrand

John Wiley & Sons, Inc.
New York • Chichester • Weinheim • Brisbane • Singapore • Toronto

12721999

ISBN: 0-471-39227-8

Printed in the United States of America.

10 9 8 7 6 5 4 3 2 1

Acknowledgments

This book would not have been written had it not been for the assistance of the National Association of Investment Clubs (NAIC). The NAIC has been an inexhaustible source of information and assistance for thousands of people who have decided to learn how to invest, build a nest egg for their future, and have a little fun in the process by starting an investment club.

Jonathan H. Strong, manager of membership development at NAIC, has been a tremendous source of information who was always willing to help out on this project in any way I requested. Bonnie Schmidt, coordinator, membership development at NAIC, was always ready to take my calls and ferret out the information I requested.

Thanks, also, to the investment club members who were willing to share information with me about their clubs and how they operate. I certainly appreciate the experts from various companies and from the financial services industry who were willing to take time to answer my questions.

As always, I appreciate the support and hard work of my agents, Nicholas Smith and Andrea Pedolsky at Altair Literary Agency in New York, for all they've done for me and my writing career during the past several years. And I thank Debra Englander for believing in this project and trusting me with this assignment.

Finally, thanks to my husband, Gary, for acting as my sounding board, idea man, editor, supporter, encourager, and calming influence. His willingness to always take the time to listen and offer his assistance is invaluable.

Preface

Wen you reach retirement age, will you have enough money saved to be able to quit work and still maintain the lifestyle you want to live? According to an analysis based on Federal Reserve data, 56 percent of households in this country are lagging behind in working toward their goal of saving for retirement. If you're part of that 56 percent, just thinking about the consequences can make you shudder. If your retirement fund is lacking when you reach retirement age, you could either continue to work until you absolutely can't work anymore due to old age and physical restraints, or you could retire, but never have any extra money to go out to dinner, attend a sporting event, or splurge on a vacation. Either way, it certainly doesn't sound like such golden years.

Instead of facing those prospects, maybe you should learn how to invest your money and start building a nest egg for your future. You can accomplish both and even add a little social activity to your life by joining or starting an investment club.

Of course, investment clubs aren't only for those who are looking forward to retirement. If you've already reached retirement age, have stopped working, and are maintaining the lifestyle you want, congratulations! That's great, but an investment club may still be a perfect investment vehicle for you. After we retire we still have plenty of years left to live. You still have to know how to invest your money so it continues to grow. And what better way to accomplish that than by getting together with your friends once a month and adding a little social activity to your retirement years?

This book will explain, step by step, how you can take responsibility for your financial future by starting an investment club and beginning to plan for the type of retirement you'd like to have. The first two chapters explain the concept of an investment club, assist you in determining whether that type of investing environment is right for you, and help you identify other potential members. Chapters 3 through 5 discuss how to create the club and determine the proper structure. Chapters 6 through 9 will show you how to find and make the investments you need to build an investment portfolio, how to conduct your club's meetings, and how to monitor your club's performance. In chapters 10 through 14 we'll discuss various investing issues and strategies, a few options your club may want to consider, and how to deal with membership changes. And in Chapters 15 through 17 we'll find out how to ensure that your members remain interested in the club through continuing education and additional social activities, and how members can build their own personal portfolios after they've gained the confidence they need to go it alone.

Whether you're in high school, at midlife, or retired, an investment club can be a great benefit. No matter what your age, it's time to take responsibility for your financial future and have a little fun at the same time. You'll be surprised how much you'll gain by gathering a few people, investing a little money, and becoming an active investor in one of the most prestigious stock markets in the world. Read on for fun and profit!

Contents

Investment Clubs: Their Popularity and Growth

W hen it comes to investing and building a nest egg for the future, many people procrastinate. They may feel they don't have the knowledge required to invest wisely, or they may fear making a mistake and losing what money they have. That procrastination, however, is the biggest mistake they can make.

Considering the dubious future of the Social Security system, we may all be totally responsible for our own financial futures with no help from the government. The U.S. government even admits that if there isn't a concerted effort to make changes to the Social Security system, it could be virtually bankrupt by 2030. But even if the Social Security system remains intact, the average retiree's check will be the equivalent of working for minimum wage. No one can depend solely on monthly Social Security payments to cover their living expenses—that would be a very meager existence.

It used to be that when we retired, we had just a few years left to live. That's not the case anymore. In this era of constant medical advances, our retirements can now stretch to 20 years or more! Without having a substantial retirement account, we may have to live those years being extremely frugal or choose to continue working well beyond the age of 65. But there's no reason why we shouldn't be able to stop working or why our lifestyles should have to be diminished when we retire. The key is to plan ahead. That means it's imperative to begin investing immediately if we want to maintain a comfortable lifestyle in our retirement years.

Many of us, however, don't invest in stocks because we're afraid of losing our money in the stock market. But yet, every day Americans pour money into lotteries with the hope of winning the big one. In July 1998 there was a Powerball lottery that was worth $295 million. The odds of winning were one in 80 million. Despite those odds, people drove for hours to reach the states where they could buy tickets, and they stood in line for up to three hours to buy those lottery tickets! The risk of losing their money was phenomenal, yet they went to great lengths to take that risk. It's true that the stock market does carry a certain level of risk, but if you take the time to find stocks that are viable, solid investments, that risk can certainly be managed.

In fact, when it comes to risk, not attempting to invest your money may be the riskiest choice you can make. Inflation constantly eats away at our buying power. Prices continue to increase. That pound of butter or loaf of bread costs more today than it did 10 years ago, and you can be sure it'll cost even more 10 years into the future. If you're not investing your money and earning a return that's higher than the inflation rate, you're losing money every year. Why not invest and at least take the calculated, well-thought-out risk of making that money grow rather than allowing it to dwindle away?

Another reason many of us put off learning to invest is that we find it to be an overwhelming task. Therefore, we take the easy way out and put our money in certificates of deposit or money market accounts because they're simple and safe. But when the deteriorating effects of inflation and the rising cost of living are factored in, those low-interest-rate investments actually reduce our future spending power. We need to turn to stocks if we want our money to grow. Consider the wide variations in the return on investment achieved during the calendar year 1999 for the following investments:

Standard & Poor's 500 Composite Index: 21.04 percent
30-Year Treasury Bills: 6.14 percent
Money Market Accounts: 4.80 percent
One-Year Certificate of Deposit: 5.65 percent

Considering that the U.S. inflation rate, based on the gross domestic product, was 1.4 percent during 1999, the Standard & Poor's 500 Composite Index of stocks earned enough to outpace inflation by 15 times. And, in fact, many investment clubs consistently beat the S&P 500 average return. With returns like that, where do you want to have your money in the future?

While no one knows if the market will continue to perform as it has in the past, typically, the general trend of the market is up. Just look at the *Dow Jones Industrial Average (DJIA)*.

Dow Jones Industrial Average {DJIA}: A mathematical calculation of the current price of 30 publicly traded stocks, which is used as an indicator for the whole U.S. stock market.

The first time that index surpassed the 3,000 mark was on May 30, 1991. By the end of 1995 it reached 5,000. In early 1997 it hit 7,000, and in 1999 it zipped past 11,000. But the DJIA isn't alone in demonstrating phenomenal performance. The *NASDAQ* has also risen to astronomical heights in a short amount of time.

NASDAQ {National Association of Securities Dealers Automated Quotations}: A computerized stock-trading system that provides up-to-date information on stocks traded in the over-the-counter market.

The NASDAQ stood at just 1,000 on July 17, 1995. On July 16, 1998, it passed the 2,000 mark. It took it less than 16 months to reach the 3,000 point on November 3, 1999. As investors became infatuated with technology stocks, the technology-heavy NASDAQ went wild, crossing the 4,000 mark after just nine more weeks and the 5,000 mark after just another nine weeks.

The move from 2,000 to 5,000 represented an increase in the total market value of all the NASDAQ-listed stocks from $2.3 trillion to $6.4 trillion. And that was during less than a two-year period. The growth in stock prices has been tremendous, but even if that growth slows, the stock market is still the place to invest your money for the future.

Learning to invest in the stock market doesn't have to be a frightening proposition. In fact, it can be fun. This book will show you how you can get together with your friends, learn how to invest at your own pace, and build a nest egg for your future. By joining or starting an investment club you can eliminate the fear and intimidation that so often accompany learning the extremely important skill of investing. Typically, most new investment club members have very little or no investment experience at all, so everyone learns together. And it seems that once the members learn, they become fairly avid investors. According to the *National Association of Investment Clubs (NAIC)*, the association that represents investment clubs across the nation, only two out of 10 new investment club members own a personal investment portfolio. After five years of membership in an investment club, nine out of 10 members have started their own personal portfolios outside of the club.

National Association of Investment Clubs {NAIC}:
A not-for-profit organization formed for the purpose of providing new investors with an investment education and increasing the level of public participation in the stock market.

The growth in the number of investment clubs in the United States is a testimonial to their popularity. In 1987 the NAIC represented approximately 10,000 investment clubs. By 2000 they represented more than 37,000 investment clubs, and that number continues to grow by 100 new clubs each month. The total portfolio value for all NAIC members in 2000 was $175 billion, with those members investing a total of $48 million in new money each month.

The primary reason for their popularity and phenomenal growth is that investment clubs create a safe environment where members can learn how to invest together and become comfortable with investing without being intimidated by investment professionals. That comfort level also helps investment club members build wealth outside of the investment club arena, because as they become comfortable with investing, they venture outside the club to begin a personal investment portfolio of their own.

This book will lay out the advantages of being an investment club member and will guide you through the steps you need to follow to start a club of your own. In easy-to-understand language, it will teach you how to:

1. Determine if an investment club is right for you
2. Find the right members who will enhance the performance of your club
3. Legally structure your club by creating a partnership agreement and bylaws
4. Determine which type of brokerage firm is best for your club to work with

5. Conduct monthly meetings
6. Build an investment portfolio by researching and buying individual stocks
7. Deal with membership changes
8. Easily handle the tax-reporting requirements of an investment club
9. Structure and operate an online investment club
10. Have fun while learning an important skill

This book will not only show you how to improve your financial future through investment club membership, but will also show you how that membership can add interest to your current social life. Ask almost any long-term investment club member and he or she will espouse the virtues of membership. Being a member of an investment club will give you the opportunity to take control of your financial future by learning how to invest, building a retirement fund for your future, and having fun in the process.

Group Investing Versus Going It Alone

Y ou know you need to start investing your money to ensure a financially secure future and you're committed to doing that. The problem is, you've never invested in stocks and aren't quite sure where to start. Then you hear someone talking about their investment club. But you couldn't be a member of an investment club if you don't know anything about investing, could you? Of course you could. In fact, once you see what an investment club is and how it works, you'll find you're the perfect candidate.

An investment club is a group of about 10 to 20 people who meet once a month, pool their investment money, and use that money to purchase stocks. At each meeting, one member comes prepared to do a stock presentation on a company he or she has researched and believes would be a good stock for the group to buy. After the presentation, the group discusses the company and asks the presenter any questions they have. At the end of the discussion, everyone votes as to whether they want to purchase that stock. Majority rules. If they vote to purchase the stock, the treasurer makes the purchase. If they decide not to purchase the stock, the treasurer deposits the money collected at that meeting into a cash account the club has established at their brokerage firm. That money will then be used the next time they vote to purchase a stock. That's a quick overview of what an investment club is and how it works.

THE THREE GOALS OF AN INVESTMENT CLUB

If you join an investment club, you should plan on accomplishing three goals:

1. *Build a nest egg:* Investment clubs meet on a monthly basis and members contribute a specified amount of money at each meeting. That money is then invested in the stock market. Investing a specific amount of money on a regular monthly basis, as investment clubs do, is an investment strategy called *dollar cost averaging.*

Dollar cost averaging: Investing a specific amount of money at regular intervals. By using this strategy, the investor buys more shares when prices are low and fewer shares when prices are high.

By using this strategy, the fixed amount of funds your club invests each month will buy more shares of a stock when its price is low. When a stock's price is high, you'll buy a fewer number shares with that amount of money. Through the use of dollar cost averaging, your money can grow over the years into a very substantial nest egg. And I do mean substantial! Consider the Mutual Investment Club of Detroit, which was formed by a group of friends in 1940. That club is still in existence. To date, the club's members have contributed $480,000 through their monthly *contributions.*

Contributions: The money that each member deposits into the club's pool of money each month to invest in stocks.

Today, that club's portfolio is worth $7 million—and that doesn't even count the $3.2 million they've distributed to club members over the years! Investment clubs that achieve longevity can build quite a nice nest egg for the members.

The goal of building a nest egg, however, should be quantified. The NAIC suggests that investment clubs should adopt the goal of doubling their money every five years. That means the club would need to achieve a compound annual growth rate of 14.9 percent—a goal that investment clubs have easily achieved, and often surpassed, over the years.

2. *Learn to invest:* Not only is an investment club a great way to build an investment account, but it's also a wonderful educational tool. Most people who join an investment club have never invested before. By researching stocks and discussing potential investments, members learn how to pick stocks and build a viable portfolio.

Most clubs also provide their members with organized educational opportunities, such as taking time at a monthly meeting to view an investment video, inviting a guest speaker to a meeting, or having a member research some aspect of investing and offer a short talk on the topic. The HY Partners Investment Club of Orlando, Florida, took an educational trip to New York to visit the *New York Stock Exchange* and get some insight as to how the stock market works. They arrived at the exchange near the end of the day so they could be there for the closing bell. It was a great educational experience. Of course, while in New York, they also managed to see a Broadway play, do a little sightseeing, and devour some fantastic meals!

New York Stock Exchange {NYSE}: Also called the Big Board, millions of shares of stock trade on this public exchange daily.

3. *Have fun and meet new people:* An investment club gives you a reason to get together with your friends once a month. At their monthly meetings, most clubs will conduct the business portion of their meeting first. That typically takes about an hour or an hour and a half. Afterwards, they have a little social hour.

In addition to having the opportunity to spend time with your friends, you'll also get to meet new people because your friends will ask their friends, who you may not know, to become members. And you never know who you might meet. Just ask Cindy Stevens. In the mid-1980s an acquaintance from the local chamber of commerce asked her if she'd like to help start an investment club.

"I finally had a job that paid decent money, so it was time to start investing for my future," says Cindy. "I jumped at the chance."

The Rochelle Investment Club in Rochelle, Illinois, that Cindy helped found had been in business for three years when Brian joined. She says he was a welcome addition to the club because he had a bit of a goofy personality and a great sense of humor. The two became friends and two years later Cindy rustled up her courage and asked Brian out.

"He told me no," says Cindy, laughing. "A couple days later he asked *me* out. I guess I had to play it his way."

The couple married in 1996, had a baby in 1997 and another in 1998. Their investment club portfolios are now their childrens' college funds. In addition to finding each other, they say they've gained great benefits from being members of an investment club.

"The club has given us the confidence we need to pick stocks and invest," says Cindy. "We've even started our own personal portfolio of stocks and mutual funds."

Brian recently got a job transfer to Minnesota, but as soon as they get settled in, they plan to look for an investment club to join there. The third goal of an investment club—have fun and meet new people—certainly worked out well for them!

The three goals of an investment club are all wonderful, but with a little work and discipline, you can accomplish all three on your own. So why bother to join an investment club? Whether you should build that nest egg on your own or through an investment club depends solely on you: your personality and how you want to invest. Both options have advantages and disadvantages you need to consider.

ADVANTAGES OF INVESTING VIA AN INVESTMENT CLUB VERSUS ON YOUR OWN

1. *Buying power:* If you have $50 per month to invest, you probably won't be able to buy individual stocks. *Commissions* on a $50 purchase could run anywhere from $8 to $30, depending on which type of brokerage firm you work with. You'd probably spend more money on commissions than on the stock you buy.

Commissions: The fees a brokerage firm charges investors to purchase or sell shares of stock. The amount charged varies widely between full-service, discount, and deep-discount brokerage firms.

But if you belong to an investment club that has 15 members, and each member has $50 to invest each month, that gives you $750 worth of buying power, making a $30 commission much less relevant. Being a member of an investment club gives you the ability to invest in individual stocks.

2. *Sharing the work:* The best way to invest your money is to use the strategy of dollar cost averaging. In an investment club, that's an easy strategy to follow. In fact, it's automatic—the club's members meet each month and invest. But if you invest in individual stocks on your own on a monthly basis, that means you have to research stocks each month to find the one you want to buy. That can involve a bit of time and effort. But if you're 12 people in an investment club, and each person is assigned a specific month, you only have to research a new stock once a year. An investment club can substantially reduce the amount of work required in building a stock portfolio.

3. *Learning in a safe environment:* As mentioned before, most people who join investment clubs have never invested in stocks. This is their first foray into the market and most are usually a little nervous about attempting a new activity they're not familiar with. If they were to begin investing on their own, they could read books or magazine articles on the topic; watch TV shows or listen to radio programs; or attend seminars—all good vehicles for learning. But they'd also have to make their own investment decisions and deal with investment professionals, some of whom may not be as understanding as they should be of a beginner who has a lot of questions. That can be very intimidating.

A group of novices learning together tends to create a much safer environment. It also gives each person access to the information the other members have already gained, and information sharing can be a great way to learn. The learning also never stops, no matter how long you're a member of an investment club. Betty Sinnock, who is a senior partner with the famous Beardstown Ladies Investment Club, once told me in an interview, "Being part of a group took away much of the fear of becoming an investor. In fact, we learn so much, we consider our monthly dues to be tuition!" I think that quote says a lot about how much you can learn by being the member of an investment club.

4. *Socialization:* Investment clubs are a lot of fun because you get to see all your friends once a month. Some clubs first attend to business at their meetings, then save time afterward for socializing.

Others will meet in a private room at a restaurant, have dinner first, and then attend to business. Either way, most clubs usually save time for socializing. In addition, clubs usually have parties during the year—a holiday party, a summer picnic, or just an annual get-together. It's a great way to get to know people who share your goal of investing for the future.

5. *A little push:* Most of us have probably decided to start an exercise regime at some point in our lives. We get the right clothes and the right equipment or we join a health club. We start out with serious dedication—and slowly lose interest until that exercise program eventually doesn't exist.

One way to keep that exercise program on track is to join an exercise group. If you and your friends all agree to meet at 7 A.M. three times a week, chances are you won't wake up and decide to stay in bed rather than go exercise, when you know you have three other people waiting for you. It's difficult to call and cancel with the excuse that you just don't feel like it.

Investing is similar. If you're buying stocks each month, you have research to do, and some months it will be easier to just forget about it than to spend the time. Or it may be more tempting to spend your investment money on a new outfit or a new tennis racket. But if you have a meeting on Monday at 8 P.M. and the other 12 members are depending on you to be at the meeting, you'll probably show up, contribute your insights, and invest your monthly contribution amount. Being a member of an investment club can help keep your investing program on track.

6. *Knowledge and confidence:* After you've been a member of an investment club for a few years, you'll have gained a lot of knowledge about investing your money in the stock market. With knowledge comes confidence. Once you've developed investment knowledge and confidence, you'll feel comfortable enough to start a personal portfolio outside of your investment club. Combining a personal portfolio with your investment club portfolio will certainly help ensure that you'll have the money you need to maintain your current lifestyle when you retire.

Those are all great advantages and may convince you that investment club membership is right for you. But where there are advantages, there are disadvantages, and you need to take those into consideration before making a decision.

DISADVANTAGES OF INVESTING VIA AN INVESTMENT CLUB VERSUS ON YOUR OWN

1. *Loss of choice:* When working with other people, you don't always get your way. Let's say you belong to an investment club and it's your month to do a *stock presentation.*

Stock presentation: A short overview—15 to 20 minutes—as to why the presenter believes a specific company's stock would be a good one for the group to purchase.

You spend time trying to find a stock that you think might be a good option, then you research the company and find that it is an absolutely wonderful company. Sales have increased each year for the past 20 years. They're making huge profits, which are also growing each year. Due to a commitment to research and development, they have new products in the pipeline. Management has a terrific track record. All the fundamentals of the company look good and the price is right.

You excitedly prepare a bang-up presentation and confidently present it at the meeting. Some of the other members love this company as much as you do, but others aren't so sure. They think it's in an industry where competition is too fierce and that the company eventually won't be able to compete because they're focusing too much on bringing new products to market, rather than concentrating on marketing the ones they already produce. You and several other members defend the company but, when it comes to a vote, seven people vote to buy it and eight people vote to not buy it. What happens? You don't buy it.

You've lost your choice as to how you want to invest your money for that month. Of course, that can't stop you from buying that stock on your own in your personal portfolio outside the club, but you won't buy it in the club portfolio. When that scenario happens, it's important to remember that a stock voted down once may not be a stock voted down twice. I've seen members present a stock, have it voted down, and a year later when it's their turn to present a stock again, present the same stock. If the stock's price has risen substantially, and still looks like it will continue to rise, you may have an even more convincing argument.

2. ***Slow moving:*** Investment clubs are slow moving because they meet only once a month. For instance, let's say your club meets on the 10th of the month, but on the 15th you see a report on TV that one of the companies whose stock your club owns has had a major catastrophe that you think may have an extremely negative impact on the company. You wonder if the club should consider selling. But your next meeting is three weeks away. By that time, the price could be cut in half.

One way some clubs resolve this problem is by including in their *club's bylaws* the ability to conduct call-in voting.

Club's bylaws: The document that lays out the specific operations of the club, such as dates and times of meetings, officer duties, etc.

That means if you see a problem, you could call each of the members, explain the problem, and each person could vote over the phone so that a quick decision could be made. That tact, however, can be very time-consuming and cumbersome. In addition, it doesn't allow for discussion, which makes it difficult to make a really educated decision.

At times, however, this disadvantage may really be an advantage in disguise. The purpose of an investment club is to invest for the long term. When a club buys a stock, it should plan on holding that stock for a long time. As you'll see in Chapter 11, a short-term problem at a company may not be reason enough to sell the stock and a quick decision may be the worst decision members can make.

3. ***Commitment and responsibility:*** This is not necessarily a disadvantage, but it is an issue that anyone contemplating joining an investment club really needs to consider. An investment club is an investment team and a team always has to work together to achieve its goal. Members have to understand that they will be responsible for attending meetings, having their contributions to the club treasurer on time, preparing stock presentations, acting as a club officer from time to time, and other duties that arise in the course of business. Anyone who isn't willing to fulfill their obligations to the other members shouldn't join an investment club.

Those are the primary advantages and disadvantages of being the member of an investment club. Now it's up to you to decide whether investment club membership is right for you. You know investing for your future is imperative if you want to be able to maintain a satisfactory lifestyle when you retire. If your investment goal is to build a portfolio of individual stocks, but you:

✔ Want to make your own investment decisions with no input from others;

✔ Prefer to learn how to invest on your own;

✔ Have no qualms about working with investment professionals;

✔ Invest enough money each month to justify paying commissions;

✔ Want to invest for the short term and buy and sell quickly;

✔ Have a get rich quick mentality;

✔ Have sufficient time to spend researching new stocks each month;

✔ Have no interest in adding activities to your social life; then an investment club probably isn't right for you.

But if you want to build a portfolio of individual stocks and you'd like to:

✔ Learn how to do that in a comfortable and nonintimidating environment;

✔ Have access to knowledge others can share with you;

✔ Invest a fairly small amount of money each month;

✔ Obtain added buying power;

✔ Share the workload of finding great stocks to buy;

✔ Gain the knowledge and confidence you need to build a personal portfolio;

✔ Meet new people and have a lot of fun; then an investment club is perfect for you.

If an investment club is right for you, chances are you'll probably have to start your own. While there are thousands of clubs in existence, it can be hard to find one because they don't advertise anywhere for new members. The best way to find an existing club is through someone you know who's already a member. Or, if you attend an investment seminar or workshop, you may have the opportunity to meet someone who is in a club. But even then, you may not be able to join. Many investment clubs are filled to capacity and even have waiting lists.

If you do find an existing club to join, be sure to research the club to make sure it meets your needs. Attend a couple of meetings so you can meet the people and see how the club operates. Review their portfolio to ensure that the stocks this club owns are stocks that you would buy for your own portfolio. Remember, when you buy into this club, you're buying a portion of the stocks that are already in their portfolio. The club you join has to fit your needs and personality, or it'll never be a comfortable fit. Consider the case of Mark and Diane Robertson (not their real names).

When Mark and Diane moved from Nashville, Tennessee to Orlando, Florida, they both considered joining investment clubs. Mark thought it would be a great way to learn more about investing and at the same time meet some people in the community. He had worked in a business environment for years and already had a base of investment knowledge. Diane, however, had been a middle-school teacher and had never really been exposed to dealing with investments.

Mark quickly found an investment club on the Internet, e-mailed the president, attended a couple of meetings, and joined that club. Diane, however, was a little hesitant. She attended one of the club's meetings with Mark. At that meeting one of the members presented the stock of a company that operated funeral homes. His pitch was that people will always be dying and it's a great profit opportunity. Diane felt uncomfortable with the whole thought of making a profit from death. She just didn't feel that this club was right for her. While Mark enjoyed the club, he was also hesitant about having Diane join. He was concerned that he might dominate her in the club and minimize her participation.

Instead of joining that club, Diane attended a NAIC investment conference with Mark, where she had the opportunity to attend an investment seminar for beginners and talk to members of other local clubs. Mark overheard her talking to a woman who invited her to attend one of her club's meetings. He said Diane's eyes lit up when the woman said that their club tries to buy only the stocks of companies that meet certain moral and ethical standards. It sounded like a perfect fit for Diane.

Diane is still weighing her options but is determined to join a club soon and begin the process of learning how to invest, starting to build an investment portfolio, and definitely having fun and meeting new friends. The care and thought she has put into finding the club that's the right fit for her will certainly pay off.

Of course, not everyone can find an investment club that's a good fit. If you can't find an existing club to join, don't worry. Starting your own club is a simple process that's extremely rewarding. If you've decided this is for you, it's time to take that first step and start calling your friends!

Gathering Your Friends

The great thing about humans is that no two people are alike. We all have unique characteristics. Some of us may be brilliant, but come off as being just a little eccentric. Some may be able to do calculus in their heads, but have a tough time trying to structure a proper sentence on paper. Some may be workaholics and get all their enjoyment from their work, while others may have a strong disdain for their work and live for the weekends, when they can play. Everyone has strengths and weaknesses and it's important that we use those strengths and weaknesses to our benefit. Since we're not all cut from the same mold, we can't all be expected to excel at the same activities.

It wouldn't make sense to ask the mathematician who doesn't like writing to write a book, just as it wouldn't be wise for the workaholic to give up his job and stay at home with nothing to do. The same issues apply when seeking out people to join an investment club. In Chapter 1 we discussed whether an investment club was right for you. When you seek out other members, you also have to consider whether they're right for you. If you don't get the right mix of people, the success of your club will be affected. When inviting people to join your club, keep the three goals of an investment club in mind:

1. Build a nest egg.
2. Learn to invest.
3. Have fun and meet new people.

Below are some issues to take into consideration when seeking out people to join your club.

1. Experience level

While most new investment club members are people who have never invested in the stock market before, there are other people who join investment clubs who are seasoned investors. It's best not to mix these two groups of people. If everyone joining the club has been investing for a while and knows the terminology and how the market works, it would be a fairly uncomfortable and intimidating environment for a novice.

One of the three goals of joining an investment club is to learn how to invest in a safe and comfortable environment. If one person is starting at the beginning and everyone else already has a working knowledge of investing, that wouldn't be very comfortable for the beginner. Conversely, you don't want to invite a seasoned investor to join a club that has all novices for members.

An investment club is a democracy. Everyone has the same amount of decision-making authority. But when one person has more knowledge than the others, that person tends to become dominant and everyone else tends to defer to that person, who eventually becomes the sole decision maker. In addition, the beginner investors often feel that as long as the one person has the knowledge required to make a decision, they don't have to bother learning. That attitude inhibits the learning process and virtually makes it a one-person club. Many clubs even include in their *partnership agreement* that people in financial professions, such as stockbrokers, financial planners, or investment bankers, can't be members of the club.

Partnership agreement: This is the document that lays out the general operations of the club, such as the purpose and the management of the club.

2. Professional members

Oftentimes, new clubs believe that having a member who is an accountant or an attorney would be an asset. While an accountant or attorney certainly wouldn't be a detriment, it is by no means necessary to include someone from those professions. There are legal, tax, and accounting issues that have to be dealt with in an investment club, but those issues are very simple and can be handled by any member. And, in fact, every member should have the opportunity to handle those issues by acting as the treasurer for the group from time to time. If one member is an accountant, the group will tend to push that person into the treasurer's position. That's not fair to anyone; the other members don't get an opportunity to learn that position, and the accountant doesn't get the opportunity to learn the other positions.

3. Array of backgrounds

It's best if you try to find members from varying backgrounds. Look to people you work with, neighbors, members of your church, other groups you belong to, or longtime friends. Try to find people who work in different industries and who hold different types of positions. Each person's expertise can become invaluable when researching companies. For instance, the person who works in a marketing position at a manufacturing firm will be a wealth of knowledge when you're discussing whether a manufacturing company whose stock you're considering buying is doing a good job of marketing itself to increase market share. The human-resources person will be able to explain the possible effects a labor strike may have on a company whose stock you own. The more diversified you can make your group in terms of expertise, the more knowledge you'll have available and the more successful you'll be at meeting the goal of building that nest egg.

With that said, there's always the exception. Take the Lady Traders of Osceola Investment Club in Kissimmee, Florida. The club consists primarily of female educators. Their members include teachers, principals, administrators, and school secretaries. All of them working in the same industry hasn't hindered their progress. They started with 25 members, and have had only three members resign during the three years their club's been in existence. Those three were immediately replaced with people who were waiting to join the club. The members all get along, have a lot in common, have built a portfolio of 12 stocks, and are learning plenty about investing. Obviously, the most important issue is that you find people who are compatible.

4. Gender, race, and family issues

Some people decide that they want the members of their investment club to be all female, or all male, or all African-American. Some clubs consist only of members of a particular family. You can structure the membership of your club any way you want, but be aware that you can change your mind later about the mix of members.

The MAJEC Investment Club of Phoenix, Arizona, was formed in 1990 by a group of women. Years later they decided to allow a man to join. The women jokingly complained, however, that as soon as the first man joined the club, the value of the club's portfolio went down. Luckily, it came right back up. The club is now comprised of six women and 12 men.

The Central Maine Investors of Augusta Investment Club started out in 1984 as a family club, and eventually expanded to include nonfamily members. Today, the club has 15 members, five of whom are original family members.

5. Level of wealth

One of the goals is to build a nest egg for your future. But what if a person already has a personal wealth that can carry him or her into and through retirement? Should that person be asked to join? Absolutely. Remember, there are two other goals and one of those, learning to invest, may be extremely important to a person of wealth. For example, a woman may be extremely wealthy, but her husband may handle all of the family's finances and investing. That can be a serious problem if her husband dies or divorces her. She needs to know how to invest her wealth to make it grow. Not having that knowledge and suddenly becoming responsible for a huge amount of money makes that person ripe for a con artist's wiles.

I once read an article about an investment club in New York that was comprised of a group of women who were all married to CEOs of major corporations. They admitted that the goal of building a nest egg within the investment club was irrelevant to them, but said that their primary objective was to learn how to invest their money just in case they found themselves alone in the future. That was a wise group of women.

6. Active participation

It's said that a chain is only as strong as its weakest link. That statement also applies to investment clubs. Everyone must be willing to work together and actively participate for the club to succeed. If one person refuses to do a stock presentation, to act as an officer, or to *monitor a stock,* that places an added burden on the other members, leading to bad feelings and dissension.

Monitor a stock: Actively following a company's performance and stock price after the company's stock has been added to the club's portfolio.

Or, even worse, if one member doesn't take responsibility for ensuring that his or her monthly contribution is in the hands of the treasurer on time each month, that can affect the other members' pocketbooks. For example, if your club has 20 members who contribute $50 each per month, you should collect $1,000 per meeting. At one of your meetings, a member presents XYZ Pharmaceuticals, whose stock sells for $16 per share. The group likes the company and votes to purchase 60 shares. Including a $30 commission, the total cost would be $990—a perfect amount for the money you have available.

But what if two members forgot to bring their $50 contributions with them? Because the total contributions you've collected for the month is $900 rather than $1,000, you'll have to buy fewer than the 60 shares the members voted to buy. How will you feel two months from now when XYZ Pharmaceuticals discovers a cure for AIDS and its stock price zooms up to $80 per share? You won't be too happy with the two members who kept you from purchasing additional shares and adding to the size of that nest egg you're building.

As you can see, it's extremely important to invite people into the club who will fulfill their responsibilities and actively participate. Look for people who exhibit those traits in their everyday life. If a person is responsive and responsible in her job, whether that job is working in an office, running a retail store, or raising children, chances are that person will also be a responsive and responsible member of an investment club.

7. Buy-and-hold investment philosophy vs. market timing

Since one of your goals is to build a nest egg, you have to determine an investment philosophy that you believe will help you meet that goal. You have two options to choose from. You can either adopt a buy-and-hold investment philosophy or your can try to do *market timing.*

Market timing: Making buy and sell decisions based on trying to determine when a stock's price is at its lowest and highest points.

If you opt to use market timing, you'll need to figure out when a stock is at its lowest price so you can buy it and when a stock is at its highest price so you can sell it. That means you'd have to be right twice. Being right once is hard enough. In fact, determining a stock's highest and lowest price is virtually impossible to do. Therefore, there have been theories developed that are designed to help market timers determine what the market as a whole will do, such as the *Kondratiev Wave Theory.*

Kondratiev Wave Theory: Theory that the economies of the Western world are subject to 54- to 60-year economic cycles that can be used to predict stock-market movements.

Nikolai Kondratiev was a Russian economist who was executed under Stalin's rule in 1938. The theory he developed in the 1920s states that there are periods that last anywhere from 54 to 60 years during which the Western world is subject to major up and down cycles. His theory incorporates information as to economic growth, war, inflation, and levels of debt. According to his theory, the United States should have an economic boom from 1992 to 2020. Books and newsletters are still published relative to this theory.

Another theory that's popular with market timers is the *Elliott Wave Theory.*

Elliott Wave Theory: A theory that projects future trends in the DJIA by counting and measuring price changes.

His theory, created in 1938, predicts market trends in the Dow Jones Industrial Average by counting and measuring its price changes. From the trends that develop, investors can supposedly determine the next broad market movement that will affect most stocks.

If you want to try market timing, these two theories may help you to predict the direction of the market as a whole. They don't, however, tell you anything about any particular individual stocks.

As you can see, market timing can be difficult and complicated. In fact, statistics show that having a long-term investment philosophy rewards you with a higher return than market timing.

With a buy-and-hold investment philosophy, an investor researches companies in an effort to find those that demonstrate good performance and that are continuing to grow year after year. The investor buys those companies' stocks based on the solid fundamentals identified. Then, as long as the fundamental reasons the investor purchased the stock remain the same, the stock should not be sold, but held long term. A buy-and-hold investment philosophy is much less complicated than market timing.

In a study, T. Rowe Price Investment Services calculated the return a $1 investment in the *Standard & Poor's 500 Composite Index (S&P 500)* would have generated over a 10-year period from June 30, 1989, to June 30, 1999.

Standard & Poor's 500 Composite Index {S&P 500}:
An index that tracks the movement of the stocks of the 500 largest U.S. public companies. Considered to be a broad gauge of stock-market movement.

They found that if an investor had left that dollar there to grow, 10 years later that dollar would have been worth $5.59. But what if the investor had decided to try to time the market by pulling his money in and out of the investment? If he had his money out of the market for just the 10 days that the market had its best performance during that 10-year period, that dollar, after 10 years, would have been worth only $3.86. If he had missed the best 40 days of the 10-year period, the dollar would have grown to only $1.90. Missing the 60 best days would have given him only $1.30. And, if he had missed the 90 best days of the decade, he would have actually experienced a loss, with his dollar shrinking to $.78 after 10 years. Obviously, timing the market is extremely difficult and minor mistakes can change your investment's performance results dramatically.

The primary reason that market timing doesn't work is that *no one* ever knows for sure if the market, or an individual stock, is going up or down. Therefore, it is virtually impossible to buy when the market is at its lowest and sell when it's at its highest. Since you can't buy low and sell high every time, why not just buy and hold? Historically, the stock market goes up over time. In fact, the Dow Jones Industrial Average went from 4,000 to 11,000 in just over four years, offering investors 25 percent annual gains. Of course, that doesn't mean every stock increased in price at that same rate but, chances are, if you bought good stocks with good fundamentals, those stocks probably increased in value. Why speculate and take a chance of buying and selling them over and over as they go up and down and paying all those commissions when you can just buy them, hold them, and make good gains? As the famous writer Mark Twain once said, "There are two times in a man's life when he should not speculate—when he cannot afford it and when he can!"

A buy-and-hold philosophy works especially well if a stock you purchase pays a *dividend*, because you'll utilize the power of *compounding*.

> **Dividend:** The portion of a company's profits that the board of directors decides to pay to the company's shareholders.

> **Compounding:** The growth of your initial investment as it earns dividends, plus additional dividends on the money previously earned.

If you reinvest that dividend, you'll be able to purchase more shares that will pay more dividends, helping you grow your investment account at a faster pace.

When finding members for your investment club, it's important to find people who share the buy-and-hold investment philosophy. If some members prefer to time the market and want to continually buy and sell stocks, while others prefer to take the long-term approach, problems will arise. Members have to understand that an investment club is not a get-rich-quick scheme. It's a time-tested investment vehicle in which members buy solid stocks of good value and hold them long term.

8. Investment objective and strategy

If your club doesn't have an investment objective, you won't know what you're aiming at. The NAIC suggests that all clubs should have an investment objective of doubling their money every five years. That means a club must achieve an average 14.9 percent compounded annual growth rate. Chances are, a club won't achieve that growth rate every year. Some years it may be lower and some years it may exceed that amount. The important issue is that you have an objective to work toward.

So, if doubling your money every three years is your objective, how do you accomplish that? You accomplish that by devising a good investment strategy.

There are several strategies an investor can follow in building a nest egg—some good and some not so good. An investor could decide to be extremely conservative and follow the strategy of putting all of her money in certificates of deposit. It's a strategy, but not a very good one. The returns she'll collect on her money will barely keep her ahead of inflation, let alone build a nest egg.

The members of your club have to agree on an investment strategy that will maximize your returns, but keep risk at a minimum. The best strategy to follow to accomplish that is to purchase *growth stocks.*

Growth stock: The stock of a company whose growth is faster than that of its competitors.

Growth stocks can help you achieve the returns you want because they exhibit faster-than-average gains in both sales and earnings over competitors and, therefore, should be worth more in five years than they are now.

Members should also agree to the strategies of investing regularly every month, keeping their portfolio diversified, and reinvesting all earnings. Following those strategies will help you take one more positive step toward achieving the goal of doubling your money every five years. We'll talk about how to follow these strategies in later chapters, but for now it's important to communicate to potential members the investment strategies that the club should be committed to follow.

Those are all issues you'll have to deal with when seeking out potential members for your club. Keep in mind, however, that when you're looking for members you don't have to find them all yourself. Maybe you'd like to have a dozen members in your club, but you don't know that many people who you think have the characteristics you're looking for. If you know three people who would be good candidates, talk to them, discuss the type of people you're looking for, and ask them to suggest others. What better way to accomplish that third goal of meeting new people than to ask your friends to invite their friends to join? If they can each suggest two or three other people, you'll have your dozen!

Finding the right mix of people is an extremely important step in starting an investment club. The Triple I Investment Club, which was comprised of women from the Chicago suburbs, learned that the hard way. The club had a small membership and wanted to increase its size. So the members invited all their friends and acquaintances to join. Some joined and others didn't.

The membership eventually grew, but the members' personalities and investment goals didn't seem to match very well. Soon, they had lots of turnover with people joining, then leaving after just a couple of months. Because of the confusion of so many membership changes, the founding members soon began to lose interest. While the club managed to stay in business for about 6½ years, they finally agreed to cash out and liquidate the club. Luckily, it was during a period when the market was doing well and the members walked away with nice little profits.

But one member of the defunct Triple I Investment Club wasn't about to give up on the concept. She convinced one of the other Triple I members and a couple of other people to work with her to start another club. This time they understood that starting a club is more than just inviting people to join so you can have 12 people contributing. They knew that personality mix and the ability to get along and join in the fun are imperative. They sought out members who they knew would have personalities that would mesh with theirs and would be committed to a long-term, buy-and-hold investment philosophy. The Wall Street Watchers were born.

Of course, no group of people will be in agreement on every issue. But as long as everyone is willing to work together, the club should survive and prosper. It's just like any other relationship—you have to work at it.

Having been in business only one year so far, the Wall Street Watchers have nine members and own six stocks. This time, they're being more discriminating as to the people they ask to join. They recruit people who they know will be committed and be an ultimate fit, rather than just trying to get a body in to get the club's membership up.

This time around, they're learning a lot and enjoying their time together. They're achieving all three goals of an investment club.

9. Local members

Look for people who live locally. It's best to only include people who live in a specific geographic region. If you meet at members' homes, you don't want everyone having to travel too far for meetings. You also don't want the member who lives far away to use that as an excuse to miss meetings.

Geography was a problem the Triple I Investment Club encountered. In trying to build up their membership, the members invited people they worked with. But in a city the size of Chicago, two people could work together downtown but live more than 60 miles apart. The club rotated meeting at members' homes, but some of the members lived fairly far away. In fact, one member lived so far away it took everyone an hour to drive to her house. It became too difficult for people to get home from work, have dinner, arrange for baby-sitters, and then drive an hour to the meeting. It simply wasn't practical. With one exception, the members of their new club all live within a five- to 10-mile radius.

While geography can be a problem, there are some clubs that allow nonresidents to join. If a member lives in another state, he simply mails in his check every month prior to the meeting. But that defeats two of the goals of being a member of an investment club: (a) learning how to invest and (b) having fun and meeting new people. It's also impossible for that member to contribute. If he can't attend meetings, he can't do a stock presentation, act as an officer, or even vote.

There may, however, be one exception when your club would agree to include a long-distance member. If an investment club has been in operation for years and has a longtime, responsible, contributing member, the other members may not want to lose that type of dedicated person. What has happened in some clubs is that after years of membership, people retired and began taking advantage of a warmer climate in another state for a few months out of the year. There's no reason your club has to lose that member because of a three- or four-month hiatus each year. You can allow that person to retain her membership. She would be responsible for sending in her monthly contribution prior to each monthly meeting and would not be able to vote at meetings if not present. Other responsibilities, such as stock presentations or hosting meetings, would have to be fulfilled during the time period the person is there and attending meetings. Even responsibilities such as monitoring stocks and holding an officer's position can be worked out. Instead of assigning those activities to one person, assign them to two members who fulfill those activities for six months each for a two-year term. For instance, the person who leaves for a few months could be the secretary from May to October two years in a row, and the other person could take that role from November to April two years in a row. Both members fulfilled a one-year term. You can't, however, have too many long-distance members because you may not have enough people present to conduct business at some of the meetings. If that happens, another option would be to suspend meetings for three months. Again, except for taxes, there are no laws governing how an investment club must operate. Flexibility may be the trait that keeps an investment club alive for years to come.

Of course, no matter how carefully you screen new members, you'll periodically end up with a member who creates difficulties. In Chapter 4, we'll discuss a few items you can include in your partnership agreement to help alleviate the problems those people may cause.

HOW MANY DO YOU NEED?

Determining how many members you'd like to invite into your club is an important issue. While you can operate an investment club with just three members, it certainly would not be the ideal situation. You need enough people to divide the work required so that it doesn't become burdensome for a few. You also want enough members so that you have a broad base of expertise.

Conversely, you probably don't want 30 people in your club, either, because you may have difficulty in finding a location for meetings that can accommodate that many. In addition, member discussions could become cumbersome with everyone trying to express an opinion. An ideal number of members ranges from 10 to 20.

If you decide you'd like to have a membership of 15 people, it's best to include an additional three or four people in your initial discussions because, inevitably, there will be people you invite who will decide that they're not interested.

EXPLORATORY MEETING

After you've identified the people you want to include in your club, it's time to conduct an *exploratory meeting.*

Exploratory meeting: The first meeting of potential investment club members, where the specifics of club membership are discussed.

At this meeting, you'll explain to the potential members what an investment club is, how it works, the advantages and disadvantages of investment club membership, and what the members' responsibilities would be. Some of the issues that are imperative for potential members to understand include:

1. An investment club is a long-term commitment. Money invested will not be withdrawn, but will remain in the club's portfolio for years.

2. The money they contribute to the club each month is considered risk capital—money that, if it's lost, won't impact their lifestyle.

3. Most clubs incur a loss or only a small gain the first year or two. It takes time to build a portfolio that shows a profit.

4. An investment club is not a get-rich-quick scheme. Members need to agree to a buy-and-hold investment philosophy.

5. There are certain commitments and responsibilities that each member must be willing to fulfill. Without that commitment, the club will fail.

After your initial presentation as to how an investment club works, the potential members will have questions. It's important that you're prepared to answer questions to their satisfaction. If you feel you're not quite equipped to handle the exploratory meeting, there are a couple of options. First, you could ask an experienced investment club member from another club to help you conduct the meeting. Another option would be to ask another club if you could sit in on one of their monthly meetings to see a club in action and learn exactly how it operates so you could pass that information on at the exploratory meeting. If they agree, ask them to schedule a few minutes for you to ask a couple of questions. Or, you could contact the NAIC and ask them if they could provide an expert who lives in your area to conduct your exploratory meeting. Whether you decide to handle the exploratory meeting on your own or choose to ask someone else to help, it's important that the meeting sets a tone instilling that an investment club is a business and is operated in a professional manner.

At the conclusion of the meeting, you can ask the potential members if they would like to commit to membership. Some may agree or decline immediately, while others may need to digest the information for a few days and let you know their decision later. Give them a deadline as to when they need to give you a definitive answer. You don't want the others who are excited about starting the club to lose their enthusiasm because they had to wait so long to get started. The best case would be that at the conclusion of the meeting, you'll have enough members to schedule your first investment club meeting, when you can start creating a club that will last for years.

Choosing the right members is an integral part of starting an investment club. According to the NAIC, a full 40 percent of new clubs are defunct within two years because they didn't have a compatible, cohesive group of people who were committed to the club's investment philosophy. A club simply can't operate when internal strife among members exists. Therefore, having the correct membership mix is a key ingredient in determining how successful an investment club will be. By choosing a diversified group of people who will be willing to actively participate and accept the responsibilities of investment club membership, you'll take the first step toward putting your club on the path to success.

Chapter

3

Structuring Your Club: The Five Decisions

N ow that you have a group of people who are committed to starting an investment club, you need to discuss five issues and make decisions concerning each one before you can start researching companies, buying stocks, and building that portfolio. It's important to understand that, except for taxes, there are really no laws governing how investment clubs are structured and operated. You're free to do whatever you please. If you want your investment club to invest in futures contracts, commodities, or government bonds, that's your choice. Almost any investment professional, however, will tell you that you're not making a very prudent choice, especially for novice investors.

This book offers advice on structuring and operating an investment club, such as meet monthly, invest in stocks, *diversify* your portfolio, and hold your stocks for the long term.

Diversify: Invest in stocks of companies that are in different industries and that are of various sizes, rather than investing only in the same industry and same-size companies.

Whether you follow that advice is your choice. For example, this book suggests that your club should elect four officers, but someone else may swear you need only three, and others will tout the benefits of five. There's a lot of flexibility in this process. Your members have to decide what's best for your club.

What you find here are options for you to consider and advice as to principles that have worked for other clubs. Whether you adopt those ideas or create new ideas is up to you. However, it's important that, no matter how you structure and operate your club, you constantly keep the three goals of an investment club in mind:

1. Building a nest egg
2. Learning to invest
3. Having fun and meeting new people

As long as you're accomplishing those three goals, whether you have two officers or 10 is irrelevant.

After conducting the exploratory meeting, you should have a group of people who are committed to becoming members of an investment club. At the first meeting the group needs to make a few decisions.

1. NAMING THE CLUB

You may think that coming up with a name for your investment club is a fairly insignificant and unimportant step in getting started but, actually, it's very important. In order to buy and sell stocks, you have to have a brokerage account. In order to open a brokerage account, you have to have an *Employer Identification Number*.

Employer Identification Number: A nine-digit identification number issued by the IRS to corporations, partnerships, or estates for tax filing and reporting purposes.

And you can't obtain an employer identification number unless your club has a name. We'll discuss how to get the employer identification number in Chapter 4. First, you have to create a name.

Have your members think about a name prior to the meeting and ask each one to come up with at least one idea. You may not use any of the suggestions, but oftentimes one name will spark an idea that will lead to other name options. Spend a little time brainstorming to come up with a name you like—you'll be using that name for a long time.

There are all sorts of ideas your club can use in creating a name. You could keep it simple and utilize your location, such as the Springfield Investment Club or the Oak Street Investors Investment Club. You could try to depict just what you foresee your members doing in the future as investment club members, such as the Stock Pickers Investment Club or the Researchers Investment Club. You could combine those two ideas and proclaim where you are and what you're doing, such as the Monthly Investors of Kane County Investment Club. Or, you could announce your meeting dates via your name, such as the Third Tuesdays Investment Club. Maybe you want to be a little more clandestine and shroud your name so no one really knows what it means, such as the Triple I Investment Club, which stands for independent, innovative investors, or the LOTS (ladies of the street), a cute acronym that evokes visions of more than just an investment club! Another option is to use terms that relate to investing, such as the Odd Lots Investment Club or the Wall Streeters Investment Club. One club in Arizona came up with the name MAJEC (pronounced magic) Investment Club. They derived the word by using the initials of the founding members.

You may quickly come up with one name that everyone likes. If so, your task was easy. The group may, however, have two or three names that various people prefer. If so, vote on the names. That's how Terri Hult, founding member and past president of the Dough Makers Investment Club of Kankakee, Illinois, says her club members decided on their name. The members brought several suggestions to a meeting, they narrowed those options down to three, then voted. The name that got the most votes won.

Creating a name for your investment club, while important, can also be a lot of fun. Get creative, throw out a lot of options, combine words from various suggestions to create new names, and fashion a name that is unique to your group. Create a name that speaks for you!

2. ELECTING OFFICERS

The number of officers investment clubs elect varies, but you'll probably want at least three, and possibly four.

President

The primary function of the president of the club is to preside over the monthly meetings. It is the president's responsibility to ensure that the business of the club is conducted in a timely manner at each meeting. If Tom insists on telling the group about the gigantic fish he caught last week, the president has to politely, but firmly, steer the meeting back to business. An investment club meeting should last one to 1½ hours. It's the president's responsibility to ensure that conversation doesn't stray and that the meetings don't turn out to be three-hour marathons.

It's also the responsibility of the president to ensure that the club is being operated in accordance with the club's partnership agreement and bylaws. A quick perusal of those documents from time to time can help the president identify any areas where the club has departed from the procedures they've established. When a question arises as to procedures, it's up to the president to either have or obtain the answer.

Secretary

The secretary is responsible for taking the minutes of the meetings and mailing them to the other members prior to the next meeting. If the members receive the minutes before the meetings, they have the opportunity to read them and can be prepared to offer any suggestions or changes. If the minutes from the previous meeting are distributed at the meeting, it takes up valuable time while members read them so they can be approved.

It's also the responsibility of the secretary to create an agenda for each meeting so everyone knows exactly what the group will be discussing and who will be fulfilling the various roles assigned at each meeting.

The secretary should also set meeting dates and locations and make various assignments in accordance with the club's procedures.

Finally, the secretary is responsible for maintaining a petty-cash fund that's used for stamps or other minor supplies required for the secretary's duties. Ideally, the money for the petty-cash fund isn't extracted from the members' monthly contributions and isn't considered a part of their *capital account*.

Capital account: The value of each investment club member's ownership in the club.

Instead, when the club is formed, each member may contribute $5.00 to the petty-cash fund. When funds run low, the secretary informs the members, who each add a couple of dollars to the fund.

Treasurer

The treasurer is the officer who deals directly with the club's brokerage firm. At each monthly meeting, the treasurer is responsible for collecting the members' monthly contributions and depositing them into the club's cash account at the brokerage firm. When the club votes to buy or sell a stock, it's the treasurer's responsibility to ensure that the trade is made. This is an extremely important duty and the treasurer must understand that he or she cannot be lackadaisical in these duties. If the members vote to purchase a stock, the treasurer must do so as soon as possible or a problem could develop.

For example, let's say a club meets on Monday evening at 7:00. They have $1,200 in their account and at the meeting they vote to buy 50 shares of a stock that sells for $21 per share. The total cost is $1,050 plus commission. The next morning the treasurer calls the stockbroker, or places the order online before the market opens. The order is filled and the club owns the stock.

But what if that treasurer got busy with other things and didn't place the order until two days after the meeting? What if, during those two days, some good news about the company was released and the stock increased in price by $3 per share to $24? It would now cost the club $1,200 plus commissions to buy 50 shares—more money than they have available. Not only will the club have to purchase fewer shares than planned, but they've lost the profit of that $3 run-up per share. How popular do you think this treasurer will be with the other members?

Obviously, it's important for the treasurer to handle all brokerage transactions as soon a possible. In fact, if a club meets on a weekday, the treasurer can call the stockbroker and take care of any buy or sell transactions during the meeting. If, instead, the club buys its stock online, the treasurer may have access to a computer and be able to place the order immediately, during the meeting.

Of course, no matter how quickly the treasurer places the orders, chances are the prices won't always be exactly what the club anticipated. If a stock closed at $21 per share on Tuesday and the club meets on Tuesday night and votes to buy that stock, even if the treasurer places the order immediately, the price may have already fluctuated and the cost may come in at maybe $21.25. For most transactions, however, if orders are placed immediately, the prices should be extremely close to the price the members expected.

Other responsibilities of the treasurer are to complete a monthly *valuation statement* that can be distributed to each member at the meeting so that they can determine the value of the club as a whole and the value of each member's capital account.

> **Valuation statement:** The document prepared monthly by the treasurer that depicts the investment club's entire portfolio and the breakdown of individual member's capital accounts.

Finally, the treasurer is responsible for handling the club's tax documents. This part of the job often frightens off a lot of investment club members, but this duty isn't nearly as daunting as some may suspect. The preparation of the valuation statement and the tax documents will be covered in Chapter 9.

Vice President of Education

Some clubs heap the responsibility of continuing education on one of the above three officers, but since this is such an important issue, it might be best to assign an additional officer to handle these duties. Remember, learning to invest is one of the three goals of an investment club member. While the educational process automatically happens as the club researches stocks and makes buy and sell decisions, it's important to supplement the learning process with more formal types of education.

The vice president of education would be responsible for formulating the educational aspects of the club. That responsibility would include arranging for speakers to come to some of the club's monthly meetings to discuss specific aspects of investing. Speakers might include the club's stockbroker, a member of another investment club, an expert in economics, a financial advisor, a representative from NAIC, or any other expert who could share investment knowledge with the group. These professionals are often willing to speak to groups at no charge. In fact, the vice president of education of the Dough Makers Investment Club not only got their stockbroker to come and speak at one of their monthly meetings, but she got the stockbroker to host a pizza party for them!

In addition to live speakers, education could also be accomplished via video- or audiotapes on investing. The vice president of education could check them out of the library, or even tape something right off the television or radio. Or, he or she may assign another club member the job of researching a specific investment topic and giving a short talk on the topic at the next meeting.

These educational presentations shouldn't be very long if they're offered at a regular monthly meeting—15 or 20 minutes, maximum. If an educational opportunity presents itself that would be lengthier, the club may want to schedule an additional meeting devoted strictly to education.

Educational presentations typically wouldn't be a regular feature at every meeting. Maybe once every three months the vice president of education could poll the members, find out what topic they'd most like to learn about, and schedule a short presentation.

If a club has four officers, the operational duties will be divided up sufficiently so that no one member is faced with an inordinate amount of work. Each officer's term of duty should be one year and the positions should be rotated among the members. Rotating those positions can sometimes be difficult. The Lady Traders of Osceola Investment Club found that some members aren't anxious to take on any officer role. Their club has been in operation for three years and the same officers have served the entire time. While those officers are certainly dedicated members who are committed to the success of their club, it's time that a few other members assume those responsibilities for a while. But each year when they ask for nominations, none is ever forthcoming. While they have added an officer or two over the years, no one has ever offered to step in and take on the existing officer roles. This year the current officers plan to insist that others take the jobs.

"It's not that we don't want the jobs or that we don't enjoy doing them," says Susan McKay, president and founding member. "It's just that you get more involved by serving as an officer."

Not only do members get more involved by serving as an officer, but they also learn a lot. To encourage others to take on officer roles, they should be ensured that the outgoing officers will take the time required to teach the incoming officers how to handle their new jobs. Howard Clarke, past president of the Central Maine Investors of Augusta, says that his club has found that, just like with any type of club, people are often reluctant to volunteer. But if you've gathered a group of people who are used to pulling together and doing what needs to be done when it needs to be done, you can usually come up with someone willing to take the officers' positions. With everyone willing to participate and with members assisting each other in learning the officer jobs, the club should run smoothly and benefit all in achieving the three goals.

3. DETERMINING MEETING TIMES AND LOCATIONS

There are lots of options here and the biggest problem you'll have is coming up with a meeting time and date that's going to be convenient for everyone. Setting a meeting date such as the 10th of every month doesn't work well because sometimes the 10th may fall on a Wednesday, but sometimes it'll be a Sunday. It's better to choose a day, such as the second Thursday of each month at 7 P.M. If the members can't agree on a specific day and time, come up with a couple of options, then vote. Majority rules. It's possible that you could even lose a member in this process because that person can't adjust his or her schedule to the day chosen. However, you have to determine a meeting date and time somehow.

After you've decided when you're going to meet, you have to decide where you're going to meet. Some clubs like to meet at the members' homes. It seems a little warmer and friendlier. And the hostess of the meeting each month may serve coffee and dessert after the business portion of the meeting while members socialize. Other clubs don't want the added work and choose to meet in a restaurant where they can have a private room and have lunch or dinner along with their meeting. Other options include a private room at the local library, a conference room at a member's place of business, or even in a room in the clubhouse at a member's apartment complex.

Wherever you meet, it's important that you have privacy and no interruptions while you're conducting business. If you're meeting at the members' homes, the hostess shouldn't be jumping up to answer the phone every 10 minutes or dealing with children. This is a business meeting and should be handled as such.

4. MAKING ASSIGNMENTS

It's important to determine a fair and equitable method of making assignments. If you're meeting in members' homes, you'll need to determine how you'll schedule those meetings. You also need to decide how you want to assign each member the responsibility of doing a stock presentation. Eventually, after you've bought stocks and built a portfolio, you'll also need to assign each of those stocks to a member to monitor that company's performance. Your members may also periodically be assigned to research a topic and present an educational report.

Assignments for all these responsibilities can be made on a volunteer basis, alphabetically by name, or by any other means the group agrees to.

The club needs to be somewhat flexible, however. For instance, let's say your club meets at members' homes and you make hosting assignments alphabetically by name. Emily's month to host a meeting turns out to be May, but she always goes to the Caribbean in May. You need to be willing to rearrange the schedule as required. Also, if you meet at members' homes, it's best not to assign a member the job of hosting a meeting and doing a stock presentation in the same month. Neither should they be assigned to present an educational report when they're already assigned to host a meeting or do a stock presentation. No member should have to handle more than one assignment per monthly meeting.

The secretary should make all of the assignments a year in advance and type a schedule of those assignments so the members know exactly when they're scheduled to handle the various duties. Figure 3-1 is a sample schedule that includes assignments for hosting meetings, doing stock presentations, and presenting educational reports with the topic assigned. Also included is a list of which member monitors which stock in the club's portfolio.

Schedule of Assignments

Member	Hosting Meeting	Stock Presentation	Educational Report	Topic	Monitor Reports
Alan	January 11	April 12			Gamex Corporation
Bette	February 8	May 10			Beeline Industries
Chris	March 8	June 14	February 8	Stock Splits	
Denise	April 12	July 12			Cedar Corporation
Emily	May 10	August 9	April 12	When to Sell	
Frank	June 14	September 13	August 9	P/E Ratios	
Gary	July 12	October 11			
Helen	August 9	November 8			
Izzy	September 13	December 13	November 8	IPOs	
Judy	October 11	January 11			Acme Company
Kathy	November 8	February 8			
Larry	December 13	March 8			Farr Corporation

Figure 3-1: Schedule of Assignments

Inevitably, all members will miss a meeting or two during the year; therefore, you should allow members the option of trading dates with each other. Having access to an annual schedule gives members ample time to determine which dates won't work for them and to arrange a trade with other club members. If members trade dates, they should be certain to keep the secretary informed so he can update the annual schedule of assignments.

5. CONSIDERING NAIC MEMBERSHIP AND REVIEWING INVESTMENT PHILOSOPHY

The National Association of Investment Clubs (NAIC) is the association that represents more than 37,000 investment clubs across the nation. You can certainly operate your club without being a member of NAIC, but the not-for-profit organization, which has been in operation since 1951, does offer some extremely useful services. Some of the primary services they offer include:

- ✔ **Better Investing:** A monthly magazine that includes articles on stocks to study, investment strategies and techniques, and investment club news. The magazine is free to NAIC members; therefore, each member of the investment club will receive a free subscription to the magazine.

- ✔ *Green Sheets:* Financial reports that provide information on various companies your members may want to research.

- ✔ *Research Forms:* Various forms and checklists club members can use when researching a company.

- ✔ *Regional Education:* The organization has more than 80 regional councils around the nation that offer seminars and classes on various investment topics.

- ✔ *Investors Congress:* Regional and national annual conventions featuring lectures, workshops, and seminars.

- ✔ *Software and Videos:* Software programs to help your club with record-keeping issues and videos on various investment club topics.

- ✔ *Low Cost Investment Plan:* A program that gives NAIC members the ability to buy stocks directly from companies without using a stockbroker.

- ✔ *NAIC Growth Fund:* A closed-end mutual fund that invests in companies by using the NAIC principles.

The NAIC even offers members credit cards, long-distance telephone credit cards, and other amenities.

Your club should discuss membership in this organization. The cost to join is $40 per year for the club, plus $14 per member. For additional information and a NAIC Membership Guide, call 877-ASK-NAIC (877-275-6242) or visit their web site at www.better-investing.org.

If you join NAIC, you'll find that they recommend four principles of investing:

1. Invest a set amount regularly, regardless of market conditions.

2. Reinvest all dividends and *capital gains* for compound growth.

Capital gains: The profits realized from the sale of stocks.

3. Buy growth stocks—the stock of companies whose sales and earnings are increasing at a rate faster than the industry average. These are stocks that you believe will be worth more in five years than they are now.

4. Diversify to reduce risk. While some stocks will do well, others may not. By diversifying your investments, the average performance of all the stocks will help you to achieve your goal.

Whether you choose to join NAIC or not, your members should definitely agree to follow these four principles. Having an investment philosophy in place will ensure that everyone is working together to achieve the club's goals.

Your club now has a name, officers, regular meeting dates and location, a schedule of assignments, and an investment philosophy. You've made great strides toward creating a club that will help you ensure a financially secure future.

The Three Documents

Now that your club has chosen a name, elected officers, and made a few other key decisions, there are three documents you'll need to prepare. One document is required before you can open a brokerage account, and the other two will outline the general and the specific operating guidelines of your club.

1. APPLICATION FOR
EMPLOYER IDENTIFICATION NUMBER (EIN)

An EIN is a nine-digit number assigned by the IRS to entities such as corporations, partnerships, or estates for tax-filing and reporting purposes. Because an investment club collects interest and dividend payments, you'll need an EIN. As was mentioned before, you can't open a brokerage account without this number. To apply for an EIN, you'll need to fill out IRS Form SS-4. You can obtain the form by calling the IRS at 1-800-TAX-FORM (1-800-829-3676). It will take seven to 15 working days to receive it. If you have access to the Internet, you can get the form off the IRS web site at www.irs.ustreas.gov or www.irs.gov, or you can pick up a copy at your nearest IRS office or at many public libraries.

The form is self-explanatory and easy to complete. Figure 4-1 shows a copy of the form and a quick rundown on which lines need to be completed and the responses you should use.

Form **SS-4** (Rev. February 1998) Department of the Treasury Internal Revenue Service	**Application for Employer Identification Number** (For use by employers, corporations, partnerships, trusts, estates, churches, government agencies, certain individuals, and others. See instructions.) ▶ Keep a copy for your records.	EIN OMB No. 1545-0003

Please type or print clearly.

1 Name of applicant (legal name) (see instructions)

2 Trade name of business (if different from name on line 1) | **3** Executor, trustee, "care of" name

4a Mailing address (street address) (room, apt., or suite no.) | **5a** Business address (if different from address on lines 4a and 4b)

4b City, state, and ZIP code | **5b** City, state, and ZIP code

6 County and state where principal business is located

7 Name of principal officer, general partner, grantor, owner, or trustor—SSN or ITIN may be required (see instructions) ▶

8a Type of entity (Check only one box.) (see instructions)

Caution: *If applicant is a limited liability company, see the instructions for line 8a.*

☐ Sole proprietor (SSN) _____
☐ Partnership   ☐ Personal service corp.
☐ REMIC   ☐ National Guard
☐ State/local government   ☐ Farmers' cooperative
☐ Church or church-controlled organization
☐ Other nonprofit organization (specify) ▶ _____
☐ Other (specify) ▶

☐ Estate (SSN of decedent) _____
☐ Plan administrator (SSN) _____
☐ Other corporation (specify) ▶ _____
☐ Trust
☐ Federal government/military
_____ (enter GEN if applicable) _____

8b If a corporation, name the state or foreign country (if applicable) where incorporated | State | Foreign country

9 Reason for applying (Check only one box.) (see instructions)
☐ Started new business (specify type) ▶ _____
☐ Hired employees (Check the box and see line 12.)
☐ Created a pension plan (specify type) ▶
☐ Banking purpose (specify purpose) ▶ _____
☐ Changed type of organization (specify new type) ▶ _____
☐ Purchased going business
☐ Created a trust (specify type) ▶ _____
☐ Other (specify) ▶

10 Date business started or acquired (month, day, year) (see instructions) | **11** Closing month of accounting year (see instructions)

12 First date wages or annuities were paid or will be paid (month, day, year). Note: *If applicant is a withholding agent, enter date income will first be paid to nonresident alien. (month, day, year)* . . . . ▶

13 Highest number of employees expected in the next 12 months. Note: *If the applicant does not expect to have any employees during the period, enter -0-. (see instructions)* . . . . . ▶

Nonagricultural	Agricultural	Household

14 Principal activity (see instructions) ▶

15 Is the principal business activity manufacturing? . . . . ☐ Yes   ☐ No
If "Yes," principal product and raw material used ▶

16 To whom are most of the products or services sold? Please check one box.   ☐ Business (wholesale)
☐ Public (retail)   ☐ Other (specify) ▶   ☐ N/A

17a Has the applicant ever applied for an employer identification number for this or any other business? . . . . ☐ Yes   ☐ No
Note: *If "Yes," please complete lines 17b and 17c.*

17b If you checked "Yes" on line 17a, give applicant's legal name and trade name shown on prior application, if different from line 1 or 2 above.
Legal name ▶   Trade name ▶

17c Approximate date when and city and state where the application was filed. Enter previous employer identification number if known.

Approximate date when filed (mo., day, year)	City and state where filed	Previous EIN

Under penalties of perjury, I declare that I have examined this application, and to the best of my knowledge and belief, it is true, correct, and complete. | Business telephone number (include area code)

     | Fax telephone number (include area code)

Name and title (Please type or print clearly.) ▶

Signature ▶   Date ▶

Note: *Do not write below this line. For official use only.*

Please leave blank ▶	Geo.	Ind.	Class	Size	Reason for applying

For Paperwork Reduction Act Notice, see page 4.   Cat. No. 16055N   Form **SS-4** (Rev. 2-98)

Figure 4-1: Application for Employer Identification Number

Line 1: Enter the name of your investment club.

Line 2: Blank.

Line 3: The name of the club's treasurer should be used here, as he or she is the person who will be handling future tax forms.

Line 4a and b: Enter the treasurer's address.

Line 5a and b: Blank.

Line 6: Enter the county and state where your investment club is located.

Line 7: Enter the treasurer's full name and Social Security number.

Line 8a: Check "Partnership."

Line 8b: Blank.

Line 9: Check "Banking purpose" and write in, "Investment club for dividend and interest reporting."

Line 10: Enter the date the investment club was created.

Line 11: Enter "December 31."

Line 12: Enter "N/A."

Line 13: Enter zeroes in all three boxes.

Line 14: Enter "Investment club."

Line 15: Check "No."

Line 16: Check "N/A."

Line 17a: Unless this exact same investment club applied for an EIN at a previous time, check "No," then skip lines 17b and 17c.

Signature Block: Fill in the treasurer's phone number, and fax number, if applicable. The treasurer's name and title should be printed where noted, and the signature and date filled in.

That's it! After you mail in the form, it will probably take about four weeks until you receive your EIN in the mail.

If you need the EIN sooner than that, you can apply by telephone by calling the tele-TIN phone number listed for your state on the form's instruction pages. The IRS representative will give you your EIN—however, you will still have to complete the IRS Form SS-4 and send it in. If the IRS has already given you your EIN by phone when you send the form in, include that number on the upper right-hand corner of the form.

In addition to the IRS Form SS-4, you need to check to find out if your state has any licensing or registration requirements for partnerships. Check with your state's licensing board, securities division, or other regulatory agency. Also, check with your county to see if they charge a minimal registration fee.

2. THE PARTNERSHIP AGREEMENT

One question most new investment clubs face is whether they should structure their club as a partnership or corporation. The answer is partnership, for four reasons.

1. *State Registration:* A partnership is less expensive to create than a corporation because, unlike a partnership, a corporation has to register with the state in which it is located and pay fees to do so.

2. *Annual State Filing Requirements:* A partnership is less expensive to maintain than a corporation because a corporation has to file annual reports with the state, whereas a partnership does not.

3. *Single Taxation:* A partnership's income flows through to the individual partners without being taxed at the partnership level, therefore, the money earned is only taxed once. A corporation's income is taxed at the corporate level and again at the individual level when the individuals receive the funds, so that any money earned is taxed twice. In addition, in a partnership any losses the club may incur in selling stock flows through to the individual members, who can use those losses on their personal tax returns.

4. *Minimal Personal Liability:* While a corporation limits the individual members' personal liability and a partnership does not, investment club members have personal liability only to the extent of buying and selling stocks through their stockbroker. As long as members monitor their brokerage account monthly, that liability is minimal.

Therefore, the partnership is the best structure for an investment club. If you're going to form a partnership, however, you need to adopt a partnership agreement that lays out the general operations of the club. That sounds complicated and legalistic, but NAIC has been extremely generous in sharing the Mutual Investment Club of Detroit's version of their partnership agreement with anyone who wants to start an investment club. The next few pages include the text of that partnership agreement. The document can also be accessed at the NAIC web site at www.better-investing.org under the heading, "Start Clubs." Please note that the following should not be considered legal or tax advice. Blanks are noted where information specific to your club would be inserted. At the end of the partnership agreement is an explanation of a few of the points you may want to consider altering from this original agreement.

Partnership Agreement of
(The name of your investment club)

This agreement of partnership, effective as of _____(date)_____, by and between the undersigned to wit:

(Names of all your club's members)

Now, therefore, it is agreed:

1. *Formation:* The undersigned hereby form a General Partnership in accordance with and subject to the laws of the State of (fill in the state where your club is located).

2. *Name:* The name of the partnership shall be (fill in the name of your investment club).

3. *Term:* The partnership shall begin on (fill in date) and shall continue until December 31 of the same year and thereafter from year to year unless earlier terminated as hereinafter provided.

4. *Purpose:* The only purpose of the partnership is to invest the assets of the partnership solely in stocks, bonds, and other securities ("securities") for the education and benefit of the partners.

5. *Meetings:* Periodic meetings shall be held as determined by the partnership.

6. *Capital Contributions:* The partners may make capital contributions to the partnership on the date of each periodic meeting in such amounts as the partnership shall determine, provided, however, that no partner's capital account shall exceed twenty percent (20%) of the capital accounts of all the partners.

7. *Value of the Partnership:* The current value of the assets of the partnership, less the current value of the liabilities of the partnership (hereinafter referred to as "value of the partnership") shall be determined as of a regularly scheduled date and time ("valuation date") preceding the date of each periodic meeting determined by the club.

8. *Capital Accounts:* A capital account shall be maintained in the name of each partner. Any increase or decrease in the value of the partnership on any valuation date shall be credited or debited,

respectively, to each partner's capital account in proportion to the sum of all partner capital accounts on that date. Any other method of valuating each partner's capital account may be substituted for this method, provided the substituted method results in exactly the same valuation as previously provided herein. Each partner's capital contribution to, or capital *withdrawal* from, the partnership shall be credited or debited, respectively, to that partner's capital account.

> **Withdrawal:** When a partner removes funds from her capital account due to resignation from the investment club. Partial withdrawals can also be made by partners who remain in the club, if approved by the other investment club members.

9. *Management:* Each partner shall participate in the management and conduct of the affairs of the partnership in proportion to the value of his capital account. Except as otherwise determined, all decisions shall be made by the partners whose capital accounts total a majority of the value of the capital accounts of all the partners.

10. *Sharing of Profits and Losses:* Net profits and losses of the partnership shall inure to, and be borne by, the partners in proportion to the value of each of their capital accounts.

11. *Books of Accounts:* Books of account of the transactions of the partnership shall be kept and at all times be available and open to inspection and examination by any partner.

12. *Annual Accounting:* Each calendar year a full and complete account of the condition of the partnership shall be made to the partners.

13. *Bank Account:* The partnership may select a bank for the purpose of opening a bank account. Funds in the bank account shall be withdrawn by checks signed by any partner designated by the partnership.

14. *Broker Account:* None of the partners of this partnership shall be a broker. However, the partnership may select a broker and enter into such agreements with the broker as required for the purchase or sale of securities. Securities owned by the partnership shall be held in

the partnership name unless another name shall be designated by the partnership.

Any corporation or *transfer agent* called upon to transfer any securities to or from the name of the partnership shall be entitled to rely on instructions or assignments signed by any partner without inquiry as to the authority of the person(s) signing such instructions or assignments, or as to the validity of any transfer to or from the name of the partnership.

Transfer agent: A company that provides the service of handling the details of shareholder accounts, such as mailing dividends, proxies, and other company documents, for a public company.

At the time of a transfer of securities, the corporation or transfer agent is entitled to assume (1) that the partnership is still in existence, and (2) that this Agreement is in full force and effect and has not been amended unless the corporation or transfer agent has received written notice to the contrary.

15. *No Compensation:* No partner shall be compensated for services rendered to the partnership, except reimbursement for expenses.

16. *Additional Partners:* Additional partners may be admitted at any time, upon the unanimous consent of all the partners, as long as the number of partners does not exceed twenty-five (25).

16A. *Transfers to a Trust:* A partner may, after giving written notice to the other partners, transfer his interest in the partnership to a revocable living trust of which he is the grantor and sole trustee.

16B. *Removal of a Partner:* Any partner may be removed by agreement of the partners whose capital accounts total a majority of the value of all partners' capital accounts. Written notice of a meeting where removal of a partner is to be considered shall include a specific reference to this matter. The removal shall become effective upon payment of the value of the removed partner's capital account, which shall be in accordance with the provisions on full withdrawal of a partner, noted in paragraphs 18 and 20. The vote action shall be treated as receipt of request for withdrawal.

17. *Termination of Partnership:* The partnership may be terminated by agreement of the partners whose capital accounts total a majority in value of the capital accounts of all the partners. Written notice of the meeting where termination of the partnership is to be considered shall include a specific reference to this matter. The partnership shall terminate upon a majority vote of all partners' capital accounts. Written notice of the decision to terminate the partnership shall be given to all the partners. Payment shall then be made of all the liabilities of the partnership and a final distribution of the remaining assets, either in cash or in kind, shall promptly be made to the partners or their personal representatives in proportion to each partner's capital account.

18. *Voluntary Withdrawal (Partial or Full) of a Partner:* Any partner may withdraw a part or all of the value of his capital account in the partnership and the partnership shall continue as a taxable entity. The partner withdrawing a portion or all of the value of his capital account shall give notice of such intention in writing to the Secretary. Written notice shall be deemed to be received as of the first meeting of the partnership at which it is presented. If written notice is received between meetings it will be treated as received at the first following meeting.

    In making payment, the value of the partnership as set forth in the valuation statement prepared for the first meeting following the meeting at which written notice is received from a partner requesting a partial or full withdrawal will be used to determine the value of the partner's capital account.

    The partnership shall pay the partner who is withdrawing a portion or all of the value of his capital account in the partnership in accordance with paragraph 20 of this Agreement.

19. *Death or Incapacity of a Partner:* In the event of the death or incapacity of a partner (or the death or incapacity of the grantor and sole trustee of a revocable living trust, if such trust is a partner pursuant to paragraph 16A hereof), receipt of notice of such an event shall be treated as notice of full withdrawal.

20. *Terms of Payment:* In the case of a partial withdrawal, payment may be made in cash or securities of the partnership or a mix of each at the option of the partner making the partial withdrawal. In the case of a full withdrawal, payment may be made in cash or securities or a mix of each at the option of the remaining partners. In either case,

where securities are to be distributed, the remaining partners select the securities.

Where cash is transferred, the partnership shall transfer to the partner (or other appropriate entity) withdrawing a portion of all of his interest in the partnership, an amount equal to the lesser of (i) ninety-seven percent (97%) of the value of the capital account in the partnership being withdrawn or (ii) the value of the capital account being withdrawn, less the actual cost to the partnership of selling securities to obtain cash to meet the withdrawal. The amount being withdrawn shall be paid within 10 days after the valuation date used in determining the withdrawal amount.

If a partner withdrawing a portion or all of the value of his capital account in the partnership desires an immediate payment in cash, the partnership at its earliest convenience may pay eighty percent (80%) of the estimated value of his capital account and settle the balance in accordance with the valuation and payment procedures set forth in paragraphs 18 and 20.

When securities are transferred, the partnership shall select securities to transfer equal to the value of the capital account or a portion of the capital account being withdrawn (i.e., without a reduction for broker commissions). Securities shall be transferred as of the date of the club's valuation statement prepared to determine the value of that partner's capital account in the partnership. The Club's broker shall be advised that ownership of the securities has been transferred to the partner as of the valuation date used for the withdrawal.

21. *Forbidden Acts:* No partner shall:

(a) Have the right or authority to bind or obligate the partnership to any extent whatsoever with regard to any matter outside the scope of the partnership purpose.

(b) Except as provided in paragraph 16A, without the unanimous consent of all the other partners, assign, transfer, pledge, mortgage, or sell all or part of his interest in the partnership to any other partner or other person whomsoever, or enter into any agreement as the result of which any person or persons not a partner shall become interested with him in the partnership.

(c) Purchase an investment for the partnership where less than the full purchase price is paid for same.

(d) Use the partnership name, credit, or property for other than partnership purposes.

(e) Do any act detrimental to the interests of the partnership or which would make it impossible to carry on the purpose of the partnership.

This Agreement of Partnership shall be binding upon the respective heirs, executors, trustees, administrators, and personal representatives of the partners.

The partners have caused the Agreement of Partnership to be executed on the dates indicated below, effective as of the date indicated above.

Name:_____ Dated:_____

Name:_____ Dated:_____

Source: National Association of Investors Corporation (NAIC)
www.better-investing.org

* * * * *

The Mutual Investment Club of Detroit's partnership agreement that NAIC shares with potential investment clubs is a great starting point. You may, however, want to take into consideration a few issues when writing this document. Below are some specific paragraphs of the partnership agreement that you may want to consider changing.

Paragraph 9: As we will discuss in Chapter 5, not all members of your investment club will necessarily own the same percentage of the club's portfolio. If members have varying levels of ownership, an issue that typically surfaces is whether members should also have varying levels of voting power (as is assumed throughout the above partnership agreement) or if the club should stipulate a rule of one person, one vote.

One school of thought is that the members who have the greatest financial commitment are probably longer-term members who have more experience, and that voting power should relate to the amount of money each member has at risk. Therefore, the person who has contributed more money should have more decision-making power.

The other argument is that all members, regardless of their level of club ownership, should each have one vote because even though each member may own differing amounts of the club, every member is putting in the same amount of work and commitment.

It's your choice how you handle this issue in your club; however, if members have varying decision-making ability, it can cause some slight complications. For instance, if the members are voting on whether or not to buy a stock and one person has a 12 percent vote and another has a 7 percent vote, it can get somewhat complicated trying to determine whether an issue passed or not. Either way, it's important to establish at the beginning which option you want to use.

Paragraph 13: While you can open a bank account for your cash funds, it's better to deposit your money in a cash account at your brokerage firm. Having your money at the brokerage firm gives you easier access when you buy and sell stocks, as we'll discuss in Chapter 5.

Paragraph 14: Whether you want to allow stockbrokers in your club is up to the group. As we discussed in Chapter 2, however, a member with that magnitude of investment knowledge may control the club and undermine the members' goal of learning to invest.

Paragraph 16: While the Mutual Investment Club of Detroit limited its size to 25 members, having that many people involved in discussions can become a bit unwieldy. Also, you need to consider the size of the location where you plan to meet. Typically, 10 to 20 members are a better parameter.

Your partnership agreement establishes the general operating procedures for your investment club. You now need to consider having the specific operations of your club in writing. The next document accomplishes that.

3. THE PARTNERSHIP BYLAWS

It's important to have the specifics of your club's operations in writing. That can be accomplished by discussing the specifics of operating your club at your first meeting, passing motions, and writing them up in the minutes of the meeting. Or, you can adopt a bylaws document, such as the sample below. Keep in mind that this document is extremely flexible and can include any information you want. The sample bylaws below is simply an example of some of the issues your club may want to include.

Bylaws of
(The name of your investment club)

Article I

Name

Section 1.1: The investment club name shall be _____.

Article II

Purpose

Section 2.1: The purpose of the investment club is to (A) teach the members the basics of investing and how to build a viable investment portfolio for their futures; (B) invest money on a regular basis and build a long-term investment portfolio; and (C) offer members an opportunity to add new friends and social time to their lives.

Article III

Meetings

Section 3.1: The club shall hold meetings on the first Monday of each month, beginning at 7:30 P.M., rotating to each partner's home, unless such date, time, or location is changed by two-thirds majority vote.

Section 3.2: Special meetings may be called by the president upon at least one week's notice to the other partners.

Article IV

Officer Duties

Section 4.1: The officers of the club shall be president, secretary, treasurer, and vice president of education.

Section 4.2: Officers shall be elected by the affirmative vote of more than 50 percent of the partner interests. Nominations for officers will be accepted at the June meeting of each year and officers shall be elected at the July meeting of each year. Officers shall serve for a 12-month term, from August 1 through July 31 of the following year. If an officer position becomes vacant during the year, that position should be filled as quickly as possible following the same nomination and voting procedure.

Section 4.3: The president shall be the presiding officer at all meetings. If unable to preside at any meeting, the president will designate another officer to be the presiding officer at that meeting. The president is responsible for appointing committees as needed, ensuring that resolutions passed by the partnership are carried out, and that the club adheres to the rules set forth in the partnership agreement and bylaws.

Section 4.4: The secretary will keep a record of the actions authorized by the partners by taking meeting minutes and distributing them to the partners. The secretary will also set meeting dates and locations and prepare an agenda and make assignments for the monthly meetings. If the club so desires, the secretary will maintain the club's and the members' membership in NAIC. She will keep an accounting of petty-cash receipts and disbursements, such cash to be used for postage and other small and routine administrative expenses.

Section 4.5: The treasurer will keep a record of the club's receipts and disbursements and partners' interests in the club. The treasurer will collect the monthly assessments (cancelled checks to be used as receipts), deposit those assessments in the club's account, and place the partners' authorized buy and sell orders with the club's broker. The treasurer will prepare the club's monthly valuation statement, listing all club assets at cost and market value, and each member's ownership value, effective as of the last business day of each month, and handle the club's tax documents.

Section 4.6: The vice president of education will be responsible for enhancing the members' investment education process by arranging for speakers, video- or audiotapes, member presentations, or other forms of education.

Article V

Contributions

Section 5.1: Each new partner shall contribute a one-time payment of $100 at the first regular meeting following acceptance as a partner.

Section 5.2: Each partner shall contribute a monthly amount of at least $20, payable at each monthly meeting, in increments of $10, up to a sum that will not increase that partner's ownership share to more than 20 percent of the club. If a partner is not able to attend a meeting, his or her contribution shall be in the hands of the treasurer by the end of that meeting. If any partner is in arrears more than two meetings on monthly payments, that partner's membership will be liquidated in accordance with paragraph 16B of the partnership agreement.

Section 5.3: Each partner shall pay his or her equal share of the partnership's annual dues for membership in the National Association of Investment Clubs. In addition, each partner shall pay an amount equal to the per-member assessment required by the National Association of Investment Clubs for annual membership.

Section 5.4: Each partner shall contribute to the petty-cash fund as needed by the secretary. Such fund will not be considered an asset of the club for purposes of calculating capital accounts.

Article VI

Membership Responsibilities

Section 6.1: Each member is responsible for attending the monthly meetings. If any member misses 50 percent or more of the monthly meetings in any 12-month period, that partner's membership will be liquidated in accordance with paragraph 16B of the partnership agreement.

Section 6.2: Each member will be responsible for researching and presenting to the club stocks for potential purchase. Presentations will be made on a rotating basis.

Section 6.3: Each member will be responsible for monitoring assigned stocks in the club's portfolio.

Section 6.4: Each member will be responsible for hosting the monthly meetings made on a rotating basis.

Section 6.5: Each member will be responsible for holding various officer positions from time to time on a rotating basis.

Article VII

Guests

Section 7.1: Members may invite guests who may be potential members to the club's monthly meeting as long as they obtain advance clearance from that month's meeting hostess. Anyone who is under membership consideration as explained in Paragraph 16 of the partnership agreement must have been a guest at at least two club meetings.

Article VIII

Voting

Section 8.1: All active partners who are in attendance at meetings will have the right to vote. There will be no proxy voting. All votes will be conducted by secret ballot with all partners having equal votes, regardless of their ownership positions. In order for an issue brought to vote to pass, it must receive the affirmative vote of the majority of the members present at that meeting.

Article IX

Brokerage Firm

Section 9.1: The investment club members will choose a brokerage firm and open an account. In addition to the brokerage account, the club will also open a cash account at the brokerage firm for the deposit of monthly contributions, proceeds from stock sales, interest, and dividends. The brokerage firm will forward account statements directly to the club's treasurer.

Article X

Portfolio

Section 10.1: Each stock the club owns should not represent more than 20 percent of the club's total portfolio value.

Article XI

Miscellaneous

Section 11.1: The partnership agreement and bylaws may be amended by the unanimous consent of the active partners.

* * * * *

The above example lays out many of the issues that should be documented before an investment club begins operations. In addition to what's included in the example and what other issues your club would like to include, there are two other items you may want to consider.

In Section 5.2 the bylaws state that a partner will be removed from the club if in arrears in contributions for more than two monthly meetings. The reasoning is twofold. First, why have a member in the club who isn't contributing financially? That totally defeats the goal of building a nest egg. Second, if all members are required to contribute at least a minimum amount at each meeting and some members are in arrears, the club will have to purchase fewer shares of the stocks they vote to purchase at each meeting—an unfair situation for all members.

Some clubs charge members a penalty for late contributions—$5 for any contribution that is one to 30 days late, $10 for contributions that are 31 to 60 days late, and removal from membership when more than 60 days late with a monthly contribution. The penalty money is deposited to the club's cash account until invested.

Section 6.1 states that any partner who misses 50 percent or more of the monthly meetings in any 12-month period will be removed from the club. Why allow someone to take up a membership spot when they don't bother to come to meetings and share in the work? However, some clubs don't feel it's a problem.

The Lady Traders of Osceola Investment Club has 25 members. About two-thirds of the members regularly attend the meetings. The other one-third does not. But yet, the members decided not to include a section in their bylaws stating that members would be terminated if they didn't attend a certain number of meetings each year. Their reasoning is that there are two areas of responsibility in being a member of an investment club. One is attending meetings, helping to make policies, researching stocks, giving stock presentations, and acting as an officer. The second is contributing money to the club. They believe that if some members want to fulfill only the second responsibility, it's not a problem. As long as those members contribute their money on time each month, they can remain a member of the club. They take the stance that those additional contributions give the other members more purchasing power and provide them with the ability to purchase stocks that sell for higher prices than they could afford to purchase without the extra money.

Another issue you could address in Article VI of your bylaws is the members' commitment to the club. The Wall Street Watchers Investment Club considered stating in the membership section of their bylaws that they expect new members to make at least a three-year commitment to club membership. While an investment club could certainly never refuse to allow a member to resign, that statement makes it very clear up front that becoming a member of this club is truly a serious commitment. The Wall Street Watchers ultimately decided not to include the statement in their bylaws, but they do verbally stress the importance of a three-year commitment to new members.

You may also want to address in this article the membership makeup of your club. If your members decide the club's membership should be all female, all male, all African-American, or fit some other specific criteria, you may want to include a statement to that effect.

Some clubs include in their bylaws a statement that a majority of members must be present at any monthly meeting in order for the club to conduct business. The reason for including that statement is that it eliminates the possibility of a few people making major decisions for the whole club. For example, what if only two people showed up at a meeting? Those two people could vote to sell all the stocks in the club's portfolio and purchase other stocks.

A reason for not including the statement in the club's bylaws is that it can be limiting. If your club has 19 members and only nine show up for a meeting, you can't conduct business. It's frustrating to prepare for a meeting, make the effort to be there, and then have to turn around and go home because not enough people were present.

Typically, in an investment club, there is no *proxy voting*. If you want your voice to be heard, you have to be present.

Proxy voting: Having another member of the club vote for you at the monthly meeting if you are absent, or forwarding your vote to the secretary prior to the meeting.

Section 8.1 states that for any issue brought to vote, it must receive the affirmative vote of the majority of the members present. It's probably best to include the phrase "of the members present." Otherwise, if a majority of the members aren't at the meeting, no voting could take place.

Section 10.1 states that no one stock should represent more than 20 percent of the club's total portfolio value. That rule will help to keep the club's portfolio diversified so that you don't end up with the risk of one stock representing 50 percent or 60 percent of the club's total portfolio value.

After the partnership agreement and bylaws are completed and signed, copies should be distributed to each member of the investment club. It's important for the members to have copies of and understand these documents, and that the club abides by the provisions contained in these agreements in a consistent manner. Not following these provisions could lead to a member taking legal action against the club.

When a member resigns from the club, it's important to have everyone sign a new copy of the partnership agreement so that the resigning member's signature is removed. When a new member joins, that person's signature should be added to the partnership agreement.

From time to time, the members should review their club's bylaws to ensure they still reflect how the members want their club to operate. Clubs grow and change, and the bylaws should reflect any new needs the club may have.

You've now completed the three documents that establish your group as a viable, operating investment club. Now all you have to do is start investing your money. It's time to take a look at the most important part of your club: the money issues.

Chapter 5

The Money Issues

While it doesn't take a lot of money to start investing and building a nest egg, each member of the club will have to come up with a minimum amount of money each month. Some may have more funds available than others so you don't want to dictate that members must invest more than they can afford.

But maybe your members can afford more than they think. It's just a matter of knowing where to find those few extra dollars. Chances are the money needed to invest each month in an investment club is money that may be wasted otherwise. If your members follow these five steps, they may discover extra funds.

1. Create a monthly budget for yourself so that you live within your means. That's an important step whether you make $15,000 a year or $150,000 a year. Without a budget or a plan, how do you know how much money you have to spend?

2. Pay yourself first. Before you spend money to go to a movie, go out to dinner, or indulge in some other activity, set aside an amount that you'll invest each month. If you don't take care of that first, it will probably be forgotten. In order to have money available to invest, you may have to forego other activities from time to time. But look to the future. If you put this year's vacation money in 100 shares of stock, that money may grow into an amount that's large enough to fund three vacations in the future. Postponing one vacation for the chance of having three isn't such a bad trade-off. If we don't indulge in instant gratification, we may have much more spending power available to enjoy in the future.

3. Let it grow. Once that money is put away in an investment account or in your investment club, never withdraw it.

4. Spend wisely. Make a distinction between what you need to have and what you want to have. If an item is just a want, it can probably wait until later. Find little ways to save money, such as taking your lunch to work rather than eating in an expensive restaurant, washing your own car rather than taking it to the car wash, or doing little repairs around your home rather than hiring a handyman to take care of them.

5. Avoid debt. Debt can really be an advantageous source of money if you're using it to purchase a home, land, or some other asset that will appreciate in value over time. Of course, if purchasing a home, find one that is priced so that you can meet the monthly payments and other expenses that a home involves, without having to scrimp. It doesn't do much good to buy a home that costs more than you can afford, and then you can't afford to enjoy living in it.

   While using debt for appreciating assets can be advantageous, using debt for depreciating assets can be a mistake. A boat or an expensive piece of furniture can depreciate to zero while you still owe money on it. For those types of items, if you can't pay cash, maybe you shouldn't buy it. When it comes to credit cards, buying on credit and paying 18 percent interest or more on that purchase simply makes the credit-card issuer rich—not you. If you do use a credit card, pay off the balance at the end of each month.

If your members follow those five steps, chances are they'll easily have the money they need for their monthly contributions.

When your club first begins operating, your members start contributing, and you begin investing, you may feel that your portfolio isn't making much progress. You're investing a small amount each month, but a portion of that money is used to pay commissions to the brokerage firm, and six months later your portfolio is worth less than the amount of money you've invested. Don't worry. Typically, most investment clubs experience a loss, or possibly a very small profit, the first year or two. But take heart. The bigger your portfolio gets, the faster it will grow. It just takes time—not a lot of money. In fact, nothing makes more money than time.

Consider the story of Gladys Holm. Holm was a single woman all her life. She worked as a secretary for a company in a Chicago suburb for 41 years. Holm's coworkers knew that she did a little investing and, periodically, she'd even ask her boss for a little investment advice. Considering, however, that at the height of her career her annual salary was just $15,000, she obviously wasn't able to invest huge amounts. Holm died in June 1996 at the age of 86. In her will, she left all her money to a children's hospital. That hospital received $18 million! Holm's story proves that it doesn't take a lot of money to build a fortune—just persistence, a willingness to do a little work to find good stocks to buy, and a long-term investment philosophy.

When it comes to determining how much money each member will contribute to the club each month, you have two options. You can have all the members contribute the same dollar amount each month, or you can allow each member to contribute the monthly amount he or she chooses, as long as it's equal to or more than whatever minimum amount the club specifies. Each option has advantages and disadvantages. Let's look at both.

EQUAL OWNERSHIP

If you choose to use *equal ownership*, the members will all contribute the same amount each month.

Equal ownership: A method of determining the amount of money each investment club partner will contribute to the club each month. While this method of each member contributing the same amount is easy to track, it can cause difficulties in adding new members to the club in the future.

The group needs to determine what that amount will be. Do they want to contribute $25, $50, $75, or more or less each month? If everyone has to contribute the same, all members will have to agree with and abide by the amount chosen.

Advantage

The advantage of using equal ownership is that it makes the club's record keeping easier. If you have 10 members who contribute $50 each per month, after one year total contributions equal $6,000. Each member's ownership is one-tenth of the whole, which is $600. Everyone owns the same portion. When the treasurer prepares the monthly valuation statement, there's very little to calculate since the members have identical ownership.

Disadvantage

Many clubs choose to use equal ownership because it makes the paperwork much easier, but they forget to look at the consequences of using this option in the long term. For instance, let's say a club has been operating for three years. With each person contributing $50 per month, after three years—ignoring market fluctuations, interest, and dividends—each member's ownership would total $1,800 ($50 per month times 36 months). At one of the monthly meetings one of the members announces that she has a friend who would like to join the club. Everyone meets the potential member and she is accepted for membership. In order to join the club, she has to ante up $1,800 so that her ownership portion will be equal to the other members. That's a lot of money! Also, except for her friend who introduced her to the club, she's handing that money over to a group of people she's met only once or twice. That scenario is difficult enough, but what happens a few years down the road when each member's ownership grows to $5,000, $10,000, and more? It'll be extremely difficult, if not impossible, to find new members who can afford or who are trusting enough to join.

While the ease of using equal ownership is very tempting, it can become extremely constricting as the club's portfolio grows. Clubs always lose members due to moves to other locations, the development of time constraints, the decision that an investment club isn't right for them, or hundreds of other reasons. Therefore, bringing new members into an investment club is always an issue clubs have to face. It's important to look at the long term and be certain that the rules and procedures you adopt today will work five or 10 years from now.

UNEQUAL OWNERSHIP

If you choose to use *unequal ownership*, members can contribute whatever amount they want each month as long as they meet the club's specified minimum.

Unequal ownership: A method of determining the amount of money each investment club partner will contribute to the club each month. While this method of each member contributing varying amounts makes tracking individual ownership more complicated, it simplifies adding new members to the club in the future.

A member may contribute $20 one month and $50 the next month. Therefore, each member's ownership will be different from the other members. The best approach to managing unequal ownership is to create *ownership units* that are equal to $10 each.

> **Ownership units:** Contribution increments of $10 that allow club members to maintain varying capital accounts.

If everyone contributes $5 each month, it will take a long time for your club to build an investment portfolio. Therefore, most clubs set a minimum amount each member must contribute each month. You may decide to set that amount at $20. Then, each month members can contribute the minimum or they can contribute additional amounts in one unit, or $10, increments. As members contribute different amounts each month, each person's ownership in the club will vary.

While ownership amounts can differ from member to member, it's best not to allow any one member to own more than 20 percent of the club. You don't want to end up with a club in which nine people own 1 percent each and the 10th person owns 91 percent!

Advantage

The advantage to unequal ownership is that whether the club has been in operation for two months or 20 years, a new member can join by purchasing two units—a $20 contribution. It's obviously much easier to entice new members when they can join for a nominal amount. They can then contribute more heavily as they become more investment savvy and comfortable with the investment club concept and fellow members.

Disadvantage

Using unequal ownership makes the individual ownership calculations somewhat more complicated because the treasurer needs to keep track of how many units each person owns, calculate what percentage of the portfolio those units represent, then calculate the value of each member's ownership. We'll discuss how to do those calculations and prepare a valuation statement that reflects unequal ownership in Chapter 9. While using unequal ownership is a bit more complicated and involves a few more cal-culations, in the long run it could save your club from disintegration if members resign.

Another issue, which we touched on in Chapter 4, involves setting up the partnership agreement. The question that often surfaces when using unequal ownership is whether all members have equal voting power or if members should vote according to their ownership percentage. It's your choice, but if you're voting on whether or not to buy a stock and one person has a 12 per-cent vote and another has a 7 percent vote, it's going to get awfully compli-cated trying to determine whether an issue passed or not. It's probably best to establish from the beginning that each member is allowed one equal vote, regardless of ownership. Even though each member may own differing amounts of the club, every member is putting in the same amount of work and commitment.

GETTING YOUR PORTFOLIO STARTED

When an investment club is first formed, it takes a while before the members' contributions build to the point that the club can begin investing. If you have 10 members and each one has decided to contribute $20 each the first month, you've collected only $200—hardly enough to make an investment. But invest-ing is what the club is all about. If you spend months meeting and presenting stocks, but you never have enough money to buy one, members may get bored. The last thing you want is for your members to lose interest. You have two options.

First, if you have a stock that meets your criteria and you'd like to pur-chase it, simply buy as many shares as you can. That may be only 10 shares, but at least it gets you in the market. It gives the members a stock to follow and will help to keep their interest. Buying that first stock can be exciting and your club should take that plunge as soon as possible.

The other option would be for each member to contribute an *initial kicker*—a certain amount just to get the club off the ground and funded.

Initial kicker: An amount of money that each mem-ber contributes to the club before it starts operating to create a cash account large enough to start buying stocks.

Maybe each person would put in $100, then begin making monthly contributions. If a club had 10 members, their kicker would give them $1,000. Combined with their first monthly contribution, they'd have enough money to purchase a stock at their first meeting.

SEEKING OUT A BROKERAGE FIRM

Choosing the right brokerage firm is important both in terms of expenses and assistance. There are three types of brokerage firms you can consider.

Full-Service Brokerage Firms

A *full-service brokerage firm* is exactly what its name implies—a firm that offers you a variety of investment services.

Full-service brokerage firm: A brokerage firm that not only fills buy and sell orders, but also gives advice and stock recommendations. Because of the additional services, it charges a higher level of commissions.

This type of broker will offer advice on potential stocks for you to buy, will help monitor your overall portfolio, and will assist you in making sell decisions. A full-service broker will make available third-party analyst reports such as *Standard & Poor's (S&P) and Value Line reports*, and the firm's own *analyst* reports.

Standard & Poor's (S&P) and Value Line reports: S&P and Value Line are companies that track the performance of various public companies and issue periodic reports. These reports are useful tools in researching stocks.

Analyst: An employee of a brokerage firm who tracks the performance of public companies and issues reports as to whether those companies' stocks should be bought or sold. The firm makes those reports available to its customers at no cost.

While these firms can offer plenty of services, you'll pay for it. Each time you buy or sell a stock, you'll pay a commission. The commissions are based on the number of shares you purchase and their price per share. Full-service brokerage firms charge the highest commissions of any type of firm. As your portfolio grows, however, you may be able to negotiate a small decrease in a full-service brokerage firm's commission rates. The larger your portfolio, the better your chances. Also, while some brokers aren't very excited about working with investment clubs because they invest fairly small amounts each month, others are more aware of the potential business an investment club can bring and are anxious to get them as clients. Remember, statistics show that after five years of membership, nine out of 10 investment club members invest outside the club and build their own personal portfolio. That means a broker who's been servicing a 10-member club has the potential of picking up nine more clients!

Discount Brokerage Firms

Full-service brokerage firms used to be the only game in town until May 1, 1975, when the *Securities and Exchange Commission (SEC)* mandated an end to all fixed commissions. That change made it possible for discount brokers to enter the scene.

Securities and Exchange Commission {SEC}:
Created by the Securities Exchange Act of 1934, it is the federal agency that protects the public against fraud and ensures full disclosure of information on securities.

When *discount brokerage firms* were first formed, they offered no services except placing buy and sell orders.

Discount brokerage firm: A brokerage firm that offers fewer services, but charges a lower level of commissions than a full-service brokerage firm.

They didn't offer analyst reports, make buy and sell recommendations, or help clients monitor their portfolios. Because of the reduced amount of service, they were able to offer lower commission rates. Investors who were willing to do their own research and make their own investment decisions could save a lot of money.

Today, the differences between full-service and discount firms aren't as black and white. Both ends of the spectrum still exist, but investors can find brokerage firms in between the two that offer all different levels of service and charge corresponding levels of commissions.

Deep-Discount Brokerage Firms

As the discount firms began to offer investors more services and charge a little higher level of commissions, a new type of brokerage firm began to spring up. The *deep-discount brokerage firm* offers investors absolutely no services except to place buy and sell orders.

Deep-discount brokerage firm: A brokerage firm that offers no additional services other than completing buy and sell transactions, which clients may have to do via computer or Touch-Tone phone. Commission charges are rock bottom.

In fact, if you use a true deep discounter, you'll never talk to a broker. You'll simply enter your buy and sell orders into a computer or Touch-Tone phone. While there's no personal touch, it's cheap. Some discounters complete trades for as little as $8.

How You Want to Trade

The method of trading your members want to use should also be taken into consideration when choosing a broker. It used to be that the only way you could make a stock trade was to pick up the phone and call your stock-broker. That's not the case anymore. Now you can also click your mouse and complete a stock trade. And online investing is quickly gaining in popularity.

According to a study conducted by Cerulli Associates, a Boston financial-research firm, there are currently 160 brokerage firms, half of which are discount firms, that offer online trading. In 1995 the value of total assets of online brokerage accounts was $27.7 billion. By the end of 1999 that number had risen to $754.4 billion. Because investors seem to like the do-it-yourself factor of online investing, Cerulli Associates predicts the total asset value of online accounts will jump to $2.2 trillion, with 85 percent of all brokerage accounts being online by the end of 2004.

Those numbers are proof that online trading has become rather enticing to most investors. However, if your club decides it wants to do its trading online, there are a few issues you need to address.

1. What are the various fees the firm charges?
2. What type of services does the firm offer?
3. What level of security does the firm offer?

Let's look at each of these issues individually.

The Costs

Stock trades completed online will be much less costly than dealing directly with a stockbroker. However, there's a lot of variation from one brokerage firm to another. You can find a lot of brokerage firms that advertise $8 trades online. But to get that price, your trade may have to meet certain criteria. Many times, due to the lack of a large amount of funds, investment clubs will purchase an *odd lot*, or fewer than 100 shares of a stock.

Odd lot: A stock transaction that involves fewer than 100 shares, which is called a round lot. The commission cost per share that many brokerage firms charge is often higher for an odd lot than for a round lot.

Some online firms will charge a higher price for an odd-lot transaction. If that's the case, and your club has mostly odd-lot trades, that can increase your costs substantially.

Some online firms will charge a flat fee plus an additional couple of cents for every share traded. Others may charge a flat fee, but tack on additional fees for special types of trades you may request, such as a *good-'til-cancelled order*.

Good-'til-cancelled order: An order to buy or sell stock that has a specific price tied to it. The order remains with the broker in the open market until it is either filled or cancelled.

Others may advertise low-cost transaction fees, but charge an additional surcharge for shipping and handling. If your account doesn't have enough activity to please the brokerage firm, you may be charged an activity fee. Or, if your members decide they want their certificates delivered to them, many firms charge to issue one. And when it comes to services, such as getting real-time quotes online or obtaining research materials from the brokerage firm's web site, that may add more charges to your bill.

The key is to make sure you understand all the fees you could possibly be charged. You don't want to open an account, start trading, and then find out that there are hidden fees that will substantially increase your costs. The time to find out about additional fees is before you open your account.

The Services

One type of service you should consider is the amount of research the firm will make available to you. Do you want to be able to access quotes from your online brokerage firm? Do you want to be able to access news stories that relate to the various companies you're following? Do you want to be able to obtain free copies of S&P reports, Value Line reports, and other analyst reports? How do you want to receive the research? Some companies will give you a choice of having them e-mailed or faxed to you. Keep in mind that there are a lot of free web sites that offer research materials on companies. If you're a customer of America Online, you can get plenty of investment information there. Some other web sites that are good resources are:

✔ www.cbs.marketwatch.com
✔ www.cnbc.com
✔ www.cnnfn.com
✔ www.msnmoneycentral.com

Don't pay your brokerage firm for the privilege of obtaining research that you can get elsewhere for free.

In addition to research, does the brokerage firm offer some type of account where your club can deposit its contributions, interest, and dividend payments? Are there minimum balances required? Does the account pay interest? What information will you be able to access via the computer on your investment club's account? You should be able to easily access your account balances and your portfolio holdings. Will all of your members be able to access the account information or only the treasurer? What types of documentation will be sent to your club's treasurer on a monthly basis? Will you receive a *year-end recap* on your account?

Year-end recap: A year-end statement that brokerage firms send to customers that recaps the activity of the account during the year, including the total amount of interest and dividend payments—information your club will need for tax purposes.

If your investment club members aren't savvy computer users, your club may need a little additional computer support. Make sure the firm has a toll-free number you can call to get help when required.

Finally, does the firm have a brick-and-mortar location where you can walk in, sit down, and actually talk to a stockbroker if you want? Many of the larger firms offer both physical locations and online trading.

Determine what services are important to your club and make sure the brokerage firm you're considering offers those services to you at no cost, or at least at a reasonable cost, before opening an account.

The Security

The last thing your club wants to happen is to have someone break into your account via the computer and start making trades or, worse yet, withdrawals. Make sure any brokerage firm you're considering uses a secure connection. You can ask that question and you can also check it out yourself by logging onto the firm's site and looking to see if there is an icon of an unbroken padlock on your computer screen, and that the address of the site starts with "https" rather than just "http." The extra "s" at the end means it's secure. With all the media attention that's been paid to the Internet and using secure sites only, it's unimaginable that a brokerage firm wouldn't have a secure site, but it doesn't hurt to make sure.

Another element of security your club may consider is *double password access*.

Double password access: Having two passwords to access an online brokerage account. One password allows the user to view the account; the second password allows the user to complete transactions

That means that all the members in the club would have the first password so that they can get online and view the club's portfolio. But only the treasurer would have the second password, which would be required to actually complete transactions. Without that second password, no one could place an order to buy or sell stock or withdraw cash. If you feel that the second level of password security is definitely required, you may want to reconsider who you've invited to be members in the club. On the other hand, having an extra level of security never hurts.

Which Type of Firm Is Best for Your Club?

One of the goals of an investment club is to learn to invest. That's accomplished by finding potential stocks to buy, researching companies, and monitoring their performance. If you're doing all the work yourselves, you really don't need a full-service brokerage firm, so why pay for services you don't need? It probably makes more sense to use a discount or a deep-discount broker.

Some new clubs, however, feel uncomfortable with their investment skills and opt to use a full-service broker for a time until they begin to trust their own decision-making ability. Other clubs prefer to stay with a full-service firm to take advantage of the additional services that are available. Terri Hult of the Dough Makers Investment Club says when their club first started, they decided to use the son of one of their members as their broker. He is with a full-service firm and they've opted to stay with him after three years of operation because they like dealing with him personally and welcome and appreciate his advice. In fact, the broker just switched jobs and the club followed him to his new full-service firm. If you feel you need that backup, go with the full-service broker. Otherwise, find a broker who's going to charge you less. The lower your commission cost, the more money you'll have available for investments.

Do your members want to complete their trades online? If so, find a firm that offers a cost-effective program that has the security level you want and charges a fair price for the services you need. Howard Clarke of the Central Maine Investors of Augusta says their club started with a full-service firm and has maintained that account since 1984. They appreciate the assistance the broker offers them. Because trading online is faster and cheaper, however, they've also opened an account with an online brokerage firm that they use for certain trades. In addition, they buy a company's stock directly from the company when possible. Their club has decided to take advantage of all the options available to them.

Locating the Right Firm

After the members have decided which type of brokerage firm to use, you need to find the specific firm you want to hire. It may be best to assign the research part of this job to one member. That member should ask the group for suggestions as to what firms to research. Members may get recommendations from friends who are investors. If no one has any ideas, you can find plenty of brokers easily enough. Brokerage firms advertise in newspapers and magazines, on radio and TV, and are even listed in the Yellow Pages.

If you want to research some of the brokerage firms online, there are three web sites you can check out that will give you a lot of good information.

1. www.gomez.com: Gomez Advisors rates more than 50 different brokerage firms that offer online investing. They rate them in several categories, including ease of use, customer confidence, on-site resources, relationship services, and overall cost. You can even choose two different firms and compare their ratings side by side. The ratings are updated on a regular basis. In addition, the site offers a screen in which consumers can post their reviews of the various companies. As always, however, you don't know who is posting the review, if that person even had experience with the brokerage firm, and if the review is honest. Read the reviews with a skeptical eye.

2. www.pathfinder.com/money/broker: This site rates brokerage firms on issues such as ease of use, customer service, system responsiveness, products and tools offered, and cost. One screen contains a form on which you can mark your preferences as to how important various services are to you and the site will find the broker that best fits your specifications.

3. www.smartmoney.com/si/brokers: This site rates brokerage firms based on trading costs, breadth of product, mutual-fund offerings, online trading, extra services, responsiveness, web reliability, and whether the firm has had any disciplinary actions taken against it. This site also offers a form you can complete with your various preferences to determine which firm would best fit your needs.

When your club has identified two or three potential firms that you may want to work with, the researching member should call them and request that they send literature that describes their services. Make sure the literature includes a commission-rate schedule. Each firm may have a web site available that includes all the information you need.

After the member has read through the literature and considered the commission rates, the field should be narrowed to one or two. If the club is considering full-service firms, the member should make an appointment to meet with the broker who will be handling the account. Most full-service brokers will offer a free half-hour consultation. If the investment club member handling this research is not the treasurer, it may be wise for the treasurer to also go to this consultation because the treasurer is the person who will be working directly with the stockbroker.

At this meeting, ask if the broker works with other investment clubs. Explain your club's investment philosophy and be sure the broker understands and agrees with that philosophy. Discuss the types of services offered, ask about their online trading services, ask for references, and then check them out.

The last step is for the member to check out any firms being considered, whether online or brick and mortar, through the *National Association of Securities Dealers (NASD)* Public Disclosure Phone Center. The number is 800-289-9999.

National Association of Securities Dealers {NASD}: The organization that enforces the rules of fair practice relative to the brokerage industry.

Give them the name of the firm, and also the stockbroker's name if you're considering a full-service firm, and they will tell you whether that firm or broker has any final and/or pending state or federal disciplinary actions. If there are no disciplinary actions, they'll tell you that over the phone. If there are, they will send you a printout. This service is free to investors. Or, you can access this information at the NASD Regulation web site at www.nasdr.com.

If you find that one of the stockbrokers or brokerage firms you're considering has had disciplinary actions taken in the past or has any pending, you may want to continue your research and find someone else. Thousands of investors lose millions of dollars every year to stock fraud. It doesn't make sense to take a chance on someone who has a questionable past. If everything checks out, the member should bring all of the findings to the investment club members and a group decision should be made.

Choosing which type of brokerage firm to use is an important step in forming an investment club. Every month you'll be giving money to that firm. You don't want to find out later that the firm is a sham or that the broker is a con artist and has run off with your hard-earned dollars. Take the time to find the brokerage firm that will fit your needs at the price you're willing to pay.

OPENING A BROKERAGE ACCOUNT

After doing a little research and having a little discussion, the investment club has narrowed its choice of brokerage firms and chosen one. It's now time to open your brokerage account, which is simply a matter of filling out a form. The primary information you'll need is the name of your club, your club's employer identification number, which we discussed how to obtain in Chapter 4, and the name and address of the treasurer. Each member of the club will need to provide an address and sign the form, giving the treasurer the authorization to place buy and sell orders with the broker. If the brokerage firms starts asking for extensive financial information on each member, that probably means they don't typically work with investment clubs. There's no reason the brokerage firm needs such detailed information about each member and you shouldn't supply it.

When opening your account, you'll need to decide whether you want the stocks you'll eventually purchase to be registered in the name of the club or in *street name*.

Street name: A brokerage account in which the brokerage firm, not the investor, is listed as the owner of the securities.

If you register your securities in street name, your club won't have to deal with the physical receipt of stock certificates. Stock certificates are negotiable instruments and must be safeguarded. That probably means storing them in a safe-deposit box—another added expense. Also, when you sell stock, due to T+3, you'll have to give your certificate to your broker within three days.

That means driving to the bank, getting the certificate, and probably driving it to the stockbroker, unless you trust the postal service to deliver it within three days.

T+3: Stands for trade plus three days, which refers to a law enacted on June 7, 1995, that reduced the settlement time for buying and selling securities from five to three days.

When securities are in street name, they are really registered in the brokerage firm's name. The broker then sends you a confirmation after each stock purchase or sale and also sends you a monthly statement depicting that month's transactions and a listing of your complete portfolio holdings.

When you register securities in street name, all of your dividends will be delivered to your broker, who will then credit them to your cash account. In addition, any reports, such as annual and quarterly reports, and proxies will be sent to your broker rather than to you. Your broker should forward those to you, but if he doesn't or if he forwards them to you long after receipt, you can solve that problem by calling the *investor relations* departments of the companies whose stock you own and ask them to add your name to their mailing list. That way, they'll send company literature directly to you.

Investor relations: A group of employees of a public company whose function is to act as a liaison between the company and the investment community, including shareholders, brokers, and analysts. Shareholders can call the investor-relations department of any public company to request company materials or to ask questions about the company.

When you open your brokerage account, your club should also open a cash account at the brokerage firm. When the treasurer collects your monthly contribution checks, she can deposit them into this account. Then, when the club purchases stock, the money can be transferred within the brokerage firm. When the club sells stock, the money can go directly to the cash account. That saves the treasurer from having to deposit checks into a bank account, then sending a check to the brokerage firm every time the club buys a stock, or from receiving a check that she has to deposit in a bank account every time you sell stock. Also, if the club buys a stock that pays a dividend, those dividends can be deposited into the account at the brokerage firm.

You've come a long way since you first decided to start an investment club. You've found members who are committed to the concept of an investment club, you've determined the structure of your club, created your partnership agreement and bylaws, and taken care of the money issues. Getting through those steps can be time consuming. The Lady Traders of Osceola Investment Club say accomplishing those steps took them the better part of a year. While it was more time-consuming than they had anticipated, they knew that if they took their time and made good decisions that it would pay off in the end. Three years later they have 25 members and have built a portfolio of 12 stocks.

Because people join an investment club to buy stocks, they can sometimes get anxious. They want to jump in and start building that portfolio before they've laid the groundwork of their club. Having enthusiasm is important, but your members also need to have patience. Without building a strong framework, the club will topple.

After you've taken the time to get your investment club structured and ready for operation, it's time to start looking for some stocks to buy.

Chapter

Learning the Ropes

S o far, we've been concentrating on structuring your investment club and getting all the documents in order. Once you have all that ground-work in place, you can start operating your club and begin focusing on one of the primary reasons you've done all this work—buying stocks. But first, let's discuss just what a stock is, where it comes from, and why it exists.

WHAT ARE STOCKS?

Stocks represent ownership—an investor's ownership of the company that issued the stock. When entrepreneurs first start their companies they get money from their own bank account or from friends or relatives, or they borrow it from banks. With loans and hard work, they struggle to survive.

After a company has been in operation for at least a few years, they become more stable and self-sufficient. They may be able to afford to oper-ate at their current size, but the entrepreneur wants to expand. While the company may be making a profit at this point, the money needed to fund an expansion can't be generated from those profits. Or maybe it's not an issue of expansion. Maybe the entrepreneur had deep pockets from the beginning and was able to build the company to a satisfactory size with his own money. But the entrepreneur has all his personal money in the operations of the company. If the company has a problem and fails, he'll lose everything. Therefore, he wants to get some of his personal money out of the company and invest it elsewhere.

When the entrepreneur decides to expand or to get some of his cash out of the company, he can go to a bank and borrow money. But maybe he just doesn't want to have debt to pay back. Maybe the bank won't give him the amount of money he wants, or the interest rate he wants, or the length of time he needs on the loan. So instead of taking on debt, he sells part of the company. He may sell 20 percent, 40 percent, or 60 percent; it depends on how much money he wants to raise. He does that by issuing shares and selling them to the public. Investors buy the initial shares through a brokerage firm and, after the shares are all sold, they start trading over a public exchange.

The price of the shares is then governed by supply and demand. The more people who think this company is a good investment and buy the stock, the higher the price will go. If you own the stock when the price increases, you have what's called a *paper profit*.

Paper profit: An investor's unrealized difference between the purchase price and the increased price of a company's stock.

You receive no real profit (money) until you sell the shares. If investors decide the company isn't a good investment, they'll sell the shares and the stock's price will decrease. If you own the shares when the price decreases, you have a *paper loss*.

Paper loss: An investor's unrealized difference between the purchase price and the decreased price of a company's stock.

Again, you don't have an actual loss until you sell the shares. When the shares trade on a public exchange, the entrepreneur doesn't receive any more money. He already sold that portion of his company and got his money. It's as if you had a car and sold it. When you sold it, you got the money the buyer paid for it. But when that person sells it, you get nothing because you already received your money.

CHOOSING A STOCK

Before your club can start buying stocks, you have to determine which stocks to buy. You do that by listening to the members' stock presentations at the monthly meetings, discussing the companies, and making a decision as to whether the majority of the members agree that a specific company is a good stock for your club to own. Doing that first stock presentation, however, can be very intimidating for most new investment club members. You can alleviate that fear by offering the members a little training in picking stocks. That can be accomplished by having the vice president of education arrange an educational meeting where a speaker can address this issue. Or you might provide the members with written information they can read at their own leisure. If your club is a member of NAIC, you may decide to purchase certain forms from them that will help you research companies. Learning how to find a stock for a stock presentation is the single most important step in achieving the second goal of an investment club: learning how to invest.

IDENTIFYING STOCKS TO BUY

There are more than 8,000 stocks available for purchase on the New York Stock Exchange and the NASDAQ combined. But it's your job to choose just one. Impossible? Not at all. There are several ways you can identify stocks that may be good investments. As always, everyone is ready to give you suggestions. You can find stock recommendations in newspapers and magazines, on TV and radio shows, from friends, relatives, or from your full-service stockbroker. Of course, many of these recommendations you may hear will be the "stock of the day." There always seems to be a stock that everyone is touting and that's extremely popular with investors. Many times, those stocks have already risen to such highs that they end up being bad investments rather than good ones. If you want to check out the most popular stock, however, you can certainly do that, but remember to remain somewhat skeptical.

Every year in its magazine, *Better Investing,* NAIC publishes a list of the 100 companies whose stocks are the most widely held by investment clubs in this country. While this list can provide you with lots of ideas as to which companies to research, NAIC certainly doesn't publish it as a list of companies whose stocks are necessarily good buys. Many of the investment clubs purchased these stocks years ago, have held on to them, and have seen their values rise tremendously. The growth prospects of those companies may not be as enticing now as they were years ago. That's why, if you're interested in a company on the list, it's always important to research it to be sure it's still at a price level that would warrant your club buying it. Just to give you an idea of what companies' stocks your fellow investment club members own, the top 10 companies whose stocks are the most widely held by investment clubs in this country as of April 2000 are listed below. Again, if you see a name that intrigues you, be sure to research the company prior to making a buy decision.

Company Name	Number of Clubs Holding this Stock
1. Intel Corporation	13,952
2. Lucent Technologies	12,350
3. The Home Depot	10,632
4. Cisco Systems	10,549
5. Merck & Co.	9,504
6. PepsiCo	9,155
7. Microsoft Corporation	7,661
8. AFLAC	7,158
9. Pfizer	7,049
10. McDonald's Corporation	6,198

Another source your members could use in finding stocks to research is investment newsletters. While some newsletters are designed to be theoretical and educational and offer only general information, others offer specific stock suggestions and even build model portfolios. Annual subscription prices can range from $30 to $1,000. Therefore, if you decide to subscribe to an investment newsletter, do a little research to ensure you're purchasing one that will fill your specific needs. Go to your public library and read through either *The Hulbert Financial Digest* or *The Hulbert Guide to Investment Newsletters,* two publications that review investment newsletters and provide an overview of the type of information each one offers. Before subscribing, request a sample copy to be sure the newsletter addresses the topics you want and is laid out and written in a language you understand.

Of course, you don't have to subscribe to an investment newsletter to come up with ideas for which stocks to purchase. In fact, it's easy for you to come up with those ideas by yourself. All you have to do is pay attention to your surroundings. That's how one woman found a stock that made her money. Her daily routine found her in her car driving the same route day after day. After a while, she noticed that one of the companies she passed every day was always spending money on improvements. They were constantly upgrading their landscaping and at one point they even doubled the size of their parking lot. It appeared to be a prosperous company so she did a little research, liked what she saw, and bought the company's stock. That stock was U.S. Surgical, and after this woman bought it, it tripled in price!

She found this stock just by paying attention to her surroundings. You can do that, too. When you go to the mall, is there one store that always seems to be excessively busy? Is there a product you use that you think is especially good? Are your children obsessed with a certain brand of clothing? Do you see a general trend in the economy, such as the aging of the population, which may point to a future boom in certain industries? Just by paying attention to your surroundings, you can identify trends and find good products that sell. Identifying those winning products is the first step in finding a good company and, therefore, a good stock to buy.

DOING THE RESEARCH

Of course, once you've identified what you believe is a good company, you have to do a little research to verify that it is indeed one you want to own. The first research step is obtaining written materials, such as the company's *annual and quarterly reports*, *10-K and 10-Q*, and *proxy*.

Annual and quarterly reports: Publications written by public companies to communicate to the investment community the company's operations for the past year or quarter.

10-K and 10-Q: Annual and quarterly financial reports a public company is required to file with the Securities and Exchange Commission.

Proxy: An invitation to a company's shareholders to attend the annual meeting. It explains what issues will be brought to a shareholder vote.

The quality of information contained in annual reports has improved during the last several years so that investors have become more comfortable with the information they find there. In fact, a survey regarding the sources of corporate information that investors trust the most was conducted by Research/Strategy/Management and Columbia University, commissioned by the Public Relations Society of America Foundation. In an article discussing the results of that survey, *Barron's* stated that out of 38 sources of information rated, corporate annual reports got the highest average score for overall credibility of investment information. Internet chat rooms received the lowest score, and while print journalism rated well, television business news ranked in the bottom third as being a reliable source. A company's annual report is a great starting point to learn about the company, its products, and services.

You can obtain an annual report and other publications directly from the company by calling its investor relations department or by visiting its web site. Or there are web sites where you can download those reports and other company information. Some of those sites are:

- ✔ www.nyse.com
- ✔ www.nasdaq.com
- ✔ www.sec.gov
- ✔ www.marketguide.com
- ✔ www.investorguide.com
- ✔ www.investorama.com
- ✔ www.freeedgar.com
- ✔ www.tenkwizard.com
- ✔ www.moneycentral.com
- ✔ www.smartmoney.com
- ✔ www.rapidresearch.com
- ✔ www.hoovers.com

When obtaining information from the Internet, be careful. There are a lot of hot stock tips available on the Internet that are extremely fraudulent. Message boards abound, even in reputable web sites. As the survey on the credibility of investment information pointed out, you can never rely on any information you find on an Internet message board. For your own safety, stick to the web sites that belong to the companies you're researching, to government agencies, or to reputable third parties that make corporate information available. NAIC's web site offers investors substantial research materials and educational information. Their web site address is www.better-investing.org.

When you've gotten all the information, read through it. Start with the annual report, which is a report the company publishes each year to tell the investment community how they performed during the past year. An annual report is typically divided into five segments.

1. *CEO's Letter to Shareholders:* This letter is a great opportunity for you to find out what plans the company's chief executive officer has in store for the company. In addition to talking a little bit about future plans, the letter will also discuss the company's past performance and any successes or failures the company had during the past year. The letter should be candid and offer potential investors insight into the company's past and future.

   A great way to determine if management follows through with the claims made in the CEO's letter to shareholders is to obtain previous years' annual reports. Read the CEO's letter and make a list of what he plans to do in following years. Then, read the next year's annual report to find out if those plans were actually executed. Follow that procedure for several years' worth of annual reports and you'll get a feel as to whether management has the ability to achieve the plans they create for the company.

2. *Business Segment Information:* This section will tell you exactly what the company does. You may think you're looking at a company that makes sweet rolls, pies, and cakes, but find out from the annual report that they also make panty hose and diapers. You'll also learn what percentage of the business each segment represents and how the company fares against its competitors.

3. *Management's Discussion and Analysis:* These are the pages that will tell you how the company has been performing from a financial point of view. Are revenues, profits, and expenses up or down? Is cash flow increasing or decreasing? Has debt skyrocketed or been

paid down? In this discussion, the past year's performance numbers will be compared to previous years.

4. *Financial Statements*: You'll find at least three financial statements in this report.

The *balance sheet* contains three primary sections: the company's assets (what it owns), liabilities (what it owes), and shareholders' equity (the difference between its assets and liabilities). This statement depicts what those numbers were at the end of the company's fiscal year and compares those numbers to one year earlier.

Balance sheet: A financial statement that looks at a company's financial status at a specific point in time, usually the last day of a quarter or fiscal year.

The *income statement* also contains three primary sections: the company's income (how much money the company took in), expenses (how much money it spent), and net income (how much it had left as profit). The statement covers a period of one year and compares the numbers to the previous year.

Income statement: A financial statement that uses income, expenses, and profit to describe how well the company performed during a specific period of time, usually one year or three months.

The *statement of changes in financial position* is a rehash of the numbers that appear on the other two statements. By rearranging the numbers, this statement tells you how much cash the company had at the beginning of the year and at the end of the year. It also explains how cash was used and where additional cash came from.

Statement of changes in financial position: Also called a cash-flow statement, it explains the difference in the amount of cash and cash equivalents the company had at the beginning and end of the year.

5. *Footnotes:* These are found at the end of the financial statements and can include information that isn't found in other areas of the annual report, such as insurance losses, accounting changes, or lawsuits pending against the company.

Footnotes: The section of the annual report that supports and explains the information found in the financial statements.

At the end of the footnotes is one more piece of information that you can take a quick glance at to determine if there are problems with this company. That's the *auditor's opinion.*

Auditor's opinion: Outside accountants' opinion as to whether the statements present fairly the financial position of the company and if the results of operations are in conformity with generally accepted accounting principles.

There are four types of auditor's opinion:

✔ The unqualified opinion is the most common. You can recognize it by the words, "the financial statements present fairly the financial position of the company and the results of its operations are in conformity with generally accepted accounting principles." While that doesn't mean the company's stock is a good investment, it does tell you that the numbers have been reported in accordance with proper accounting standards.

✔ The qualified opinion can be recognized by the words, "subject to the resolution of" or "the statements are consistent except for." That means the auditors were dissatisfied with one piece of information in the statements. You might want to find out what that piece of information is by reading the annual report or by calling the company's investor relations department and find out if it could have a major impact on the company's future.

✔ The disclaimer opinion can be recognized by the words "unable to express an opinion." Auditors will issue this type of opinion if, for some reason, they couldn't verify the company's numbers. If the auditors can't verify the numbers, you probably don't want to depend on the information included in those financial statements.

✔ The adverse opinion can be recognized by the words "do not present fairly." This means the auditors didn't think the numbers in the statements depicted the company's actual performance. This is not a company whose stock you want to own.

Chances are the only opinion you'll ever find in an annual report will be the unqualified opinion. Typically, if the auditors have a problem with the reporting of any information, they'll discuss it with the company and management will fix the problem so that the information does conform to generally accepted accounting principles. The auditors will usually work with management so that they can give the company an unqualified opinion. If, however, you do find one of the other three types of opinions, you might want to call the company and find out why, or toss out that company's reports and find another one to research.

After you've read through all the verbiage in this report, set it to the side and we'll come back to it later to look at the financial statements.

Now read the company's quarterly reports. Because annual reports are published only once a year, companies issue quarterly reports every three months just as an update as to what they are doing. These reports are short and usually contain just a letter and the three financial statements.

The 10-K and 10-Qs will include almost the same information you found in the annual and quarterly reports, but these reports won't be as pretty—no glossy paper, colorful pictures, or fancy charts. While the company uses its annual and quarterly reports as marketing tools to try to get investors to buy their stock, the 10-K and 10-Qs are reports that the company is required to file with the SEC—no need to be slick with them! Even though most of the information is the same, it doesn't hurt to quickly scan these reports. You may find revealing information that wasn't in the glossy version.

The final report is the proxy. This is the report the company sends to its shareholders when inviting them to attend the company's *annual meeting* and to vote on certain issues.

Annual meeting: A once-a-year meeting of a public company's shareholders, at which management presents an overview of the company's past year and discusses future plans.

You'll find a lot of good information here. The proxy is required to include a performance chart, which compares the company's performance against its peers and certain indices, such as the S&P 500. In addition, the proxy includes short bios and the salary levels of top executives. If you see that management personnel are earning gigantic salaries but the company's performance is far below its peers, you might want to find out why. Review how management is paid. The most positive situation for investors is that management people are paid modest salaries with big bonuses that are tied to performance.

The proxy will also tell you how many shares of the company's stock management and the directors each own. If they own none of the company's stock, that's not a good sign. If they think their company's stock is such a great investment for you, why don't they invest in it themselves? If they do own shares, that means they have a financial stake in the company's performance and will be committed to doing what's best for the company. The percentage amount the executives own will be very different for different size companies. Management and directors who own 1 percent of General Motors have a much larger financial exposure than the management and directors who own a 10 percent stake of a small company. Look at the size of the company and be sure that management has a substantial holding of its own stock.

When you've finished reading through all of the company's materials, you're going to have a pretty good idea as to what this company is. You'll know what their primary business is and what products or services they offer. You'll have a feel for who their competition is and whether this company has competitive advantages or disadvantages. You'll know what share of the market they have, who their customers are, how they distribute their products, and what their plans are for the future. From reading the verbiage in the reports, you'll have a little information about the company's financial performance, but you need to do an analysis of the company's past performance, which will help you predict their future performance..

There are two types of analysis that can be used when analyzing a company's financial performance and trying to determine how that company's stock price will perform in the future. One option is *technical analysis*.

Technical analysis: Identifying trends and predicting a stock's price movement through the study of its volume and price in the marketplace.

In doing this type of analysis, you study the stock's volume and past price and try to predict how the market and the stock's price will move in the future. Technical analysis is based on the assumption that stock prices and the stock market, in general, follow certain patterns. If those patterns can be identified, you can determine the future direction of the stock's price and the market as a whole.

For instance, one of the less complicated theories used in technical analysis is the *advance-decline theory*.

Advance-decline theory: Theory used in technical analysis to determine the general trend of the stock market by comparing stocks that are increasing in price to those that are decreasing in price.

This theory looks at the total number of stocks that trade during one day on a specific exchange, such as the New York Stock Exchange or NASDAQ. It then compares how many of those stocks increased in price from the day before and how many of those stocks decreased in price from the day before and computes the difference. By calculating these numbers on an ongoing basis, technical analysts try to determine a pattern and, therefore, the direction of the market. If, over a period of time, there are more stocks whose prices are advancing, then it's considered a *bull market*. If there are more stocks whose prices are declining, it's considered a *bear market*.

Bull market: A market in which stock prices are increasing or are already very high.

Bear market: A market in which stock prices are declining or are already very low.

Of course, that tells you absolutely nothing about a specific company's stock to help you evaluate it for your presentation to your club.

Technical analysis looks at the market as a whole to predict trends, rather than at individual companies. It involves dealing with lots of charts and computer programs and is usually used by professional analysts. Many experts in the investment community believe this type of analysis simply does not work.

The other type of analysis, which tends to be easier to understand and, frankly, more realistic to most people, is *fundamental analysis.*

Fundamental analysis: Predicting the future movements of a stock based on an analysis of the company's financial statements, past performance, and current strategies.

In fundamental analysis, we look at the fundamentals of the company. That means we're going to analyze the company's financial statements to help us determine their future earnings and dividends. Fundamental analysis focuses on issues such as earnings, cash flow, return on equity, and even the industry in which the company operates to determine whether the company's true valuation is reflected in its stock price. That information suggests just how well the company, and its stock price, will do in the future. Fundamental analysis will help us identify stocks that are undervalued and that will, hopefully, increase in price.

Since we're not professional analysts, it's best that we stick to fundamental analysis. Of course, we're not going to do a full-blown fundamental analysis like a professional security analyst would do, but we can at least learn some of the basic ratios that you can calculate to help determine the future of the company's stock.

It used to be that if you wanted to know what these ratios were for a specific company, you had to calculate them yourself. That's not the case anymore. You can now easily find these ratios already calculated for you in the company's annual reports, in several third-party reports, and on a multitude of investment-research web sites. In fact, most annual reports have charts that track the most important performance numbers and ratios over a 10-year period. These charts are invaluable in spotting trends or discovering blips in a company's past. It's easy to look at the chart and determine whether key numbers, such as sales and net income, have been increasing each year. Despite having most of the ratios already calculated, it's good to know how the calculations were done so that you have a better feel for what the numbers mean and where they came from.

Let's start with ratios that are calculated from the balance sheet. The balance sheet is the financial statement that depicts where the company stood, financially, on a specific day. In the case of the annual report, that specific day is the end of the company's fiscal year. For the majority of companies, that's December 31.

Current Ratio

Current assets divided by current liabilities

The *current ratio* is a measure of a company's liquidity.

Current ratio: A ratio that determines how many times a company's current liabilities could be paid with its current assets.

It is calculated by dividing the company's current assets by its current liabilities. The result of that calculation tells you how many times the company could pay off its liabilities that will come due during the next year if it converted all its liquid assets to cash. A current ratio of less than 1.5 to 1 may mean the company could run out of cash and have a problem continuing to operate. It's important to compare this number to other companies in the same industry to get a feel as to whether the company's current ratio is in line, because a good current ratio can vary from one industry to another. Industries in which companies have small inventories and easily collectible accounts receivable can safely operate with a lower current ratio than companies that have a greater proportion of their current assets in inventory and sell their products on credit. The higher a company's current ratio, the better—to a point. If a company has so much cash lying around that it has an extremely high current ratio, management needs to put that cash to better use—spend some of it on research and development or expansion.

Working Capital

Current assets minus current liabilities

The *working capital* ratio is calculated by using the same numbers as the current ratio. It is current assets minus current liabilities.

Working capital: Ratio that depicts a company's available liquidity.

This ratio tells you how much cash or cash equivalents the company would have left free and clear if it paid off all its current debts with its current assets. A company needs to have sufficient funds at its disposal in case financial problems should occur. If a company is growing, its working-capital number will be higher this year than it was the previous year.

Debt-to-Equity Ratio

Total debt divided by shareholders' equity

With the *debt to equity ratio*, we're looking at how much total debt the company has relative to its shareholders' equity.

> **Debt-to-equity ratio:** A ratio that measures leverage by comparing a company's total debt to its shareholders' equity.

To calculate this number, divide the company's total debt (short and long term) by its shareholders' equity. The lower the number, the stronger the company. If a company has a high debt-to-equity ratio, that debt and its interest payments may inhibit the company from growing. If they already have too much debt, they won't be able to borrow more money if they need it for expansion or to sustain them through difficult economic periods.

Once again, there's not one number that you can identify as being the best debt-to-equity ratio because it depends on the industry. If the company is in an industry that's very capital intensive because they have to buy huge pieces of machinery or build gigantic manufacturing plants, they'll have a higher debt-to-equity ratio. But companies that don't have to make big capital outlays to do business, such as consulting firms or temporary personnel agencies, should have smaller debt-to-equity ratios. Therefore, when judging this number, it's important to compare it to other companies in the same industry.

Let's now look at the ratios we can calculate from the income statement, the document that shows us the company's income, expenses, and profit.

Earnings Per Share (EPS)

Net income divided by number of shares outstanding

Earnings per share tells you how much money the company made in earnings during the year on a per-share basis.

Earnings per share {EPS}: A measure of how much money a company made during a specified period of time on a per-share basis.

It's calculated by dividing the company's earnings (also called net income or profits) for the year by the number of shares outstanding. The number represents how much money the company had left on a per-share basis after it paid all its expenses. This is money the company can use for funding expansion, conducting research and development, or even paying dividends to its shareholders.

Companies' EPS numbers are widely reported in the press and can seriously affect a company's stock price. Prior to the company releasing its annual EPS number, security analysts who follow the company make an estimate as to what they believe the number will be. The analysts offer their predictions and finally narrow it down to what's called a *consensus number.*

Consensus number: The number that a group of analysts agrees to as their projection for a specific public company's earnings per share for a specific period of time.

That consensus number is the one that's reported in the media as to what the analysts expect for a company's EPS number.

Companies, however, never make projections as to their EPS numbers—only the analysts do. When the company releases its number, if it is above the analysts' estimates, their stock price may soar. If it's below, their stock price may plummet. Companies' stock prices have been known to drop several points in a day simply because the company missed the analysts' projections by one penny.

Then, there's what is called the *whisper number.*

Whisper number: The earnings-per-share number an analyst really wants a company to report, despite the analyst's prediction of a lower number.

The analysts may announce a consensus number of $1.67 per share for a company, but as an aside or (as the name implies) in a whisper, add, "but they better come in at $1.69." If the company hits the $1.67 mark, their stock price may still drop because they didn't hit the whisper number. In addition to the consensus number being reported in the press, the whisper number is also usually reported. And, of course, where there's a need for information, there's a web site that supplies it. The web site where investors can find the most recent consensus and whisper numbers for most public companies is www.whispernumber.com.

Earnings per share is obviously an important number. Steadily increasing earnings are a sign of good management and should drive the price of the stock steadily upwards. If earnings increase one year, decrease the next, then remain stagnant, management is having a problem with consistency. Look for the consistency of earnings over a five- to 10-year period. If a company's number of outstanding shares has remained the same, steady increases in EPS depict growth and a potentially rising stock price. Decreases in this number may be the result of decreasing sales or increasing expenses, which could result in a stock price drop. If you see that there are major changes in the number from one year to the next, find out why.

Price/Earnings Ratio (P/E)

Price per share divided by earnings per share

The *price/earnings ratio* tells you how much an investor is paying for every dollar of earnings the company makes.

Price/earnings ratio: A ratio that depicts how many times a company's annual earnings per share a stock is selling for in the marketplace.

For example, if a company has a P/E ratio of 15, that means that the company's stock price is 15 times its earnings per share. P/E is calculated by dividing the company's per-share stock price by its earnings per share. If a company has a high P/E ratio, it's considered expensive because you're paying a high price for the amount of profit the company is making. A low P/E ratio indicates the stock is cheap.

But what is expensive and what is cheap? By looking at the P/E ratio, you'll get a better feel as to the value of a stock than by looking at its price.

Let's say company A and company B are in the same industry, but company A's stock sells for $20 per share and sports a P/E of 45. Company B's stock sells for $70 per share and has a P/E of 12. Despite company A's price being lower, it's still the more expensive stock of the two. That's because for you to purchase the $20 stock of company A, you have to pay 45 times more than what that company is earning on a per-share basis. But you can buy the $70 stock of company B for only 12 times what the company is earning. With the $70 stock of company B, you're paying a lower amount for each dollar's worth of earnings.

The average P/E ratio for the S&P 500 has changed over time and has ranged from as low as six to as high as 34. Currently, the S&P 500 average P/E ratio is about 31. But if you look at stocks of companies that are in different industries, you can't really tell if one stock is cheaper or more expensive by the P/E ratio. That's because every industry is different. The high-tech industry tends to have P/Es that are higher than the average of the S&P 500, whereas the financial-services industry tends to have much lower P/Es. Companies that are in their infancy also tend to have higher P/E ratios than older, more mature companies because new companies are expected to grow quickly and mature. Also, investors are willing to pay a higher price for a stock when they believe that company has a higher potential of generating a much greater level of profits in the future.

When looking at P/E ratios, you need to compare the ratio of the company you're researching with that of other companies in the same industry. If you're researching a bank stock and find the P/E ratio to be 22, but the other bank stocks you look at sport P/E ratios between 10 and 12, you need to question why the one you're considering is so high. Why are investors willing to pay 22 times this bank's earnings per share to own it while they're only willing to pay 10 or 12 times earnings per share for other banks?

The answer to that question is that investors may believe that the bank with the 22 P/E ratio has greater potential for future earnings. For some reason, they're expecting the bank to increase its earnings dramatically, which would result in a lowering of the P/E ratio that would be more in line with other banks. However, if that increase in profits doesn't materialize, chances are the stock price will tumble, bringing the bank's P/E ratio in line with other banks. When looking at P/E ratios, always compare the P/E of the company you're researching with that of other companies in the same industry.

Return on Equity

Net income divided by shareholders' equity

Return on equity tells us how the company is performing by telling us what our return on investment is.

Return on equity: A ratio that shows what percentage return a company is realizing on its net worth.

If we purchase a certificate of deposit that pays 6 percent interest with no compounding, our return on investment is 6 percent. To calculate this same number for a company's stock, divide the company's net income by the shareholders' equity. If return on investment is less than the current interest rate, the company isn't performing very well. In fact, management could liquidate the company, invest the money in certificates of deposit, and be better off financially. And they wouldn't have to be working at running a company every day! The number should be significantly higher than current interest rates. Again, you need to look at this number over a period of five to 10 years and also compare it to other companies in the same industry.

Dividend Yield

Dividend per share divided by price per share

Because an investment club buys growth stocks, the majority of the companies in its portfolio will probably not pay a dividend. Stocks that pay large dividends are considered income stocks, not growth stocks. But some growth stocks do pay small dividends and, if someone is offering even a 2 percent *dividend yield* on your investment, it's a nice little bonus.

Dividend yield: This number is the percentage return that the company's dividend represents relative to its current price.

The dividend yield tells you the return you're getting, from the dividend payment only, on your stock at its current price. The dividend yield on stocks can be found in newspaper listings, but understanding the numbers behind the calculation can be helpful.

While these are all good ratios and statistics that can help you determine whether a company's stock is a good buy, the list is not all-inclusive. You could spend hours with calculator in hand crunching numbers, if you want. But too much information can be confusing. It makes more sense to focus in on a few key ratios.

By this time, you probably have a pretty good feel as to whether you like this company. So far, however, the company's management has written every document you've read about the company. In fact, many of the reports you've read are used by the company as marketing tools to try to get investors to buy their stock. Obviously, the company wants to put on its best face in these reports. Therefore, the information will be somewhat slanted toward the positive. When reading corporate reports, be sure to read between the lines. They may state that they reduced costs by cutting their work staff by one-fifth. Reduced costs are great, but will the other four-fifths of the staff still be able to handle the workload? And if so, why did the company have such a large staff to begin with?

You can clarify some of these questions by including in your research documents that have been published by third parties. Many brokerage firms have analysts on staff who follow various industries and write reports on companies within those industries. If you're using a brokerage firm that has staff analysts, you can ask your broker for copies of these analysts' reports that are written about the companies you're researching. Even with these reports, however, you have to be careful.

Sometimes a brokerage firm can have a conflict of interest with a client. Let's say that ABC Brokerage Firm has a division that does investment banking and helps to bring companies public. Claudia Cake Corporation hires ABC Brokerage Firm to help them do their IPO by pricing their initial shares and selling them during the subscription process. Claudia Cake Corporation is now a customer of ABC Brokerage Firm and, hopefully, they'll get more business from them in the future when they do secondary offerings.

After the IPO, the stock is selling in the marketplace and ABC Brokerage Firm's analyst decides to write an analyst report on the company so the firm can hand it out to their clients. But the analyst finds that Claudia Cake Corporation isn't doing very well. Sales and earnings are down and they just lost a big contract with one of their longtime customers. But the analyst knows that if he says anything very negative in his report, the management of Claudia Cake Corporation won't be very happy because the report could cause the price of their stock to go down. In fact, company management may be so upset that when they have more investment-banking business, they may not use ABC Brokerage Firm. Of course, the brokerage firm doesn't want to lose that business. So maybe the analyst will try to make the report a little more positive than he should.

Another reason the analyst doesn't want to upset company management is because the company may cut off his information flow. Analysts get a lot of information about companies directly from management. They talk to them on the phone, have personal meetings with them, and attend analyst meetings the company sponsors. But if an analyst writes a negative report about a company, management may never be willing to give that analyst any information again. An analyst without direct communication to companies can't do his job.

When an analyst writes a report on a company, he makes recommendations as to whether investors should buy or sell the company's stock. Some analysts have so much power that as soon as they issue a report on a company, that company's stock reacts. A negative report can drive a company's stock price down.

If you review analyst reports, you'll discover that you almost never see a sell recommendation. The analysts have adopted all sorts of terms they use, such as accumulate or hold, but sell isn't in their vocabulary very often. They've learned to walk a very fine line in an effort to keep the companies happy, but yet offer investors information that's useful. But the pressure brought on an analyst by the companies he covers can be severe.

One blatant example is that of Marvin Roffman, a food and gaming analyst with Janney Montgomery Scott. On March 20, 1990, Roffman was quoted by the *Wall Street Journal* as saying that he was pessimistic about the future of Donald Trump's Taj Mahal casino in Atlantic City. Trump was livid about the comment. He threatened to sue the brokerage firm unless it agreed to fire Roffman or force him to issue a public apology.

Roffman issued the apology, but Trump still wasn't happy. He insisted that some specific points be added to the apology. Roffman not only refused, but he publicly retracted his apology. The next day he was fired. In retaliation, Roffman sued Trump for $2 million plus punitive damages for defamation and interfering with his employment contract. He received an undisclosed settlement.

Analysts can have a lot of pressure placed on them to write positive analyst reports. Some stick to their guns, others crumble. It's been reported in the press that some analysts even admit to having a two-tiered rating system for the companies they cover. They keep a buy rating on a company's stock and report that to the general public, then tell their favorite investors to sell the stock. The group that is told to sell is kept fairly small to prevent word from getting back to the company that's being rated.

While an analyst's report can be helpful to you in your research, you have to analyze the report somewhat to determine whether you believe the information is valid. When reviewing a brokerage-firm analyst's report, try to decide whether the logic the analyst has used in reaching his conclusions is correct. Weigh the advice the analyst gives and combine that advice with the information you've gleaned from the company's annual report and other documents. Never rely on one piece of information or one recommendation.

Another type of research report investors can utilize when researching companies is that written by analysts who work for companies such as Value

Line and Standard & Poor's. The analysts at these companies analyze public companies and write reports as to their thoughts on the past performance and the future of the company and how it compares to others in the same industry. These companies have no reason to slant the information they report to either the positive or the negative side because they have no other relationship with the companies they're analyzing that would cause a conflict of interest. Therefore, it's always important to include these types of reports in your research. Most public libraries carry both the Value Line and the Standard & Poor's reports.

Figures 6-1 and 6-2 show examples of both publications for the Walgreen Company.

The Value Line report is a one-page synopsis of the company. The analysts who write these reports typically specialize in one industry and follow several companies in that industry. Some of the report information is based on the analyst's judgment. Other portions of the report are historical data.

The information that is based on the analyst's judgment includes the three-year projections as to price and annual total return. The analyst who wrote the above report projects that the high and low prices for Walgreen Company during the period 2002 to 2004 will be $35 and $25, with an annual total return ranging from a loss of 4 percent to a gain of 4 percent. Those numbers were determined by an economic model based on the analyst's estimates about the company's future, its industry, and certain company characteristics. Other numbers that are in italics—such as the annual rates of change, including earnings per share, and dividends per share predicted for future years and future-year estimates—that appear in the chart in the middle of the page are also projections. The write-up at the bottom of the page is based on the analyst's opinion he has formed after researching the company.

In the bottom right-hand corner of the report are four measurements that Value Line includes in each report. The first is a rating of the company's financial strength. The highest rating is an A++ and the lowest rating is C. Also included is a rating of the stock's price stability, which is measured on a scale of 100 to zero. The third measurement is the company's price growth persistence, again rated on a scale of 100 to zero. And, finally, it includes an earnings-predictability rating, which is also based on a scale of 100 to zero. On some reports you'll find the rating to be "nmf," which means that there is no mentionable figure available.

The Standard & Poor's report for Walgreen Company appears in Figure 6-2.

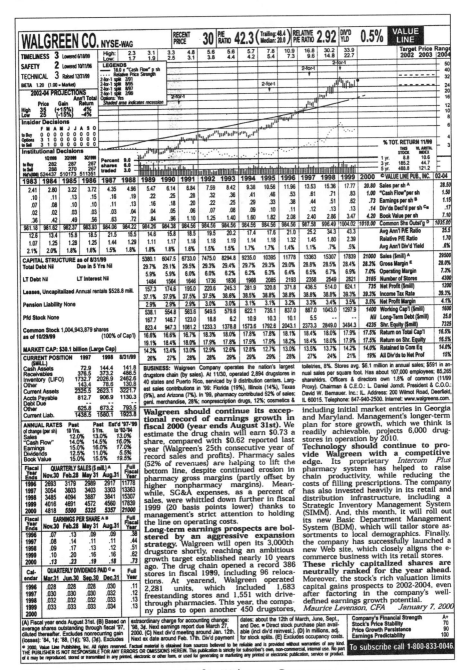

Figure 6-1: Value Line Report for Walgreen Company
Copyright: The Value Line Investment Survey

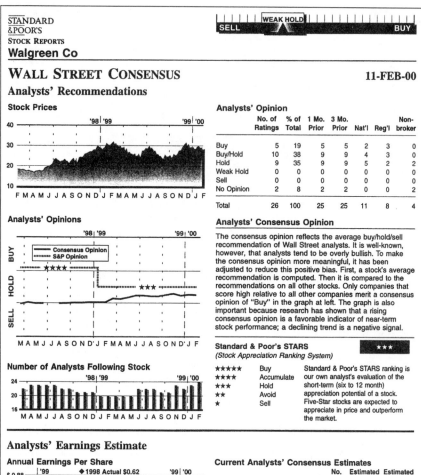

Figure 6-2: Standard & Poor's Report for Walgreen Company *(continued)*
Source: Standard & Poor's

STANDARD
&POOR'S
STOCK REPORTS

Walgreen Co.

12-FEB-00

INDUSTRY OUTLOOK

The S&P Retail Drug index fell 25.1% in 1999, versus an increase of 18.8% in the S&P Super 1500. Early in 1999, the retail drug chains were hurt by the threat of increased competition by a host of Internet start-up drug sites. While this concern ultimately subsided as many of the Internet drug sites were acquired by retail chains and pharmacy benefit managers (PBMs), the industry has continued to languish. More recently, the drug chains have been pressured over concerns whether an Internet pharmacy order belongs to the retail drug chain where the order originated or the PBM. While we believe these concerns are overblown, it is likely that it may take a few months before momentum flows back into the group. Also potentially damaging to the industry, we see a push by supermarket chains into the pharmacy business as a concern in the long term. As a result of these factors, we believe the drug chain industry will continue to underperform the market in the next year.

Longer-term prospects will continue to be buoyed by: consumers' fundamental interest in health and personal care; an aging population; the higher number of drugs coming off patent to more readily available over-the-counter (OTC) status; and an increasing use of drug ther-

apies versus hospitalization. The demographics of an aging society indicate prescription usage increases. Pharmacy margin pressure is stabilizing as some of the larger chains have refused to participate in unprofitable third party plans.

Competition will remain intense as more retail segments recognize the customer draw and profitability of pharmacy sales. Supermarkets and discount store operators have added pharmacies and beefed up their assortments of health and beauty aids departments (H&BA). The combination of sharper pricing by the competition, increased low-margin, third-party payment plans, and lower drug-price inflation is forcing chains to focus on generating more aggressive growth in their core businesses and finding ways to broaden into specialized areas. Since the challenges imposed by these competitors will intensify, the industry is fashioning a more proprietary identity that is based on comprehensive selections of basic H&BA items, OTC products, and in-and-out shopping convenience. Also, capital investments in technology and distribution efficiencies to keep costs in line have become a priority.

Industry Stock Performance
Related S&P 1500 Industry Index

Retail (Drug Stores)

Month-end Price Performance As of 01/31/00

INDUSTRY: RETAIL (DRUG STORES)
*PEER GROUP: DRUG STORES

Peer Group	Stock Symbol	Recent Stock Price	P/E Ratio	12-mth. Trail. EPS	30-day Price Chg %	1-year Price Chg. %	Beta	Yield %	Quality Ranking	Stk. Mkt. Cap. (mil. $)	Ret. on Equity %	Pretax Margin %	LTD to Cap. %
Walgreen Co.	WAG	29⅝	46	0.65	-2%	-4%	0.97	0.5	A+	29,810	19.7	5.8	Nil
CVS Corp.	CVS	39⅝	26	1.55	5%	-25%	0.91	0.6	B-	15,528	15.6	4.7	8.2
Drug Emporium	DEMP	4⅛	NM	-0.58	-1%	-35%	0.40	Nil	B-	54	7.1	0.8	47.5
Duane Reade	DRD	27½	12	2.26	21%	-16%	NA	Nil	NR	473	NM	3.2	93.0
Horizon Pharmacies	HZP	6¼	NM	-0.55	83%	-39%	NA	Nil	NR	36	NM	NM	39.8
Longs Drug Stores	LDG	20¾	12	1.76	-18%	-45%	0.27	2.7	B+	814	10.3	3.2	2.1
Phar-Mor Inc	PMOR	3½	NM	NA	38%	-47%	NA	Nil	NR	43	NM	0.5	NA
Rite Aid	RAD	7¼	10	0.73	-7%	-84%	1.06	6.4	B+	1,861	4.9	1.6	51.8

Figure 6-2: Standard & Poor's Report for Walgreen Company *(continued)*
Source: Standard & Poor's

STANDARD
&POOR'S
STOCK REPORTS

Walgreen Co.

11-FEB-00

NEWS HEADLINES

■ **01/03/00**   NEW YORK (Standard & Poor's)--Jan 3, 2000, WALGREEN CO., announced 1Q EPS $0.13 vs. $0.10. Results are adjtd. for Jan. '99 2-for-1 stk. split.

■ **11/22/99**   UP 1 3/4 to 29 3/8... Merrill upgrades to near term accumulate from neutral... Co. unavailable...

■ **11/22/99**   1:45 pm... WALGREEN (WAG 29-1/8) UP 1-3/8, MERRILL UPGRADES TO NEAR TERM ACCUMULATE FROM NEUTRAL... Analyst Mark Husson tells salesforce views hiatus in stock price performance since Feb. as aberration... Now believes that steady march up hill of outperformance can resume... Comfortable that WAG has won war with pharmacy benefit mgmt cos. over Internet scripts... Adds WAG's Internet volume continues to grow, is now at over $20M/year run rate on prescriptions alone, amongst leaders of .com pack... Notes market pays large premiums for strong mgmt, clean numbers, finl conservatism, consistent EPS growth - matrix of which WAG is king./J.Freund

■ **10/05/99**   NEW YORK (Standard & Poor's)--Oct 4, 1999, WALGREEN CO., announced 4Q EPS $0.16 vs. $0.15 and annual EPS $0.62 vs, $0.54. Results are adjusted for Jan. '99 2-for-1 stock split. Results exclude loss of $0.03 from acctg. change related to the cost of business process reengineering activities. Results for 4Q '98 incl. charge of $14.1M from LIFO provision and after-tax gain of $22.9M or $0.02 per share from the sale of the company's 14 long-term care pharmacy facilities.

■ **10/04/99**   10:30 am... STILL HOLD WALGREEN CO. (WAG 25***)... FY Q4 EPS $0.16 vs. $0.13, in-line with S&P guidance... Revenues up 18.7%,

boosted by 20% increase in pharmacy comparable sales, 13% same store sales jump, addition of new units and relocation of units... In future, WAG should benefit from improvement in third party pharmacy margins, improved overhead leverage and 450 planned unit openings in FY 00 (Aug.)... Still see $0.75 in FY 00... Although strong performer, WAG not cheap at 49X expected $0.51 free cash flow and 33X our expected FY 00 EPS estimate. /R.Izmirlian

■ **06/28/99**   10:50 am... STILL HOLD WALGREEN CO. (WAG 29***)... FY Q3 EPS $0.16 vs. $0.13, $0.01 above our estimate, aided by better gross margins than expected... Revenues up 18%, boosted by 20.2% increase in pharmacy comparable sales, 12.3% same-store sales jump, addition of 268 new units or relocated units... Going forward, WAG should benefit from improvement in health plan pharmacy margins and increase in planned FY 00 (Aug.) openings to 450 units... Boosting our FY 99 and FY 00 EPS $0.02 and $0.05, respectively, to $0.62 and $0.75... Although strong performer, WAG not cheap at 57 times expected $0.51 FY 00 free cash flow. / R.Izmirlian

■ **06/28/99**   June 28, 1999, Walgreen Co., announced May '99 3Q EPS, $0.16 vs $0.13 and 9 mos. EPS, $0.46 vs $0.39 . Results for 9 mos. '98 exclude charge of $0.03 per share from the cumulative effect of an accounting change. Results adjtd. Jan. '99 for 2-for-1 stk. split.

■ **05/20/99**   UP 3/4 to 26 3/8... Merrill upgrades to near term accumulate from neutral... Co. notes Merrill comments...

■ **05/20/99**   12:00 pm... WALGREEN

(WAG 26-5/8) UP 1, MERRILL UPGRADES TO NEAR TERM ACCUMULATE FROM NEUTRAL... Analyst Mark Husson tells salesforce while all 3 drug retailers have similar comps, EPS growth potential, believes WAG stands head and shoulders above peers in capital management... Notes co.'s 19% return on investment gives him confidence its stepped up capex program will allow it to generate mid- to high-teens EPS increases for medium term... Says co. has highest inventory yield in sector, enjoyed 2 years of steady improvements while peers experienced declines... Notes shares off 30% from their highs... Sees $0.60 FY 99 (Aug) EPS, $0.70 FY 00... Has $30 target./B.Brodie

■ **03/29/99**   1:20 pm... STILL HOLD WALGREEN CO. (WAG 29***)... Q2 FY 99 EPS $0.20 vs. $0.17, in line with S&P estimate... Revenues up 14.6%, boosted by 18.4% increase in pharmacy comparable sales, 9.4% same store sales jump, addition 80 new units... Q2 was first time since 1994 gross margins were stable year-over-year... suggests gross margin deterioration from third party sales waning... See 17% EPS growth in FY 99 (Aug.) due to new stores, further SG&A leverage and stabilization of gross margins... Despite continued solid performance, more than adequately valued with P/E of 50, EPS growth rate of 16%-17%. /R.Izmirlian

■ **03/29/99**   March 29, 1999, Walgreen Co., announced Feb. '99 3 mos. EPS of $0.20 vs $0.17 and 6 mos. EPS of $0.30 vs $0.26 for same period a year ago. Results are as reported adjusted for Feb. '99 2-for-1 stock split. Results for 6 mos. period of 1997 excls. charge of $0.03 per sh. from acctg. change.

Figure 6-2: Standard & Poor's Report for Walgreen Company *(continued)*
Source: Standard & Poor's

STANDARD & POOR'S STOCK REPORTS

Walgreen Co.

12-FEB-00

Business Summary - 06-JAN-00

Walgreen (WAG) has a long history of financial success: the company has gained prescription market share in all but one of its 50 leading markets within the past five years. In FY 99 (Aug.), Chicago-based WAG, the largest U.S. retail drug store chain in terms of revenues and profitability, posted its 26th consecutive year of record sales and earnings. Sales increased 17% in FY 99, to $17.8 billion. Earnings before special items advanced 22%, to $624 million.

In 1909, the company's founder, Charles Rudolph Walgreen Sr., purchased one of the busiest drug stores on Chicago's South Side, and transformed it by constructing an ice cream fountain that featured his own brand of ice cream. The ice cream fountain was the forerunner of the famous Walgreen's soda fountain, which became the main attraction for customers from the 1920s through the 1950s. People lined up to buy a product that WAG invented in the early 1920s: the milkshake.

The company has long resisted the merger fever that has spread through the drug store industry. Instead, WAG has stressed internal growth strategies: large-scale infiltration of new markets, and relocations of units to free-standing stores; and convenience, including 24-hour operations and drive-through pharmacy service.

At August 31, 1999, WAG operated 2,821 drug stores in 39 states and Puerto Rico, with large concentrations of stores in Florida, Illinois and Texas. Internally, the company is growing faster than any other drug store chain. It opened 386 new or relocated drug stores during FY 99, while closing 114 units. All new stores are freestanding buildings located at major intersections, as opposed to shopping centers and strip malls. Within the past five years, approximately 60% of WAG's stores have been opened or remodeled, and more than 50% offer drive-through prescription service. WAG plans to open 450 units in FY 00, with a goal of a total of 6,000 stores by FY 10.

Pharmacy sales account for about 52% of total sales. The company, which was already a leading dispenser of prescriptions in the U.S., boosted pharmacy sales 23% in FY 99 (with a gain of 19% for comparable drugs).

Recent technological advances include satellite linkage to all stores and facilities, point-of-sale scanning and implementation of the strategic inventory management system (SIMS), uniting all elements of the purchasing, distribution and sales cycle. This will reduce inventory, improve in-stock positions and provide quicker reaction to sales trends. The Intercom on-line pharmacy system links all stores with headquarters and one another.

Healthcare Plus, WAG's pharmacy mail-order subsidiary, offers sales, marketing and operational support for third-party retail and mail-order prescriptions through two facilities. The company has also formed a pharmacy benefits manager, WHP Health Initiatives, targeting small to medium-size employers and HMOs.

Per Share Data ($) (Year Ended Aug. 31)	1999	1998	1997	1996	1995	1994	1993	1992	1991	1990
Tangible Bk. Val.	3.47	2.86	2.40	2.08	1.82	1.60	1.40	1.25	1.10	0.96
Cash Flow	0.82	0.72	0.60	0.52	0.46	0.41	0.35	0.32	0.28	0.25
Earnings	0.62	0.54	0.44	0.38	0.33	0.28	0.25	0.22	0.20	0.18
Dividends	0.13	0.13	0.12	0.11	0.10	0.09	0.08	0.07	0.06	0.05
Payout Ratio	21%	23%	27%	29%	30%	30%	30%	29%	29%	28%
Prices - High	$33\frac{7}{8}$	$30\frac{1}{4}$	$16\frac{7}{8}$	$10\frac{7}{8}$	$7\frac{7}{8}$	$5\frac{3}{4}$	$5\frac{5}{8}$	$5\frac{5}{8}$	$4\frac{7}{8}$	$3\frac{3}{8}$
- Low	$22\frac{5}{8}$	$14\frac{3}{4}$	$9\frac{5}{8}$	$7\frac{1}{4}$	$5\frac{3}{8}$	$4\frac{1}{4}$	$4\frac{3}{8}$	$3\frac{3}{4}$	$3\frac{1}{8}$	$2\frac{1}{2}$
P/E Ratio - High	55	56	38	29	24	20	23	25	24	19
- Low	37	28	22	19	17	15	18	17	16	14
Income Statement Analysis (Million $)										
Revs.	17,839	15,307	13,363	11,778	10,395	9,235	8,295	7,475	6,733	6,047
Oper. Inc.	1,226	1,024	872	750	652	574	511	451	405	355
Depr.	210	189	164	147	132	118	105	92.1	84.3	70.4
Int. Exp.	0.4	1.0	2.0	2.0	2.0	3.1	6.8	16.2	19.1	19.3
Pretax Inc.	1,027	877	712	607	524	458	400	353	312	281
Eff. Tax Rate	39%	39%	39%	39%	39%	39%	39%	38%	38%	38%
Net Inc.	624	537	436	372	321	282	245	221	195	175
Balance Sheet & Other Fin. Data (Million $)										
Cash	142	144	73.0	9.0	22.0	108	121	226	135	214
Curr. Assets	3,222	2,623	2,326	2,019	1,813	1,673	1,463	1,439	1,247	1,187
Total Assets	5,907	4,902	4,207	3,634	3,253	2,909	2,535	2,374	2,095	1,914
Curr. Liab.	1,924	1,580	1,439	1,182	1,078	1,051	884	889	684	632
LT Debt	Nil	Nil	Nil	Nil	Nil	11.0	17.0	31.0	136	163
Common Eqty.	3,484	2,849	2,373	3,634	1,793	1,574	1,379	1,233	1,081	947
Total Cap.	3,559	2,938	2,486	3,779	1,935	1,758	1,569	1,462	1,393	1,266
Cap. Exp.	696	641	485	365	310	290	185	145	202	192
Cash Flow	834	726	600	519	453	400	350	313	279	245
Curr. Ratio	1.7	1.7	1.6	1.7	1.7	1.6	1.7	1.6	1.8	1.9
% LT Debt of Cap.	Nil	Nil	Nil	Nil	Nil	0.6	1.1	2.1	9.8	12.9
% Net Inc.of Revs.	3.5	3.5	3.3	3.2	3.0	3.1	3.0	3.0	2.9	2.9
% Ret. on Assets	11.5	11.8	11.1	10.8	10.4	10.4	10.0	9.9	9.7	9.7
% Ret. on Equity	19.7	20.6	19.7	10.8	19.0	19.1	18.8	19.1	19.2	19.7

Data as orig reptd.; bef. results of disc opers/spec. items. Per share data adj. for stk. divs. Bold denotes diluted EPS (FASB 128)-prior periods restated. E-Estimated. NA-Not Available. NM-Not Meaningful. NR-Not Ranked.

Office—200 Wilmot Rd., Deerfield, IL 60015. **Tel**—(847) 940-2500. **Website**—http://www.walgreens.com **Chrmn & CEO**—L. D. Jorndt. **Pres & COO**—D. W. Bernauer. **SVP & CFO**—R. L. Polark. **VP & Treas**—J. A. Rein. **Investor Contact**—Rick Hans. **Dirs**—V.A. Brunner, W. C. Foote, J. J. Howard, C. D. Hunter, L. D. Jorndt, A. G. McNally, C. Reed, J. B. Schwemm, W. H. Springer, M. M. von Ferstel, C. R. Walgreen III. **Transfer Agent & Registrar**—Harris Trust & Savings Bank, Chicago. **Incorporated**—in Illinois in 1909. **Empl**— 107,000. **S&P Analyst:** Robert J. Izmirlian

Figure 6-2: Standard & Poor's Report for Walgreen Company *(continued)*
Source: Standard & Poor's

STANDARD &POOR'S
STOCK REPORTS

Walgreen Co.

NYSE Symbol **WAG**

In S&P 500

12-FEB-00

Industry:
Retail (Drug Stores)

Summary: WAG, the largest U.S. retail drug chain in terms of revenues, operates more than 2,800 drug stores in 39 states and Puerto Rico.

S&P Opinion: Hold (★★★)	Recent Price • 29%	Yield • 0.5%
	52 Wk Range • 33⅞-22⅝	12-Mo. P/E • 45.6

Quantitative Evaluations

Outlook
(1 Lowest—5 Highest)
• 1

Fair Value
• 24⅜

Risk
• Low

Earn./Div. Rank
• A+

Technical Eval.
• Neutral since 1/00

Rel. Strength Rank
(1 Lowest—99 Highest)
• 58

Insider Activity
• Neutral

Earnings vs. Previous Year
▲=Up ▼=Down ▶=No Change

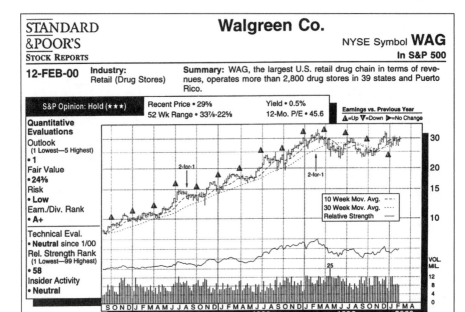

10 Week Mov. Avg. — —
30 Week Mov. Avg. · · · ·
Relative Strength ——

OPTIONS: ASE

Overview - 06-JAN-00

Sales are expected to increase about 19% in FY 00 (Aug.), fueled by the opening of 450 new or relocated stores, pharmacy sales gains in excess of 20%, and incremental sales gains for WAG's developing Internet site. Strong pharmacy sales will be driven by an aging population, new drug introductions, moderate drug price inflation, and entry into new markets. Gross margins could narrow, as WAG becomes more aggressive on pricing, in order to continue to gain market share from other drug, supermarket, and mass merchandise retailers. Gross margins could also come under pressure from an increase in third party prescriptions sales as a percentage of total pharmacy sales. Operating margins should widen, aided by improved payroll expenses, more efficient advertising, and greater sales leverage. We estimate EPS growth of 22% for FY 00, to $0.75, from $0.62 in FY 99.

Valuation - 06-JAN-00

We rate the shares hold, as their premium valuation is balanced against WAG's continued strong financial results. The shares were recently trading at 32X our calendar 2000 EPS estimate of $0.90, nearly 2X the projected long-term EPS growth rate of 17%, and at a 45% premium to the shares of other drug chains that we cover. These extreme valuations would probably warrant a lower rating for most other drug store chains, but WAG's high multiples can be justified by its long history of providing stable earnings growth, and its industry leading ROE. While WAG's gross margins are likely to narrow, due to more aggressive pricing, this strategy has enabled the company to continue to boost its market share, despite increased competition from other retail channels. It is likely that lower gross margins will be outweighed by increased gross margin dollars, due to greater sales.

Key Stock Statistics

S&P EPS Est. 2000	0.75	Tang. Bk. Value/Share	3.47
P/E on S&P Est. 2000	39.5	Beta	0.97
S&P EPS Est. 2001	0.87	Shareholders	64,476
Dividend Rate/Share	0.14	Market cap. (B)	$ 29.8
Shs. outstg. (M)	1006.2	Inst. holdings	50%
Avg. daily vol. (M)	1.766		

Value of $10,000 invested 5 years ago: $ 56,663

Fiscal Year Ending Aug. 31

	1999	1998	1997	1996	1995	1994
Revenues (Million $)						
1Q	4,016	3,485	3,054	2,693	2,406	2,118
2Q	4,691	4,094	3,603	3,179	2,807	2,499
3Q	4,571	3,887	3,403	2,990	2,617	2,336
4Q	4,560	3,841	3,303	2,918	2,565	2,283
Yr.	17,839	15,307	13,363	11,778	10,395	9,235
Earnings Per Share ($)						
1Q	0.10	0.09	0.08	0.07	0.06	0.05
2Q	0.20	0.17	0.15	0.13	0.11	0.10
3Q	0.16	0.13	0.10	0.09	0.08	0.07
4Q	0.16	0.15	0.11	0.09	0.08	0.07
Yr.	0.62	0.54	0.44	0.38	0.33	0.28

Next earnings report expected: late March

Dividend Data (Dividends have been paid since 1933.)

Amount ($)	Date Decl.	Ex-Div. Date	Stock of Record	Payment Date
0.033	Apr. 14	May. 19	May. 21	Jun. 12 '99
0.033	Jul. 14	Aug. 18	Aug. 20	Sep. 11 '99
0.034	Oct. 13	Nov. 10	Nov. 15	Dec. 11 '99
0.034	Jan. 12	Feb. 16	Feb. 18	Mar. 11 '00

A Division of The McGraw·Hill Companies

Figure 6-2: Standard & Poor's Report for Walgreen Company
Source: Standard & Poor's

The Standard & Poor's report also offers the reader a lot of historical information, including lots of numbers, a business summary, and even news headlines from the past year. The overview and valuation sections of the report offer the analyst's opinion as to how well the company will perform in the future. This report also includes an industry outlook and a comparison of the company's performance to its primary competitors. At the end of the report is a review of the consensus opinion of several Wall Street analysts.

You may note when reviewing these two reports that a few numbers may differ from one report to the other. That's due to the methods each company uses in reporting the numbers. For example, Value Line makes adjustments for situations that affect the numbers, but are only onetime events. They then explain the adjustment in the footnotes. For the most part, the numbers from one report to the other will match.

While these two reports contain most of the same basic information, reading both of them gives you the advantage of getting the opinions of two different analysts who have researched the company. The analysts' research, it's important to note, includes not only the same materials you've read in your research, but also discussions with company management, field trips to company sites, and the opportunity to attend company-sponsored analyst meetings. But even with the additional access to the company, analysts aren't always right. Therefore, these reports should be used as supplements to your own research, not as an answer.

When you finish this process, you'll have a feel as to whether you're comfortable with this company and whether you believe it's a stock that you want to present to your investment club members.

If you find it's not a stock that you believe would be a good buy for your club, find another company to research. The point of this exercise is not to research a stock and present it. The point is to recommend a good stock to buy to the other club members. That may mean researching two or three before you find the right one. Therefore, it's important to start thinking about what stock you want to present to the members far in advance. You don't want to start your research a few days before your presentation and find that the stock you picked is not one you like after you begin researching it. You'll probably only have to research a stock once a year. Make sure you take the time and make the effort required to find a good one.

Chapter

Creating a Winning Presentation

inding and researching a company's stock that you want to present to your investment club can be somewhat time-consuming. But because investment club members take turns making presentations, you'll probably only have to do it about once a year. That's not much of a time commitment, considering that you're investing money in new stocks every month.

When determining which company should be researched and presented each month, some clubs choose to make that a group decision. After they decide on a company, they assign it to a member who does the research and presents the stock to the group.

Some clubs create a stock-selection committee, which is comprised of two or three members. Those members decide which stocks they want to consider, do the research, and then present the chosen company's stock to the other members. If the club votes not to buy the stock, the same members remain on the stock selection committee and begin the process over again. Those members remain on the committee until the club votes to purchase a stock the committee presents.

Other clubs just assign a member the job of doing a presentation and that member can choose which stock to research and present. The members of the Central Maine Investors of Augusta discuss various industries, choose which industry they want to study, then have someone volunteer to choose a company within that industry to present. By narrowing it down to a specific industry, they've found that there will usually be one or two members who have knowledge in that area who will volunteer.

The HY Partners Investment Club of Orlando, Florida, has developed an unusual method. When the club first started, one member was assigned to research a company and present it to the group each month. But they found that method to be very stressful. Most of the members were just learning about investing and didn't feel very comfortable doing individual presentations. They decided, instead, to have one member each month pick two companies for the group to research. The procedure they follow is for the member to announce the names of the two companies at the monthly meeting. Then, during the next month, all the members research those two companies. At the next meeting, they discuss their research, then make a determination as to whether they want to buy either company's stock. Their method creates a bit more work for the members because everyone has to do research every month, but they find it to be a more comfortable method of finding stocks to buy. They feel that through this process they gather more information and make more informed decisions.

When determining which stock to present, some clubs also put price caps on the stocks they'll consider buying. For instance, they may state in their bylaws that the club will only consider purchasing stocks that sell for $25 per share or less. The reason they set the limit is that the lower price allows them to purchase more shares. Also, brokerage firms charge less per share in commissions if you buy a round lot (100 shares) than if you purchase an odd lot (less than 100 shares), so by purchasing a lower-priced stock, they'll probably save on commissions. The club can also purchase new stocks more often because it takes less time to save up the money required to buy a lower-priced stock.

By using this strategy, however, the club takes the chance of missing out on some great stocks that could give them tremendous returns. Most investors would prefer to purchase 50 shares of a $50 stock that moves up to $80 per share for a profit of $1,500, than to purchase 100 shares of a $25 stock that moves up to $35 per share for a profit of $1,000. In that case, saving a little bit of money on commissions is irrelevant. Whether you set price caps on the stocks you consider purchasing is up to you, but if you decide to use them be sure to state that in your bylaws.

THE OVERVIEW

Now that you've found the absolutely best company in the world and you're excited about the future prospects of its stock, it's time to convince your fellow investment club members that they should vote to buy this stock. It's time to develop a presentation that will make your fellow members love this stock as much as you do.

While a presentation doesn't have to be long—only 15 or 20 minutes—it does have to be convincing. If you're going to be convincing, you have to be interesting. Just spouting off a bunch of numbers and a few statistics isn't going to convince anyone to buy a stock, no matter how great its prospects. You have to offer information that is meaningful and that will make your audience raise their eyebrows in wonderment as to how you found such a great buy.

Start your presentation with an overview of the company. If this is a company most people aren't familiar with, you may need to be a little more detailed in your overview. If this is a company, like Microsoft, Walgreen's, or McDonald's, that everyone knows, your overview can probably be rather short. If, in your research, however, you've found that the company produces a product or offers a service that you weren't aware of, chances are the other club members aren't aware of it, either. Be sure to include that in your overview.

Explain what the company does and how well it does it by incorporating the numbers you've identified in your research into your presentation. Use specifics in your presentation. Don't just say the company produces paper products, has increasing sales, and is expanding. Instead, use statements such as:

- ✔ This company produces three-quarters of all the paper products used in the United States.

- ✔ The company increased its sales by 50 percent during the last five years, from $500 million to $750 million.

- ✔ The company, which funds its expansion from its own cash flow, plans to build another manufacturing facility within the next two years.

Discuss management's past performance relative to sales, earnings, and stock-price growth. Use some of the ratios you calculated in your research, discuss how the ratios compare to previous years, and compare your company to others in the same industry. Talk about the company's customers, its market share, and why the company's industry will continue to grow. Discuss whether the company's customers are only domestic or if the company sells to customers around the world, giving this stock an international flavor. If the company isn't selling its products or services in other countries, does it have plans to expand internationally? Include information on the competition and why the company you're presenting is better than its competitors. Explain why you think this company's future looks bright and, if possible, incorporate economic statistics. For example, if you're discussing a company that builds and operates retirement homes, try to find out the projected growth rate of the retirement population in the United States.

Discuss the company's current involvement with the Internet—both in terms of buying their raw materials or selling their products. If they're not utilizing the Internet, do they have plans to do so? Incorporate information from third-party reports and statements that security analysts have made about the company. If there's something unique about the company or its product, discuss that.

INCLUDING INDUSTRY-SPECIFIC INFORMATION

You also need to include a short discussion as to the nuances of the industry that this company is in. There are certain issues that are pertinent to specific industries that help detail the company's performance. Below is a list of some of the major industries in this country and some of the issues that you should explain to the club's members when presenting a company that does business in that industry.

> ✔ *Banking:* One issue that pertains to banks and not to companies in other industries is credit quality. Banks make their profits by lending money to borrowers. Therefore, they have to make sure that the individuals and companies they lend money to will have the wherewithal to pay the money back.
>
> Include in your presentation information about the bank's level of nonperforming loans, which you can find in the footnotes to the financial statements. If that number is increasing, that's a problem. Discuss how this bank's number compares to that of other banks of the same size. Also, check the bank's income statement for *charge-offs*. Every time a bank writes off a loan, that money is lost. Compare the current year's amount of charge-offs to past years to determine if they've increased or decreased. Include a comparison of charge-offs reported for the bank you're presenting as compared to its industry peers.

Charge-offs: Loans that the bank has funded but now deems to be uncollectible.

Also, explain any nuances of the industry to the club members. For instance, banks tend to have lower P/E ratios than companies in other industries because they have lower growth rates. Also, banks typically have higher dividend yields than companies in most other industries. In fact, half the return investors usually receive from a bank stock is related to its dividend.

✔ *Energy/Utilities:* If you're presenting the stock of a company in the energy and utilities industry, you'll need to explain to the other members how the specific company you're presenting fits into the industry as a whole. According to Sue Becht, vice president of investor relations at Duke Energy Corporation, due to deregulation and the ability of companies to take advantage of other opportunities, many industry changes have taken place. There are really three distinct types of companies you can consider within the framework of the energy/utilities industry.

1. *Utilities:* These are the companies that focus on the distribution of energy to a specific region—the types of companies that sell their products directly to consumers. Because these companies are regulated by the states, their income and growth are fairly steady and predictable. Also, these companies typically pay fairly substantial dividends. Therefore, the stocks of these companies don't demonstrate much volatility.

2. *Wholesalers:* These are the companies that build huge electric generators and sell their products to municipalities or gigantic corporations that use so much electricity that they can buy directly from the wholesalers. Wholesalers never sell directly to the consumer.

   These companies can demonstrate extremely volatile earnings and growth because their business is very cyclical. In August their sales will probably spike up due to the demand for air conditioning, while in April their sales may be at their lowest point, as most regions have no need for air-conditioning or heating. Therefore, investors in this type of company have to be prepared to deal with a lot of volatility in the company's stock price.

3. *Energy:* These are the companies that seek out earnings growth by focusing on many aspects of the industry. They'll generate power, own processing facilities, own pipelines, take advantage of privatization, and become involved in a multitude of industry areas. They offer new products and services and base their focus

on the world's demand for energy and the earnings-growth prospects that are available. These companies are not regulated by the states, but because they are so diversified within the industry, their earnings and growth are not as volatile as those of the whole-salers. Duke Energy Corporation fits into this third category.

Becht suggests that investors determine their ability to handle volatility in their investment portfolios before deciding which area of this industry they want to consider. Since investment clubs focus on growth stocks, the third group of companies within this indus-try would probably be the best fit.

✔ *Insurance:* There are four pieces of information that are specific to the insurance industry that you should include in your presentation. Two of those issues relate to the number of policies the company sells and renews each year, and the other two issues relate to the two types of income that insurance companies earn.

1. *New Sales:* New sales are extremely important to insurance com-panies because, unlike other industries in which a sale is typically a onetime revenue, new sales often represent sales for several years to come as customers continue to renew their policies. New sales depict a potential for continued growth.

2. *Persistency Rate:* This number, which can be found in the compa-ny's annual report, represents the percentage of existing policies that customers renew each year. Renewals are important in that they demonstrate a satisfied customer base that will, hopefully, renew their policies for years to come. Obviously, the higher the persis-tency rate, the better.

3. *Premium Income:* Insurance companies have two sources of income. The premium income is the money the company makes by selling insurance products each year. Hopefully, this number increases year after year, demonstrating increased revenues from the company's product sales.

4. *Investment Income:* The other way an insurance company makes money is through investment income. When they collect the premium income from their customers, that money must be invested so that it grows, and hopefully earns more money than the company will have to pay out in insurance claims.

If an insurance company is increasing its new sales, renewing policies from previous years' sales, and garnering a large spread on the amount of money it's earning from its investment income versus its payouts, it's showing good growth relative to industry specifics.

✔ *Pharmaceuticals:* The most important issue that's specific to the pharmaceutical industry is what's called its pipeline. How many new products is the company working on that will eventually come to market and start generating a profit? Discuss what products are in the pipeline, what diseases the drugs will treat, and how many people have those diseases. If it's a new wonder drug that treats diabetes, sales should be strong. If it's a new drug that treats a rare disease that a small number of people experience, the drug probably won't contribute much to sales.

Also, consider where the new drugs have progressed to in the pipeline. The pharmaceutical industry categorizes new products into five different phases:

1. *Preclinical:* This means the drug is in the very early stages and is still being researched. Statistics show that only about one in 5,000 products in the preclinical stage will make it to market.

2. *Phase I:* These products are farther along in the research stage. In this phase you can expect about one drug in 500 to make it to market.

3. *Phase II-A:* Typically, about one drug in 50 that makes it to Phase II-A will make it to market.

4. *Phase II-B:* If a drug makes it to this phase, it has a one in five chance of becoming a marketable product.

5. *Phase III:* A drug that makes it this far has a better than one in two chance of making it to market. In fact, Merck Pharmaceuticals has lost only one product that made it to Phase III in the past 10 years.

Compare the number of products that you think will make it to market with the number of patents the company has expiring. Hopefully, they have new products available to patent to replace the expiring patents, which give the competition an opportunity to step in. A patent lasts 20 years, but that time begins as soon as the company applies for the patent and starts working on the product. Therefore, by the time the product comes to market, a good portion of the patent protection is already used up.

In addition, when presenting a pharmaceutical company's stock, you'll want to talk about the company's quality of researchers and the consistency of their investment in research. The annual report will include information about the backgrounds of the senior researchers. Make sure they have fairly impressive backgrounds. And, finally, report on the company's research expenditures. If they've suddenly reduced the amount of money they spend on research, that may mean problems in the future.

✔ *Retail:* Most retail company stocks that you may present will probably be companies that are already known by most of your investment club's members. But despite being familiar with the company, there are certain issues that you should report on that are important to retail companies.

According to Richard A. Freeman, director of the investment banking division, specializing in retail, at Salomon Smith Barney in New York City, the most important issue to address when presenting a retail company is comparable store sales—sales on a per-store basis. Are the comparable store sales positive or negative? If positive, by how much? If they are less than 5 percent, that's not impressive. If they are more than 5 percent, that is impressive.

Report also on total revenues, known as top-line growth. If revenues aren't increasing from year to year, the company isn't growing. Next, report on the company's bottom-line growth or earnings. Earnings should be growing at a pace that is at least equal to, and preferably faster than, the revenue growth. Of course, a retail company can increase its earnings by cutting costs, but there always comes a point when costs can't be cut anymore. And in the age of the Internet, when consumers have access to more information than ever before, increasing prices for the company's products in an effort to grow top-line sales also becomes more difficult.

Freeman points out that the most important aspect for a retail company is growth. He says there are three ways a retail company can grow its business:

1. *Increase revenues by adding more stores:* This is the slowest and most expensive way for a retail company to grow.

2. *Increase revenues by improving productivity:* This can be done through upgrading—better lighting, merchandise, signage, additional products or services. This can be a difficult way to achieve growth.

3. *Increase revenues and earnings by acquisitions and mergers:* This is the fastest and easiest way to achieve growth. However, it can be very expensive.

If the company you're presenting is demonstrating growth, report on which method it is using to achieve that growth.

When it comes to presenting retail-company stocks to your investment club, it's easy to become somewhat blind to the underlying business of the company. You may have shopped at the company's stores for years and been happy with their products and services. Therefore, you just assume that it's a good company and that its stock would be a good buy. But even if you're familiar with the company's retail outlets, you still need to look at the underlying business and determine if this company is growing, how it's growing, and if you believe that growth will continue.

✔ *Technology:* This is one of the fastest-changing industries your investment club can possibly consider for potential investment. But to overlook this industry would be a huge mistake. There are wonderful technology companies whose stocks hold the promise of great returns through capital appreciation. When presenting these companies' stocks to your club's members, there are certain issues that are important to address.

David Readerman, CFA and director of Internet strategy for Thomas Weisel Partners in San Francisco, California, has been researching technology stocks for 17 years and has seen several major technology cycles. He says that there are four areas that are most important to consider when presenting your research on a technology company to your investment club's members.

1. *High-Quality Management:* While having a quality management team in place is important in any industry, it's especially important in the technology industry. So many new technology companies are started because someone has a great idea for a hot technology product. But that isn't enough. Management has to know how to attract and retain high-quality, high-energy people. They have to be able to focus on designing, building, shipping, and supporting great products globally. That means management has to put in place an active research and development group and back that up with a highly competent support and service organization.

2. *Viable Business Model:* Some companies flourish by selling only automobiles, only sportswear, or only food products. But a technology company can't depend on selling only one product. Cars, tennis shoes, and breakfast cereals don't become obsolete, but technology products become obsolete in a matter of months. A technology company with one product and no research and development is a company that's probably headed for liquidation.

3. *Competitive Analysis:* Having no competition would be a great environment in which to exist for most companies. But if a technology company has no competitors, maybe the reason is that they don't have a product that anyone really wants. Having competitors validates that there is a market for the company's products. After you identify the competition, you need to determine how the company you're presenting to the other members will win in the long term against that competition.

4. *Financials:* Very few new technology companies start out showing a profit or demonstrating strong cash flow. While short-term losses are acceptable, you need to report to the other members just when and how the company plans to break even, then generate positive cash flow and profits.

    When presenting a technology company to your club's members, if you can successfully address the above four issues in your presentation, you've probably found a good technology stock that will serve your club well over the long term.

✔ *Telecommunications:* When presenting a telecommunications company's stock, report to the other members which sector of the telecommunications industry the company is in. Do they provide local phone services or wireless services, manufacture equipment, or is it a network company? Or, does this company offer several of those services? Keep in mind that some areas of this industry grow faster than others. For example, the voice transmission business currently grows fairly slowly while the data and wireless businesses demonstrate rapid growth. Also, consider how the company is positioned relative to the Internet. Mergers are also rampant in this industry. If the company is fairly small, could it possibly be a takeover target of a larger company that's in the same business, but has a hole in its service coverage that the company could fill? The primary considerations in presenting a telecommunications company is to report on the company's business, size, and position in the industry as a whole.

USING HANDOUTS

If you want the other investment club members to remember the facts of your presentation, it's important to have handouts. You may not, however, want to give them out until after you've completed your presentation. There's nothing more frustrating than being excited about the company you're presenting, but as you speak you find that instead of listening to you, the other members are flipping through pages and reading. Complete your presentation, then pass out any handouts you have. Give the members a couple of minutes to peruse them, then ask for discussion.

Some of the handouts you might want to provide are copies of the company's Value Line or S&P report. Or maybe the CEO wrote a particularly insightful letter in the annual report that you'd like the members to read. You may even want to use a yellow marker to highlight some of the more pertinent information. Or maybe there was an interesting chart in the annual or quarterly report or proxy that you'd like the other members to see. You could even type up your own listing of company highlights that you think are important. Whatever you use, it's usually good to be able to give the other members something that they can look at and take home with them. Who knows? They may love your presentation so much that they want to go home and buy this stock for their personal portfolios.

MAKING YOUR PRESENTATION FUN

A stock presentation doesn't have to be dry and boring. Think of creative ways to pique the other members' interest. For example, if you're presenting a company like Hershey's, bring a bag of Hershey's Kisses and/or Hugs and let the members sample the company's products as you do your presentation. Maybe you decided to do a presentation on a company called Palm because you have one of their Palm Vx machines that handles e-mail, stock quotes, and other functions, and you think it's a great product. Bring your machine to the meeting and demonstrate it. Maybe you decide to present Procter & Gamble Company. Gather up a sampling of their soaps and cleaning products, put them in a basket, and bring them to the meeting. If you decide to present Applebee's International, try to get a copy of one of their restaurant's menus or a copy of a carryout menu, and bring that to the meeting. Are you presenting Walt Disney Company? Wear Mickey Mouse ears while you do your presentation! Do whatever it takes to get your audience's attention and get them interested in this great company you've found.

One woman in my club did a stock presentation on the retail store Gap. She went to one of the Gap stores, asked for a dozen small Gap shopping bags, and put her handouts in the bags. She could have gone one step farther and worn clothes she bought at Gap and modeled them at the meeting. Anything you can do to bring the company to the meeting with you will make the company come alive and help you convince the other members that the product and the company are both good buys.

THE DISCUSSION PERIOD

At the end of your presentation, there should be a discussion period. Inevitably, no matter how much information you've included in your presentation, the other members will have questions. Make sure you bring all of your research materials to the meeting in case there's a question you can't answer and you need to look it up.

Be prepared for questions that you may consider negative. If your club invests in this company's stock, everyone in the club will have a stake in it. They just want to make sure that their money is being invested wisely. It's important that you don't become defensive when someone asks you a negative question. The other members aren't attacking you with their questions; they're just trying to clarify information to be sure that this is a company they want to invest in.

Be open to what the other members have to say. In fact, the discussion period is one of the great advantages of an investment club because you can utilize the other members' expertise. For instance, if you presented a company whose products are patented, you may not have considered what happens when the company's patents run out. The member who works in a similar type of company may be able to explain what happens to companies and their products when patents run out and the competition steps in. That one little piece of information may make you change your mind about this company. Having the opportunity to share experience and expertise may save you from investing your money in a company that could have major problems in the future.

The HY Partners Investment Club, which often invites guest speakers to the club's monthly meetings, even asks the opinion of the speaker who's attending that meeting. It's important, however, that if you decide to include the opinion of an outsider, that you don't let that person make the decision for you. Don't think that just because this person is an investment professional that she knows more than you do. Your members are the ones who have done the research and, chances are you know more about this company than she does.

Most clubs make a decision whether or not they want to buy a stock right after the presentation and discussion. However, the members of an investment club can make their own rules. Bob McClow of the MAJEC Investment Club in Phoenix, Arizona, says their club won't buy a stock the first month someone introduces it to the club. Their reasoning is that they want to give the other members an opportunity to think about the presentation and do a little research of their own on the company. They've had stocks that sounded like good buy candidates during the presentation, but after several members spent time doing a little more research, they found a problem. They typically make a buy decision the second or third month after a stock has been presented. Of course, during that time lag, the price of the stock may move up. Then, if the members decide they like the stock, they may have to pay more to buy it than if they had purchased it immediately after the presentation. They believe taking that risk is worth taking the time to do additional research.

In most clubs, however, if the members like the stock, someone will make a motion to purchase a certain number of shares after the discussion is complete. Other motions may alter the original motion until a motion is finally seconded. You're then ready for the group to vote.

THE VOTE

If your club has chosen to use secret ballots when they vote, you'll never know how many members or which members voted for or against the stock. The secretary will simply announce whether or not the vote passed.

If the group votes not to buy the stock you've presented, don't worry about it. The voting has no reflection on you, only on the stock. If you haven't convinced them to buy the stock and you still like the company months later when it's time for you to do a presentation again, present the same company. If you do, however, be sure you start your research from scratch. The company will have issued new quarterly and 10-Q reports and maybe even new annual, proxy, and 10-K reports. Get those reports and redo your research. Recheck the S&P and Value Line reports. The status of companies can change over time. Make sure it's still a company you like. If the company is voted down a second time, you may want to move on to another company for your next presentation, as listening to a presentation on the same company year after year would become somewhat tedious for everyone.

GETTING OVER THAT FIRST HURDLE

Presenting your first stock to the group can be a little nerve-racking. But every member will go through it and there's no reason to believe that the other members won't be supportive. As long as you've done your research, made the presentation fun and interesting, and remain open to questions and discussion, you'll get through it with no problem at all. In fact, you'll probably start looking forward to the next time you can present a stock.

Chapter

Conducting Monthly Meetings

You've come a long way since you've decided to start your investment club. The initial setup of your club has been a bit of work, but now that you've got the groundwork laid it's time to start enjoying yourself. It's time for your first regular monthly meeting.

As we go through the steps of how the meeting should be conducted, let's assume that your club has been in operation for one year and has built a portfolio of four stocks: PepsiCo, Merck & Company, Citibank, and Sun Microsystems.

STARTING THE MEETING

If, when writing your bylaws, the club decided that meetings would be held on the third Tuesday of each month at 7 P.M., then the meeting should start at 7 P.M. If latecomers know you'll wait for them, they'll be late for every meeting and they'll show up later every month. But if they have to walk in as business is already being conducted, they'll be on time next month.

It's important that you satisfy all three goals of an investment club at every meeting—learning, investing, and having fun—but you need to have a plan for doing that. You need an agenda. Without an agenda, no one knows how the meeting will be conducted. It's important to remember that an investment club is a business and should be conducted as one. Having an agenda will also help members to keep focused so that the meeting doesn't get offtrack and turn into a four-hour ordeal. If people get offtrack or if someone begins a long dissertation that doesn't necessarily add to the conversation, it's the president's job to politely steer the meeting back on track.

Having an agenda can help. When the secretary sends the previous meeting's minutes to the members, the agenda for the next meeting should be included. Figure 8-1 shows a sample agenda.

1. President calls the meeting to order.

2. Secretary's Report
   Approval of minutes from last meeting

3. Treasurer's Report
   Collection of contributions
   Approval of treasurer's valuation statement

4. Educational presentation
   What Are Stock Splits, by John Smith

5. Reports from stock monitors
   Citibank—Bette
   Merck & Co., Inc.—Peter
   PepsiCo, Inc.—Gary
   Sun Microsystems, Inc.—Joan

6. Stock presentation
   Walgreen Company, by Mary Jones
   Discussion
   Vote

7. Old business
   Update on speaker for October meeting

8. New business
   NAIC dues
   Next meeting assignments

9. Adjournment

Figure 8-1: Sample Agenda

The president should call the meeting to order on time. The first order of business is to approve the minutes from the previous meeting. All members should have the minutes and should have already reviewed them. Any corrections should be discussed and noted in the following month's minutes. If there are no changes, someone should make a motion that the minutes be accepted, another member should second the motion, and a vote should be taken.

While it's important that your meetings are orderly and follow certain procedures, don't get too hung up on formalities. You don't need to have a copy of *Robert's Rules of Order* by your side or become an expert on how to make a motion. The primary issue is that your meetings are conducted in a professional and businesslike manner.

THE MONEY ISSUES

The next order of business is to collect the members' monthly contributions and review and approve the treasurer's report, which is the club's valuation statement. The details of how to prepare the valuation statement will be covered in Chapter 9. The treasurer should collect the members' contributions for that month, total them, and announce how much has been collected. The secretary should note that amount in the minutes.

The treasurer should then distribute the valuation statement. The valuation statement is informational in that it outlines the value of the club's entire portfolio, including any cash that's not yet invested. It also breaks the portfolio down as to what percentage and dollar amount of the club each individual member owns—their capital accounts.

In addition to the valuation statement, the members should also have access to the most recent month's brokerage statement. The treasurer can either give each member a copy or, if making copies is a problem, simply give out the original statement and allow members to pass it around. By perusing the brokerage statement each month, you can be certain that your treasurer is following the club's wishes. It's not that you don't trust your treasurer, but this is a business, and all businesses understand the importance of checks and balances. By following certain procedures, you can help ensure that one of your members won't run off with your hard-earned money. Just because you know the other members of your club doesn't mean a problem can't develop.

Since its inception in 1951, NAIC has recorded 21 cases of fraud in which one member of a club, usually the treasurer, absconded with the other members' money. One of the more well-publicized cases happened in the 1960s when an investment club, whose members were all from the same family, was defrauded. The father was the treasurer of the club and he took off with the money!

Another case of fraud was perpetrated by James Dufficy, head of Alexa Group, who told the members of his "investment club" that they should trust him and let him make all the investment decisions. When he told them he was going to invest the club's money in a computerized stock-option strategy that would give them a better return than the Standard & Poor's 500 index, the club members agreed. But no such strategy existed and Dufficy had already diverted 40 percent of the club's money to his own account before he was caught. He was sentenced to six years in prison for bilking 50 of his fellow investment club members out of a whopping $950,000!

Fraud is a frightening prospect when it comes to investment clubs. If it would make your members more comfortable to have your members bonded, NAIC offers this service via Old Republic Insurance Company. The coverage protects your investment club's portfolio against theft of the club's funds by one of the partners. The insurance must be renewed every year.

The insurance, however, probably isn't necessary if your club members are diligent about reviewing the monthly brokerage statements and even auditing the treasurer's books once a year. When you review the monthly brokerage statement, check to be sure that any business the club transacted in the prior month is noted. If the members' contributions from the previous meeting totaled $650, was $650 deposited to the account? Are there any unauthorized withdrawals that show up on the statement? If the members voted to sell 100 shares of Kmart and buy 50 shares of Wal-Mart Stores at the last meeting, are those transactions reflected on the statement? If not, you need to ask your treasurer a few questions.

If anyone has any questions regarding the valuation or brokerage statement, those questions should be directed to the treasurer. If there are no questions or discussions, a motion should be made that the club accepts the treasurer's valuation statement. Someone should second the motion, and the president should ask for approval from the other members. Typically, on votes such as this, a count of raised hands or the sound of a verbal agreement is sufficient.

EDUCATION

The next item on the agenda is education. As discussed before, your club probably won't have a formalized educational segment at every meeting. Many clubs offer this segment at every third or fourth meeting. The educational portion needs to be kept short so that your meeting doesn't get too long. A 10-minute report from a member or a short video are possibilities. On the preceding sample agenda, John Smith, one of the club's members, has agreed to research the topic of *stock splits* and explain to the club how they work and what they mean. A short review can easily be done in 10 minutes.

Stock split: An increase in the number of shares issued by a company without any change in its financial position. A two-for-one stock split doubles the number of shares outstanding and cuts the price per share in half.

If the vice president of education periodically wants to arrange for a speaker to do an hour-long presentation, that should probably be done at a separate meeting, unless your members agree in advance to having a longer presentation at a monthly meeting. If your club brings in speakers, however, find someone who will be interesting and informative.

When looking for speakers, be sure to tap your membership. You may find out that a member's cousin is a securities analyst, or that another member's best friend works in the investor-relations department of a company whose stock your club is considering purchasing. Your club members may be a wealth of information and contacts when it comes to scheduling educational events. For instance, the Wall Street Watchers managed to convince one member's husband, who was an executive from the international marketing group of McDonald's Corporation, to attend one of their meetings and talk about the company. At another meeting a member's husband, who worked for a broadband communications company, discussed that industry.

THE PORTFOLIO

Your club currently owns four stocks in its portfolio. As each stock was purchased, a member was assigned to follow that stock's progress. When assigning stocks for monitoring, it's a good idea to assign a different member to a stock other than the person who presented it. Oftentimes, a person who presented a stock becomes married to it. If there's bad news, human nature is such that if it's my stock, I may sugarcoat the bad news because I don't want to say anything negative about a stock that I convinced the group to buy. Another member who didn't bring the stock to the group will probably be more objective.

These monitoring reports should be kept short. In fact, the reports may or may not even be required from month to month. The member who's following Citibank may have no report in September because the stock is steadily increasing in price and there's been no major news or announcements about the company. But in October, the member may have received the company's third-quarter report. At that meeting, he would discuss the highlights of the company's last quarter, including revenues and income. When he receives the quarterly report, he may also want to check the most recent S&P and Value Line reports to see if the analysts have had any changes in their thinking about the company. Or the member may not have received the company's quarterly report, but there's been news about the company in the newspapers. Or maybe the stock's price has dropped or increased significantly. Prior to the meeting, the member may want to call the company's investor-relations department and find out what their story is as to the change in the stock's price. Whether there's no news on a company or an annual report has just been issued, these monitoring reports should take only a few minutes each.

To monitor stocks properly, investment club members should become regular readers of publications such as the *Wall Street Journal, Barron's, Business Week,* or *Forbes.* Those types of business publications will help members keep current on significant happenings at the companies they're following.

Members can follow their stock's price activity on a daily basis in any major newspaper. The listings are fairly straightforward. And if you subscribe to *Barron's,* which is published only on Saturday, you can glean a whole week's worth of price activity, plus other interesting information, including analysts' earnings estimates for the current and the next year. Figure 8-2 shows a section from the New York Stock Exchange Composite List in *Barron's* showing the listing for Wal-Mart Stores.

Barron's
New York Stock Exchange Composite List

1	2		3	4	5	6	7	8			9
Mkt.	52-week			Tick	Vol			-----Week's-----			Net
Sym	High	Low	Name	Sym	100s	Yld	P/E	High	Low	Last	Chg
s	70.25	38.88	Wal-Mart	WMT	614424	.5	36	49.31	43.44	44.38	-3.38

	-----------------------EARNINGS-----------------------				DIVIDENDS	
10	11	12	13	14	15	16
Latest	This	Next	Latest	Year	Latest	Rec.
Full Year	Year	Year	Qtr.	Ago	Divs.	Date
01/00 1.28	1.45	1.67	Jan .43	.35	q.05	12-17-99

Figure 8-2: Barron's New York Stock Exchange Composite List

Column 1: A small "s" indicates a stock split or stock dividend amounting to 10 percent or more during the last year. In Wal-Mart's case, they had a stock split during the past 12 months.

Column 2: $70.25 was the highest price Wal-Mart traded at during the past year, and $38.88 was its lowest price.

Column 3: The name of the stock this listing depicts.

Column 4: The company's stock symbol.

Column 5: The volume. During this week, 61,442,400 shares of Wal-Mart stock traded hands. The volume numbers must be multiplied by 100. Volume, for most companies, stays within in a certain range. If volume is suddenly unusually high, there is probably news about the company in the media that investors are reacting to.

Column 6: The current yield Wal-Mart investors receive based on the stock's current price. It's calculated by dividing the company's latest 12-month dividend by the last current market price. If you purchased the stock at a price different than this day's price, your yield would be higher or lower.

Column 7: This number tells you that the price of one share of Wal-Mart stock is 36 times higher than the amount of money Wal-Mart earned on a per-share basis this fiscal year.

Column 8: These numbers depict the highest and the lowest prices the stock traded at during the past week and the price at which it closed at the end of the trading week.

Column 9: This number tells you that the stock was down $3.38 from the previous week's close. Wal-Mart stock would have closed at $47.76 the previous week.

Column 10: Wal-Mart's earnings for the company's fiscal year ending January 31, 2000, were $1.28 per share.

Columns 11 & 12: These numbers are projections as to the company's earnings for the current and the following fiscal years.

Column 13: This column tells you that Wal-Mart had earnings of $.43 per share for the most recent quarter ending January 31.

Column 14: This number tells you what the company's earnings per share were for the same quarter one year ago. Wal-Mart increased its earnings by $.08.

Column 15: This tells you that the most recent quarterly dividend was $.05 per share.

Column 16: This is the date an investor must be a shareholder of Wal-Mart stock in order to qualify to receive the most recent quarter's dividend.

The *Barron's* listing can give you a lot of information for the company you're monitoring, relative to stock price, earnings, and dividends, with one quick glance. But if you want more up-to-date information, you can get that, too. Just turn on your TV to CNBC. See those two bands at the bottom of the screen that keep scrolling along? That's a *ticker,* and you can find any stock you want on that ticker and see its trading price with just a 15-minute delay.

Ticker: A continuous reporting of stock transactions as they occur—with a slight delay. Found on certain television stations and in brokerage-firm offices.

The top band is white and represents the stocks that trade on the New York Stock Exchange (NYSE). The bottom band is blue and represents stocks that trade on the American Stock Exchange (AMEX) and on NAS-DAQ. That band will show a list of AMEX stocks for a short time, then switch to the NASDAQ stocks. The stock market opens each weekday at 9:30 A.M. and closes at 4:00 P.M., eastern standard time. During that time, the *stock symbols* and their current prices are shown as the various stocks are traded.

Stock symbols: Shortened designations (usually one to four letters) that represent a public company.

Just above the two ticker bands is a box that tells you at what level the Dow Jones Industrial Average and the NASDAQ are trading. During non-trading hours, the bands run the stocks in alphabetical order, according to their stock symbols, with their closing prices for that day.

When reading the ticker, you may notice that all the stocks on the top band, the NYSE stocks, have symbols that consist of one to three letters. Sometimes, a lowercase *p* may be added to the symbol to denote a preferred stock, which we'll discuss later in Chapter 13. Or, if stocks have different classes, a period and an additional letter may be added on the end to denote that special class. On the bottom band, the AMEX stocks also consist of one to three letters, but the NASDAQ stocks consist of four, or sometimes five, letters to denote a stock that is not a common stock.

Therefore, if you want to know at what price Lucent Technologies is trading during the day and you know it's a NYSE stock, it will be on the top band. The symbol is LU. Below are two examples of what LU may look like when it goes scrolling by and what it means.

LU 100@36.50—If the number of shares is less than 1,000, the actual amount is shown. This listing would mean that 100 shares of Lucent Technologies traded at $36.50 per share.

LU 10.5K@36.50—If the number of shares is 1,000 or more, the number will appear with a *K* and must be multiplied times 1,000. Therefore, this listing would mean that 10,500 shares of Lucent Technologies traded at $36.50 per share.

As you can see, the ticker is easy to read once you know the symbols and the volume designations.

From time to time on the TV screen above the ticker you may see the words "Curbs in," meaning that trading curbs are in effect at the NYSE. These *program trading curbs* were adopted by the NYSE in response to the huge market downturn that occurred in October 1987.

Program trading curbs: Restrictions placed on stock transactions by the Securities and Exchange Commission when the market reaches a specific milestone. Used to reduce market volatility.

The NYSE says the curbs are used to "reduce market volatility and promote investor confidence." When you see that curbs are in place, don't worry. They exist to manage index arbitrage, which has nothing to do with trades made by individuals.

With all the information available via newspapers, TV, and the Internet, it's very simple to follow a stock's current price. Therefore, members should always know the current price of the stocks they're monitoring when they come to the monthly meeting.

As the club's stock portfolio grows, each member will probably be required to monitor more than one stock. One member can monitor three or four stocks, which should be more than sufficient to cover a club's portfolio.

THE STOCK PRESENTATION

The next order of business is the stock presentation. On this agenda, Mary Jones is presenting Walgreen Company. It's wise to include the name of the company being presented on the agenda so that prior to the meeting, if other members hear news about that company or have information available, they have the opportunity to bring that information with them and share it during the discussion period. The presentation should take about 15 to 20 minutes, then be followed by the discussion period, during which time the other members can ask questions or add information they may have.

At the end of the discussion, it's time to decide whether the group wants to purchase shares of Walgreen Company. If a member believes they should purchase 50 shares, she'll make a motion—"I move that we purchase 50 shares of Walgreen Company." Someone will second it, or maybe someone else will suggest that they buy 100 shares of the stock. The group should discuss how many shares they want to buy and, of course, check with the treasurer to ensure they have enough money and also that they will be able to cover commissions. Once a number of shares has been established, someone should make a final motion and another member should second it. It's now time to vote.

There are two options when it comes to voting. The president can call for a show of hands. Or you can vote using a secret ballot by having the secretary pass out slips of paper on which the members vote yes or no. The best option is to use a secret ballot. Here's why.

Let's say Mary presented Walgreen Company because she did all the research and decided the company was in an industry she thought would flourish in the future, because the aging baby boomers will need pharmaceuticals. She found that Walgreen Company is the leader in its industry, with good growth and excellent prospects to continue that growth. Management is stable and has done a good job, and all the ratios point to a bright future.

Mary is extremely excited about presenting this stock because she believes she's done a good job and found a winner. Before the meeting she tells John how much work she's done in researching this stock and how excited she is about it. When she presents the stock, however, John isn't nearly as excited about it as Mary. He believes competition is going to increase tremendously, that people will obtain their pharmaceutical needs through other means, such as the Internet, and that the company will lose market share. He decides he doesn't want to invest the club's money in this stock. When the president calls for a show of hands of those who vote to buy the stock, Mary turns to John with a big smile. Will John vote no? Will he be concerned about hurting Mary's feelings? Will he vote yes just because he thinks Mary will be upset with him because he voted not to buy the stock?

By using a secret ballot, Mary won't know who voted for or against the stock. In fact, if the motion passes, Mary doesn't have to know anyone voted against it. The secretary can simply announce that the motion passed. There's no need to announce that there were 14 votes for and one vote against.

If the group decides not to buy the stock that's presented, or if they have additional cash, they may want to discuss purchasing additional shares of a stock they already own. If they have 50 shares of Citibank, and the person who monitors the stock had a great report, they may want to add to that position. Or if the person monitoring Merck & Company had a negative report, they may now want to discuss selling that stock. At some meetings, you may have discussions regarding a couple of your holdings, or you may have no issues to address.

FINISHING UP

It's now time to discuss any old business or new business the members may feel is important. Old business includes unresolved issues, such as an update from the vice president of education as to the availability of a speaker the club discussed inviting to a special meeting, or a review of who's bringing what dish to next weekend's potluck picnic. New business may include an announcement from the treasurer that everyone needs to bring money for their annual NAIC dues next time, or a request from the secretary for additional money for the petty-cash fund.

At the conclusion of those discussions, the president should announce the next meeting's assignments, then adjourn the meeting. The entire meeting should have lasted between one to 1½ hours. If meetings are stretching out to two hours or beyond, the president needs to start curtailing discussions and ensuring that members stay focused on the business at hand.

After the meeting is adjourned, it's party time, if you'd like. Bring out that pizza. Cut that chocolate cake. Put up that pot of coffee. This is your opportunity to chat with your friends, get to know each other better, and have a little fun. But beware! You may be surprised to find that despite the fact that the meeting has been adjourned, rather than talking about recent movies, your tennis game, or your child's preschool, the discussion continues to focus on interesting stocks, the strength of the economy, or the growth of certain industries. When members get excited about investing, there's no stopping them!

Chapter

Keeping the Records

The club's record keeping is primarily the responsibility of the treasurer. At some point, however, every member will fill the position of treasurer. Therefore, it's important that every member understand what record keeping is required and how it's done. There are two different areas of record keeping the treasurer needs to be concerned with: monthly valuation statements and tax documents.

MONTHLY VALUATION STATEMENTS

The treasurer keeps track of the investment club's assets—stocks and cash—by preparing a monthly valuation statement. This statement keeps the members informed as to what stocks the club owns in its portfolio, when those stocks were purchased, what price was paid for each of the stocks, and what those investments are worth as of the date of the valuation statement. It also includes information as to how much cash the club has in its brokerage cash account.

The second half of the statement reflects how much of the total club's assets each member owns. These statements can be prepared by hand or, if the club is a NAIC member, they can purchase software that can help the treasurer produce the statements.

Dating the Statement

The valuation statement depicts the club's assets as of one specific day. Therefore, the members need to choose what date the statement will reflect.

That day probably won't be the day of the monthly meeting because the treasurer wouldn't even be able to start preparing it until the day of the meeting, after the stock market closes. You need to allow the treasurer sufficient time to prepare the statement. For example, if your club meets on the second Thursday of each month, the valuation statement may be dated as of the last business day of the previous month. Whatever date the club chooses, you may want to include that exact date in Section 4.5 of your club's bylaws.

Portfolio Value Section

The first section of the valuation statement depicts the club's total portfolio value. Figures 9-1 and 9-2 show a sample of the portfolio value section of a monthly valuation statement for two consecutive months as depicted by NAIC in their manual, "Starting and Running a Profitable Investment Club."

Valuation Statement

As of July 31, 2001

Portfolio Value

Company	No. of Shares	Purchase Date	Cost per Share	Total Cost	Price per Share This Date	Total Value
Moore Steel	20	7/15/01	$5.58	$111.60	$5.125	$102.50
Cash on hand						8.45
Total value of club this date						$110.95
Total number of valuation units to date						12.00
Value of each unit this date ($110.95 divided by 12 units)						$ 9.25
Number of units each $10.00 deposited at July meeting will purchase ($10.00 divided by $9.25)						1.081

Figure 9-1: Valuation Statement
Source: National Association of Investors Corporation (NAIC)
www.better-investing.org

This is the valuation statement of a new investment club. As you can see, the club has, to date, purchased only one stock. Let's look at each column of their July valuation statement separately.

✔ **Company Name:** This is the name of the company whose stock the club purchased.

✔ *Number of Shares:* This is the number of shares the club purchased of each company's stock in each individual transaction. This statement has only one line item.

✔ *Purchase Date:* This is the date the club purchased the shares—information that will be required for tax purposes when the shares are sold.

✔ *Cost Per Share:* The club paid $5.58 per share for Moore Steel Company. That amount includes the commissions the club paid to purchase the stock. On this valuation statement, the treasurer adds the commission to the total cost of the shares and divides it by the number of shares purchased to calculate the cost per share. If you prefer, you could use the actual cost per share, then multiply it by the number of shares to get a total share cost. You'd then need to include an additional column called "Commissions" and add the total share cost and the commission to determine your total cost. However you choose to handle the commission charge, it's important that it's included.

✔ *Total Cost:* This column represents the total cost of the 20 shares of stock plus commissions (20 times $5.58).

✔ *Price Per Share This Date:* This is the per-share price of the stock as of the close of business on the date of the valuation statement. This information can be found in almost any newspaper.

✔ *Total Value:* This column represents the current value of all the shares you purchased in this transaction of that particular company. The total value of Moore Steel Company is $102.50 (20 times $5.125).

To determine the club's total value, you need to add in the club's other asset—cash. Include a line for cash on hand, which is the balance of the club's cash account at the brokerage firm as of the statement date, then total the column to determine the club's total value as of the date of the statement. At the end of July the club had $8.45 in its cash account, giving the club a total value of $110.95.

At the club's first meeting, the 12 members contributed $10 each. Therefore, the club consisted of 12 valuation units. But the price of Moore Steel Company's stock decreased from $5.58 per share to $5.125 per share, making the total value of the stock $102.50. With the $8.45 in the cash account, the clubs total assets equaled $110.95. If you divide the club's total assets by the 12 valuation units, the per-unit value is $9.25 ($110.95 divided by 12).

At that meeting, however, the members contribute another $10 each. Remember that the unit value, to date, is worth $9.25. Therefore, that $10 contribution can purchase 1.081 units ($10.00 divided by $9.25).

Now let's look at the club's valuation statement at its next month's meeting. Because they voted to buy another stock in July, they now have two stocks listed on the August meeting's valuation statement. (See Figure 9-2.)

Valuation Statement

As of August 31, 2001

Portfolio Value

Company	No. of Shares	Purchase Date	Cost per Share	Total Cost	Price per Share This Date	Total Value
Moore Steel	20	7/15/01	$5.58	$111.60	$5.50	$110.00
XG Products	22	8/16/01	4.91	108.02	4.25	93.50
Cash on hand						20.30

Total value of club this date	$223.80
Total number of valuation units to date	24.972*
Value of one unit ($223.80 divided by 24.972)	$ 8.96
Number of units $10.00 purchases ($10.00 divided by $8.96)	1.116
Members' total investment	$240.00

*The "total number of valuation units to date" of 24.972 is derived as follows:

Valuation units as of beginning of July meeting	12.000
12 members deposit $10.00 each at July meeting, each purchasing 1.081 units (12 x 1.081)	12.972
Total units at beginning of August meeting	24.972

Figure 9-2: Valuation Statement
Source: National Association of Investors Corporation (NAIC)
www.better-investing.org

On this month's valuation statement, the club owns 20 shares of Moore Steel Company, which now has a current price of $5.50, for a total value of $110.00. It also owns 22 shares of XG Products, which has a current price of $4.25, for a total value of $93.50. The club owns two stocks. Therefore, there are two line items.

Sometimes an investment club will purchase a company's stock and later decide they like the stock so much, they want to purchase more. To make the record keeping easier and to help at tax time, the treasurer should make each purchase a separate line item on the valuation statement. For instance, if your club purchases 50 shares of Walgreen Company in February, then purchases another 50 shares in July, the valuation statement should reflect two purchases of 50 shares each, rather than one holding of 100 shares.

After you list the club's two stocks, you have to add in the $20.30 in the club's cash account. This club has a total value of $223.80.

Once again, the 12 members contribute $10 each. But each $10 purchases 1.081 units (based on the July statement). Therefore, 12 times the 1.081 units equals 12.972 units. Add the 12.972 units purchased with the July contributions to the 12 initial units, and the club has a total of 24.972 units.

On the August valuation statement, the total value of the club is $223.80. Therefore, each unit is worth $8.96 ($223.80 divided by 24.972 units). Now, the number of units that $10 can purchase is 1.116. But the members' total contributions to the club are $240 (12 members times $20 per member). Just like most new investment clubs, this one has experienced a small loss of $16.20. It often takes a new club one or two years before it really starts generating a comfortable profit.

The above statements depict the value of the club's total portfolio, but each member will want to know how much his or her share of the club is worth.

Value-Per-Member Section

While the members want to know what the total value of the club's assets are and the breakdown of stocks it owns, they also want to know what portion of those assets belongs to each of them individually. In Chapter 5 the members decided whether they wanted to use equal or unequal ownership in their club. While unequal ownership is the best choice in the long run, we'll look at how this section of the valuation statement would look under both scenarios. Figure 9-3 shows the second part of the valuation statement, assuming the club uses equal ownership.

Value Per Member

August 31, 2001

Total Club Value:	$223.80
Number of Members:	12
Value Per Member:	$18.65

Figure 9-3: Value Per Member

That's pretty straightforward and simple. If the total value of the club is $223.80 and there are 12 members who have all contributed the same amount of money and, therefore, each own the exact same percentage of the club, each member's value is $18.65 ($223.80 divided by 12).

Now, let's look at how the treasurer would prepare the value-per-member section if your club uses unequal ownership. (See Figure 9-4.)

Value Per Member

July 31, 2001

Member	July Investment	July Units	Total Units	Current Value Per Unit	Total Value
Alan	$10.00	1	1	$9.245	$9.245
Bette	$10.00	1	1	$9.245	$9.245
Chris	$10.00	1	1	$9.245	$9.245
Denise	$10.00	1	1	$9.245	$9.245
Emily	$10.00	1	1	$9.245	$9.245
Frank	$10.00	1	1	$9.245	$9.245
Gary	$10.00	1	1	$9.245	$9.245
Helen	$10.00	1	1	$9.245	$9.245
Izzy	$10.00	1	1	$9.245	$9.245
Judy	$10.00	1	1	$9.245	$9.245
Kathy	$10.00	1	1	$9.245	$9.245
Larry	$10.00	1	1	$9.245	$9.245
	$120.00	12	12		$110.94

Figure 9-4: Value Per Member

In July each person contributed $10, which purchased one unit. Since this is the first month of operation, each person owns one unit, total. Due to a drop in the price of the one stock the club owns, the value of one unit of the investment club is $9.245 ($110.95 divided by 12 units). Therefore, each person's total value is $9.245. Now, let's move to August. (See Figure 9-5.)

Each person purchased one unit in July. In August each person contributed $10 and that money purchased 1.081 units. So now each person owns 2.081 units. The value per unit is currently $8.96 (223.80 divided by 24.972 units). Therefore, each person's value in the club is $18.65.

As the months go by and members begin to contribute varying amounts, the chart will eventually depict different numbers for each member.

The above valuation statement reflects one way of keeping the club's books. If you find that another method fits your club's needs better, by all means, use that method. The point is, the treasurer needs to report the current status of the club's assets to the members every month. As long as that's accomplished, it doesn't make any difference how you arrange the information.

Value Per Member

August 31, 2001

Member	July Investment	July Units	August Investment	August Units	Total Units	Current Value Per Unit	Total Value
Alan	$10.00	1	$10.00	1.081	2.081	$8.96	$18.65
Bette	$10.00	1	$10.00	1.081	2.081	$8.96	$18.65
Chris	$10.00	1	$10.00	1.081	2.081	$8.96	$18.65
Denise	$10.00	1	$10.00	1.081	2.081	$8.96	$18.65
Emily	$10.00	1	$10.00	1.081	2.081	$8.96	$18.65
Frank	$10.00	1	$10.00	1.081	2.081	$8.96	$18.65
Gary	$10.00	1	$10.00	1.081	2.081	$8.96	$18.65
Helen	$10.00	1	$10.00	1.081	2.081	$8.96	$18.65
Izzy	$10.00	1	$10.00	1.081	2.081	$8.96	$18.65
Judy	$10.00	1	$10.00	1.081	2.081	$8.96	$18.65
Kathy	$10.00	1	$10.00	1.081	2.081	$8.96	$18.65
Larry	$10.00	1	$10.00	1.081	2.081	$8.96	$18.65
	$120.00	12	$120.00	12.972	24.972		$223.80

Figure 9-5: Value Per Member

TAX DOCUMENTS

April 15 is a notorious date in this country because it's tax day. With some exceptions, we all have to file and pay our taxes by this mid-April date. Partnerships, however, do not pay taxes at the partnership level. Instead, the partnership income earned in the form of dividends, interest, and capital gains is passed through to the individual partners, who are then responsible for claiming that income on their personal tax returns.

Despite the fact that the partnership itself does not have to pay taxes, it does have to file tax forms with the IRS every year. The forms your club is required to submit to the IRS are IRS Form 1065 (U.S. Partnership Return of Income, including Schedule D) Capital Gains and Losses, and a Schedule K-1 for each member of the club. Each member must also receive a copy of his or her individual Schedule K-1. These forms can be obtained from your nearest IRS office, at many local libraries, can be ordered from the IRS by calling 1-800-TAX-FORM, or can be printed from the IRS web site at www.irs.gov or www.irs.ustreas.gov.

These tax forms are strictly informational in that they notify the IRS as to how much your investment club realized in *short-term gains and losses, long-term gains and losses*, dividends, and interest during the year. If the forms are not filed each year, the individual members of the club could face an IRS penalty.

Short-term gains and losses: Profits and losses incurred from selling an asset that was held one year or less.

Long-term gains and losses: Profits and losses incurred from selling an asset that was held more than one year.

It's important to understand that the club only realizes capital gains or losses when a stock they own is sold. For instance, if the club purchased 50 shares of ABC Company at $26 per share and the stock is now trading at $51 per share, even though the club has a $25 per share gain on that stock, there's no tax due until the stock is sold. If they still own the stock they have a paper profit, which is not taxable. When the stock is sold they have a capital gain, which is taxable.

Because the IRS delineates between short- and long-term gains and losses, the treasurer needs to keep track of how long the club owned each stock it sold during the year. That information will be needed when filling out the club's tax returns. That information, however, can be found on the confirmations the club receives from its brokerage firm for its purchases and sales of stocks.

When it comes to taxes, it's important to understand that the individual partners will typically have to pay tax on income they don't receive. In Chapter 3 we discussed that one of the four principles of investing suggested by NAIC is to reinvest all dividends and capital gains. Therefore, if the club sells a stock and makes a profit of $800, that money won't be divided up among the members to take home with them. Instead, that $800 will be placed in the club's brokerage cash account and will later be used to purchase another stock. Because the club realized a profit from that sale, however, taxes must be paid. Each member will pay tax on his or her share of that $800 gain, but won't receive the money. Each member's share of the taxable income is determined by his or her individual capital account.

For example, if one member owns 8 percent of the club's assets, and the club has an $800 gain, that member's portion of the taxable gain would be $64 (8 percent times $800). The same is true with dividends. When a company whose stock the club owns pays a dividend, that money goes into the club's cash account to be reinvested in more stocks. Taxes, however, must be paid on that dividend and are allocated based on each member's level of ownership. The members' individual tax information is distributed to them on the Schedule K-1 that the treasurer prepares for each member. This form is informational for the members and does not have to be sent to the IRS with the members' personal tax returns because it's already been filed by the treasurer with the club's tax forms.

In addition to the federal IRS tax forms, clubs may be required to file state or local tax forms. The treasurer should check with the appropriate taxing authorities to determine if there are any state or local tax requirements where your investment club is located.

The tax forms investment clubs are required to file are fairly self-explanatory. If, however, the treasurer feels uncomfortable with this task, it may be well worth having a tax advisor assist. The Dough Makers of Kankakee, Illinois, had their taxes done by an accountant and, like many clubs, felt it was well worth the $100 they were charged. If you have an accountant complete your tax forms the first year, the treasurer could possibly use those initial forms as a model and complete future years' tax forms with no problem. Or, your club could purchase a copy of the February issue of the NAIC magazine, *Better Investing,* which typically includes an article that offers line by line instructions on filling out the required tax forms.

At some point, every member of your investment club will fill the office of treasurer. Oftentimes, members hesitate to take on this role because they believe it's too complicated. But with a little training from the exiting treasurer, it's a job that can be done fairly easy. And it's a great way to get a little experience in dealing with a brokerage firm—experience that will help when you start your own personal investment portfolio!

10

Chapter

The Nuances of Building a Stock Portfolio

Congratulations! You've created an investment club, you're investing in the stock market, and you're building a nest egg for your future. You've made a lot of progress, but as your club meets from month to month, there are various nuances to investing in stocks that will surface that you need to know about. Some of these nuances present you with great opportunities. Some offer you additional options in your quest to increase the size of your portfolio. Others may be investing options that you need to understand so that you'll know to keep your distance. You probably won't want to get involved in those aspects of investing. Some of these topics represent potential problems you need to be able to identify in case they raise their ugly heads. And some others are options you need to know about so you can get recourse if you do find yourself embroiled in a dispute. Let's look at some of the issues you may find yourself dealing with after you've starting amassing a stock portfolio.

INVESTMENT ISSUES

Dividends

We previously defined a dividend as the portion of a company's profits that the board of directors decides to pay to the company's shareholders. For example, if you purchased a stock for $20 per share and that company's board of directors decides to pay its shareholders a 4 percent dividend, you'll receive $.80 per share from that company every year. Most companies divide that $.80 into four equal payments so that you'd receive $.20 per share every three months. If your club owns 100 shares, you'll get $20 every three months. It's not a lot of money, but if you own several stocks that pay dividends, it can add up. Also, that's another $20 you can invest that can also start collecting dividends. And you never know when the company might increase their dividend payment.

You might wonder why a company would give money every quarter to its shareholders. The reason is that they want their shareholders to be happy. If the company pays a steady dividend, more investors may be willing to buy the stock. The more investors who buy the stock, the higher the price will move. Two years from now the company may want to raise more money by selling more stock. If shareholders are happy with the stock's progress, they'll probably be willing to buy more. But if shareholders aren't happy, they won't be interested in buying more stock and the company won't be able to raise more money through a *secondary public offering*, which may hinder the company from expanding or making acquisitions.

Secondary public offering: A company's issuance of stock subsequent to its initial public offering.

Another reason management wants investors to keep buying their company's stock and drive the price higher is because management personnel typically own big chunks of the stock. Therefore, just like any other shareholder, they want the price to increase so they can make money. Dividends are just one more tool management can use to keep shareholders interested in their stock and convince them to buy it. The future growth of the company, and probably a good portion of the management personnel's wealth, depend on happy shareholders driving the price of the stock upward.

Of course, not all public companies pay dividends, but that doesn't mean those companies don't want happy shareholders. It just means that those companies believe they can put the money to better use and still make their shareholders happy. Here's the theory.

Companies that are fairly new or that are in fast-moving industries probably won't pay dividends because management needs all the money they have available to fund the company's growth, build the business, expand, and research new products. But shareholders don't mind that the company doesn't pay a dividend, because if management uses that money to grow and the company does well, its stock price will increase. An increasing stock price always keeps investors happy!

The companies that typically pay dividends are older, more well-established companies in mature industries. Those companies have gone through their years of rapid growth and can probably now fund the slower rate of growth they'll experience from their own cash flow and still have enough money to pay a dividend. Therefore, they may not see such rapid increases in their stock prices, but a nice, steady dividend is certainly a plus for investors.

A company that's a good example of providing its shareholders with steady dividends for years is General Electric. Not only have they paid their shareholders a dividend every year for the past 24 years, but the dividend has been steadily increasing. Figure 10-1 shows that dividend's growth during the past few years relative to the S&P 500 index dividend growth.

That's the type of dividend payments investors like to see. It's important to remember, however, that dividend payments are not an indication as to whether a company's stock is a good or bad investment. You can only make that determination by researching the company's fundamentals.

If your club decides to purchase a stock that pays a dividend, you need to understand how the dividend payments are made. There are four terms you'll need to know—*declaration date*, *record date*, *ex-dividend date*, and *payment date*.

Declaration date: The day a public company announces the amount of its dividend for that quarter.

Record date: The day on which the company closes its books for the quarter. Any investor recorded as a shareholder on that day will receive that quarter's dividend.

Ex-dividend date: The first day on which someone purchasing a company's stock would not receive the most recently announced dividend.

Payment date: The day a public company actually pays its quarterly dividend.

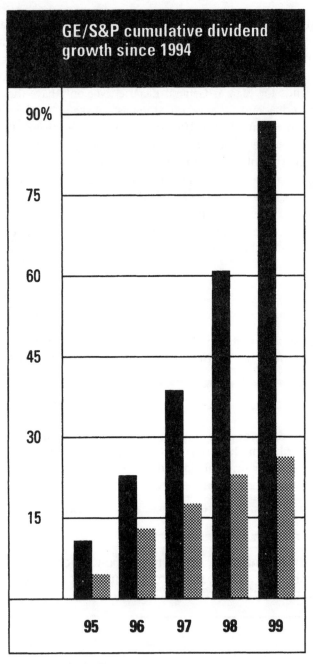

Figure 10-1: General Electric Dividend Growth Since 1994
Source: General Electric Company

Declaration date: This is the day the company announces how much the dividend will be for that quarter. On this day, it will also inform the public as to the record, ex-dividend, and payment dates.

Record date: This is the exact date on which you must be a shareholder in order to receive that quarter's dividend. You may be a shareholder for only one day out of the quarter, but as long as that day is the record date, you'll get the dividend. Conversely, you could own the company's stock for almost the whole quarter, but sell it just prior to the record date, and you won't get the dividend. If you want to receive a company's dividend, this is an important date to note.

Ex-dividend date: This is the last day you can buy a company's stock and still receive the dividend for that quarter. Earlier, we discussed T+3, or trade plus three days, which means it takes three days for a trade to close after you buy or sell a stock. When you instruct your stockbroker to buy a stock for you, she purchases it and tells you what the exact price was. That price is locked in, but you're not really considered the owner of that stock until three days later. Consequently, if you buy a stock the day before its record date, you won't get the dividend. But if you sell a stock the day before the record date, you'll still get that company's dividend payment because it takes three days for that sale to finalize.

Payment date: This is the day the company sends out dividend checks or credits the dividend to the shareholders' accounts.

While these are dates your club may want to consider when buying and selling dividend-paying stocks, you shouldn't let a dividend record date drive your investment decision. For example, let's say your club meets on April 8 and decides to sell 100 shares of a stock that's been in your portfolio for a while, but hasn't performed. One of the members mentions that the stock's record date is April 14 and that the club's dividend payment would be $30. The members decide it would be silly to sell just before they're about to collect a $30 dividend payment, so they decide to hold off on the sale until after the ex-dividend date. But two days later, the price of the stock drops two points. The club then sells the stock. They'll collect the $30 dividend, but they ended up selling the stock for $200 less than if they had sold it as soon as they made the decision to do so. Of course, the opposite could have happened. They could have decided to wait to sell the stock and the price could have increased by two points. The club would then have collected the $30 dividend and sold the stock for an extra $200. The problem is, you never know until it's too late whether the price will increase or decrease. All you can do is weigh your options and make the best decision you can.

Dividend Reinvestment Plans (DRPs)

Another option many dividend-paying companies offer their shareholders is *dividend reinvestment plans* (DRP—pronounced "drip").

Dividend reinvestment plan {DRP}: A plan in which the company offers investors the option of having their dividend used to purchase additional shares of the company's stock, rather than receiving the dividend in cash.

AT&T was one of the first companies to offer its shareholders a DRP, in 1971. Today, almost all dividend-paying companies offer their shareholders some form of a DRP. If your club enrolls in a company's DRP, instead of paying you a quarterly dividend in cash, it purchases more of its stock and credits that stock to your account. The advantages are that some companies purchase this stock for their shareholders at a slight discount to the current market price and charge their shareholders either reduced commissions or no commissions at all. Also, when the company purchases shares for your DRP account with your dividend, if there is money left over because there's not enough to buy one more share, the company will credit your account with a fractional share. Be aware, however, that there may be a few fees involved with DRP plans, but typically they are minimal. Also, with DRPs it's important that you keep accurate records of all of purchases and any sales because you'll need that information at tax time.

Cash Option Plans

In addition to their DRP, some companies also offer a *cash-option program* in which shareholders have the option of sending additional money to the company at regular intervals.

Cash-option program: Program offered by companies in which shareholders participating in the DRP can mail in regular cash contributions for the company to purchase additional shares of the company's stock for the investor.

The company then uses that money to buy the shareholder even more shares of the company's stock without having to go through a stockbroker. Before becoming involved in any company's cash-option program, you should call their investor-relations department and ask for information as to how the plan works and what fees may apply because each company's plan is different.

After you've enrolled in a company's dividend-reinvestment plan, if you have questions regarding payment of your dividend, or if you have a problem with your dividend payment, you'll get a faster response if you call the company's transfer agent rather than the company's investor-relations department. It's the transfer agent's job to manage the company's shareholder records, including their dividend-reinvestment and cash-option programs. The transfer agent can assist you in requesting and canceling stock certificates, providing you with information about your dividends, and any other account questions you may have. The transfer agent's name, address, and phone number can be found in the company's annual report.

Direct Stock Plans (DSPs)

Some major corporations now offer investors the opportunity to buy even their initial purchase of the stock directly from the company at a reduced cost through a *direct stock plan*.

Direct stock plan: Plan offered by companies in which investors can purchase their initial shares of stock directly from the company.

If you choose to use this option, call the company and get the details of how their plan works, including any expenses you'll be charged and the initial investment required to open an account.

Another way to buy without a broker is NAIC's Low-Cost Investment Plan, through which NAIC members can purchase various companies' stocks at a reduced commission cost.

Keep in mind that when you purchase stock through a broker, the minute you place the order the stock is purchased. Therefore, you have a good idea as to what your cost per share will be. When you use other methods, such as cash-option programs, direct stock-purchase programs, and

NAIC's Low-Cost Investment Plan, however, your stock is not purchased until your check is received. That can take a few days at best and the price of the stock can fluctuate so that you're never quite sure what your price will be.

With these programs, because the stock is held in an account with the company, your club will have to sell the stock it accumulates directly through the company by submitting instructions in writing to the transfer agent. Or, you can have the company issue your club a stock certificate and you can sell the shares through your broker. Again, whether you have the company sell the shares or you request a certificate, it will take several days before the stock will be sold. Unlike selling your stock through a broker, you won't know what your the price will be when the actual sale takes place.

If you're interested in these types of services, the web sites listed below may provide you with the information you need to make a decision.

✔ www.netstockdirect.com: This web site provides a list of companies that offer DRPs and DSPs and provides plan summaries.

✔ www.dripcentral.com: This web site offers lots of resource materials regarding DRPs and DSPs.

✔ www.dripinvestor.com: This is the web site of Charles Carlson, who writes the *DRIP Investor Newsletter*. In addition to being able to request a list of stocks that offer DSPs, investors can also request a free sample copy of his newsletter.

✔ www.moneypaper.com: Through this site you can obtain information on various companies' DRPs. It also offers a newsletter and gives investors the ability to purchase their initial shares of stock through this organization, but you must be a subscriber to the service.

All of these programs are good options in building an investment portfolio, but it's important to understand how each program works and what fees you'll be charged.

Stock Splits

At one of your monthly meetings the treasurer hands out the valuation statement and you notice an error. In the portfolio value section of the statement, the listing for Cisco Systems shows the club owns 100 shares. But the club only purchased 50 shares of that stock. During the discussion period, you politely point out to the treasurer that he made an error. The treasurer explains that in the last month Cisco Systems' stock split two for one and the club now owns 100 shares. What happened?

What happened is that Cisco Systems doubled the number of shares your club owns of their stock! But don't get too excited. At the same time they doubled your holdings, they cut their stock price in half. The total value of your Cisco Systems stock is still the same.

If your club owns 50 shares of a stock that trades for $60 per share, your total value in that stock is $3,000 (50 shares times $60 per share). After a two-for-one stock split, the number of shares the club owns increases to 100, but the price per share decreases to $30. The value of your stock is still $3,000 (100 shares times $30 per share). Companies can split their stock in any way they want. Our example is a two-for-one stock split, but many companies opt to do a three-for-two, a three-for-one, or any other combination they want. But if the value of your stock holding remains the same after a stock split, why bother?

Investors who bought GE stock in 1925 paid $337 for one share. Seventy-five years later that one share would have been worth more than $235,000, hardly a price many investors could afford. To keep their stock affordable, GE split its shares nine times during that 75 years, as depicted in Figure 10-2.

General Electric Stock Splits

Due to stock splits, one share of GE stock purchased in 1925 would have increased to

Date of Split	Split Ratio	Number of Shares
1926	4 for 1	4
1930	4 for 1	16
1954	3 for 1	48
1971	2 for 1	96
1983	2 for 1	192
1987	2 for 1	384
1994	2 for 1	768
1997	2 for 1	1,536
2000	3 for 1	4,608

Figure 10-2: General Electric Stock Splits

Due to those stock splits, one share of GE stock purchased in 1925 would have turned into 4,608 shares valued at approximately $51 per share by June 2000, for a total value of more than $235,000. By using stock splits, GE was able to keep their stock affordable so more people could buy it. And the more people who invest, the higher the company's stock price increases.

In many instances, companies will combine the announcement of a stock split with an increase in its dividend payment. For instance, if a company pays a $.60 dividend and splits its stock two for one, that dividend will also split two for one, making the dividend $.30 per share. But the company may increase it to $.32 per share at the same time as the split. That increased dividend may help attract even more investors.

A stock split may be a positive sign that a company is doing well, and because the postsplit price is more affordable, and more investors can buy the stock, there's a chance the price may increase. But investors shouldn't buy a stock based on rumors of a stock split. What ultimately drives a company's stock price is performance. If a company's earnings are declining, they're losing market share, and management isn't turning that around, they can split their stock all they want and most investors still won't buy the stock. A good example of that was CompUSA.

On April 22, 1996, the company split its stock two for one, making the postsplit price $15.16. Three years later, that stock was selling at $6.125. Obviously, the investment community didn't think it was a good investment, despite the stock split. It's the company's performance that investors need to focus on because that's what drives the price up to levels that allow the company to do a stock split.

Reverse Stock Split

A variation of the stock split is the *reverse stock split*.

Reverse stock split: A decrease in the number of shares issued by a company without any change in its financial position. Used as a ploy to increase the company's stock price.

If a company's stock is selling at $4 per share and you own 100 shares, your stock has a total value of $400 ($4 times 100 shares). If the company does a four-for-one reverse stock split, you'll then have 25 shares that sell for $16 per share, which still has a value of $400 ($16 times 25 shares). Not many companies use the reverse stock split, but when you see one that does, it probably isn't a good sign. We said that companies split their stock to make it more affordable. So why would a company want to use a reverse stock split to increase the price of its stock? The reason is that stocks that sell for under $5 are called microcap stocks and are considered to be very risky. Therefore, most investors stay away. By doing a four-for-one reverse stock split the company now sports a stock price that more investors would consider.

If the only way a company can increase its stock price is by relying on a ploy such as a reverse stock split, it's probably not performing very well, and probably not a stock your investment club wants to own. Once again, viable companies increase their stock price by demonstrating good performance.

Initial Public Offerings (IPO)

The first time a company creates stock and sells it to the public through the brokerage community, it is called an *initial public offering*, or an IPO.

Initial public offering (IPO): The process through which a company legally creates stock and sells that registered stock to the public for the first time.

If a company is popular in the investment community and investors believe the stock will do well, an IPO's volatility can be unbelievable. That's been the case with many of the Internet stocks that have gone public. Consider the case of Netscape Communications Corporation. Netscape made its IPO debut on August 8, 1995, and came to market at $28 per share. That first day of trading saw Netscape's shares rise to a high of $75 and finally close the day at $58.25. When e-Toys first hit the market it soared from $20 to $80 in one day, then eventually dropped back to around $12 per share.

Or what about Palm, which sells the popular Palm Vx and touts itself as offering Internet access anywhere, anytime. The company first went public on March 2, 2000. The IPO price was $38 per share. When the stock first started trading, it hit $160 per share and dropped back to $80 per share the next day. The really amazing part of this IPO was that 3Com Corporation was the sole owner of Palm and in the IPO, 3Com sold only 5 percent of Palm. But within the first day of trading, that 5 percent was worth more in *market capitalization* than 3Com, which owned the remaining 95 percent of Palm. Sometimes, investors have to accept that the stock market just doesn't make sense!

Market capitalization: A valuation placed on a company that's calculated by multiplying its number of shares outstanding by its current stock price.

Despite the absurdity of it all, wouldn't it have been great if your club had owned a couple hundred shares of Netscape or Palm when they first hit the market? It would have been great, but it would also have been impossible.

When companies do an IPO, they do so through an *investment banker*.

Investment banker: A brokerage firm that helps companies bring their stock to the public.

The investment banker helps the company determine the number of shares they'll sell and figure out what the price will be. Then the shares are allocated to specific brokerage firms that will sell the shares to the public. These firms sell the shares to their customers prior to the stock being listed and sold in the marketplace over an exchange. This selling period is called the *subscription period*.

Subscription period: The period of time when the brokerage firms sell the initial shares of a company's stock to investors prior to it trading on a public exchange.

After the subscription period, the stock starts selling over an exchange, where investors can trade it just like any other stock.

But IPOs have sort of an Old Boy network. The first problem investors face is that the brokerage firms that get IPO shares to sell during the subscription period sell them only to their customers. So if you're not a customer of that brokerage firm, you can't buy those shares. But even if you are a customer of that brokerage firm, you still may not be able to buy those shares.

When a brokerage firm gets an allocation of an IPO stock that the investment community thinks is going to zoom up in price as soon as it starts trading, every customer of that brokerage firm wants to get their hands on some of those shares. But the brokerage firm has only so many shares to sell. If one of their customers has a $1.5 million account and trades tens of thousands of dollars worth of stocks each week, and your investment club has a $22,000 account and trades about $600 worth of stocks a month, and you both want shares to an upcoming IPO, who do you think will get those shares? I'd say the guy with the $1.5 million account has an excellent chance. Is that fair? No, but no one said life was always going to be . . . well, you know.

That doesn't mean, however, that an investment club can never get IPO shares. Let's look at another scenario. This time the brokerage firm is allocated IPO shares of a company that the investment community thinks is pretty dismal. The analysts have so little interest in it, they don't even cover it. There's no hype about it in the media. Nobody cares. But the brokers have been allocated a certain number of shares that they have to sell during the subscription period. Of course, the guy with the $1.5 million brokerage account isn't interested. Neither is the woman with the $750,000 account. These are the IPO shares that your investment club could probably get access to. But don't expect these shares to hit the market at $28 per share and zoom up to $75. Instead, they may hit the market at $28 per share, then drift down to $24.

Typically, for smaller investors, such as most investment clubs, the IPO shares they have access to are shares that no one else wants. But take heart. In some cases, the IPOs that everyone wants aren't necessarily that great anyway. Just because the brokerage community thinks an IPO will do well doesn't mean it will. Popular IPOs are often extremely volatile and become overpriced quickly. An explanation of why such high volatility occurs was reported in a March 27, 2000, *Business Week* article that stated that in some cases, the investment bankers who help take companies public bring those companies out at lower prices than the market will bear. The articles states, "They do it to please institutional clients, who buy at the offering price and then sell into the initial runup." Whether the allegation is true or not, the fact remains that many IPOs are volatile and the average investor can lose a lot of money by trying to participate in a stock when it first hits the market.

If your club is interested in a specific IPO, you're probably better off taking a wait-and-see attitude. Wait until the stock starts trading on an exchange, give it a year or so to work out all the hype, then research the company to determine whether the stock's price represents the true value of the company and decide if it's a stock the club wants to buy. When it comes to IPOs, the old song title "Fools Rush In" often applies.

INVESTING STRATEGIES

Diversification

There's an old saying: "Variety is the spice of life." While that's true of life, it's also true of investing in stocks. Except that in stocks, variety is called *diversification*.

> **Diversification:** Investing in stocks of various types of companies, including those in different industries and of different sizes.

Diversification is important because it substantially reduces the amount of risk that is inherent in your portfolio. There are two types of risk investors face when entering the stock market: market risk and firm risk.

Market risk, which accounts for 30 percent of total risk, is the risk you take that the market as a whole will take a major downturn. That type of movement in the market cannot be reduced by diversification because market movements affect all stocks. Therefore, it can't be avoided.

Diversifying by Industry

Firm risk, which accounts for about 70 percent of the total risk your club will have to deal with when buying stocks, relates to specific companies and to the industries those companies represent. As the company or industry changes or as investors' perception of the company or industry changes, firm risk increases or decreases. Diversifying your stock holdings can reduce that risk. Therefore, if you reduce firm risk, you're basically left with only 30 percent of the total risk that exists in stock-market investing.

For example, if your investment club owns the stocks of Wal-Mart Stores, Gap, Kmart, and Target, and the retail industry encounters problems, chances are your whole portfolio will take a nosedive. But if your four stocks are Wal-Mart Stores, Lucent Technologies, General Motors, and Abbott Laboratories, and the retail industry has a downturn, only one of your four stocks will probably be affected.

Diversifying by Company Size

While diversifying among various types of industries is important, there's another aspect to diversification you need to consider. Your club should also diversify its portfolio by company size. The investment community breaks companies down into four different size categories.

Large-Cap Stocks

Large-cap stocks: Stocks of companies whose total number of outstanding shares multiplied by the company's current stock price equals more than $5 billion.

Typically, the larger a company, the less risk that's associated with its stock. Large companies are more stable because they have reserves set aside so they can withstand economic downturns. They also have the resources required to fight their competition. Because these companies are so large, there are plenty of analysts who cover them and there is widespread media coverage. Obtaining information on these companies is easy. Also, because these companies have so many shares outstanding, they are very liquid, making it easy to buy and sell their stock. Their stock prices are also not very volatile because the companies don't demonstrate fast growth; they've already achieved their spurt of growth and are now growing at a more steady and consistent pace. Therefore, while a large-cap company offers low risk, it also offers fairly low rewards—maybe a dividend plus steady growth, but not spectacular growth.

Small-Cap Stocks

Small-cap stocks: Stocks of companies whose total number of outstanding shares multiplied by the company's current stock price equals $1 billion or less.

Because of the company's size, small-cap stocks are considered to be more risky than large-cap stocks. Oftentimes, being new companies, they may not even be making a profit due to start-up costs, marketing costs, and research expenditures. Therefore, they have no reserves or resources available to help them weather an economic downturn or to fight their competition. If a major problem arises, they could face their demise. Because these companies are small, they don't attract the attention of the media or of analysts, so coverage on them may be minimal. The number of shares outstanding will be much smaller than the number of shares a large-cap company has outstanding. Therefore, the small cap's stock will be less liquid and more volatile. But if a small-cap company gets through its infancy and performs well, the rewards can be great. A small cap's stock price has a much greater chance of doubling, or more, than that of a large-cap company's stock. Therefore, small-cap stocks offer the potential for higher rewards, but also carry higher risk.

Midcap Stocks

Midcap stocks fall somewhere in between the large and small caps. They don't carry as high a risk level as the small caps do, but are not as low risk as the large caps. The midcaps offer more potential for price appreciation than the large caps, but not as much as the small caps.

Midcap stocks: Stocks of companies whose total number of outstanding shares multiplied by the company's current stock price equals between $1 billion and $5 billion.

Microcap Stocks

Microcap stocks: Stocks of extremely small companies. The stock's price is typically around $5 per share or less.

Microcap stocks carry an extremely high level of risk. These are the stocks of companies that have no track records, and probably generate no revenues or profits. In fact, they may not even have any prospects of ever generating revenues or profits. These stocks sell at very low prices—sometimes even less than $1—and typically sell for not much more than $5 per share. Because of their low prices, they're also called penny stocks. These companies have no media or analyst coverage and are not very liquid. In fact, with many of the microcap stocks, it's difficult to even obtain the price at which they're currently trading. Microcap stocks are the types of stocks that con artists use to defraud investors out of their money by using a scam called *pump and dump.*

Pump and dump: A scam in which a con artist pumps up the price of a microcap stock by recommending it to investors, then dumps his own shares when the price increases, leaving the investors with fairly worthless stock.

They convince unsuspecting investors that the company has a great future and that its stock is about to take off. When those investors start buying the stock on the con artist's recommendation, the price starts to rise. As soon as the price increases several points, the con artist sells his shares for a huge profit. After he's dumped his shares, he stops touting the stock and the price falls dramatically. The con artist makes a lot of money and the investors lose their money. Microcap stocks offer an extremely high level of risk, but unfortunately, not much chance of any reward.

When diversifying your club's portfolio, you should include small-, mid-, and large-cap stocks. While the small-cap stocks add a little risk to your portfolio, they also offer the potential for higher reward. By including large-cap stocks, that high risk of the small caps is balanced with stocks that offer lower risk but also a little lower reward potential. Midcap stocks offer a good blend of both risk and reward potential. When it comes to microcap stocks, avoid them at all cost! Why take on such a high level of risk when the potential of reward is negligible?

No matter what size company your club is considering, it's always important to research them to ensure it's a stock your club wants to own. By finding and purchasing good companies that represent the various size categories, you'll create a portfolio that consists of a good mix of potential risk and reward.

Diversifying by Going Global

Another way you can diversify your portfolio is by going outside of the United States. One option in doing that is to purchase the stocks of big U.S. conglomerates. While they're still U.S. companies, they probably conduct a large amount of their business in other countries. For instance, there aren't many countries you can venture into without seeing a McDonald's. Owning multinational companies is an easy way to add a little international flavor to your club's portfolio.

There is another option, however, your club could consider if it wants to venture outside the United States and buy shares of companies in other countries. Your club can purchase *American Depositary Receipts (ADRs)*.

American Depositary Receipts (ADRs): Certificates sold over U.S. stock exchanges that represent shares of foreign companies.

Buying foreign stocks directly from another country would be very difficult. For instance, if you wanted to buy stock in Nestle's, which is domiciled in Switzerland, you'd have to find a stockbroker in Switzerland and try to deal with the language differences. In addition, you'd have to figure out how to change your U.S. dollars into Swiss francs.

But thanks to financier J.P. Morgan, there's an easier way. In 1927 Morgan decided there should be a simple way for Americans to buy the stocks of foreign companies, so he created ADRs. He purchased shares of foreign companies, deposited them at the foreign office of a U.S. bank, then issued a receipt, or ADR, that traded on a U.S. stock exchange in dollars. By using ADRs, U.S. investors could purchase shares of foreign companies directly from their stockbrokers without having to deal with the language barriers or the currency differences.

It's important to note that one ADR doesn't necessarily equate to one share of the foreign company's stock. An ADR may represent several shares or just a fraction of a share of the underlying foreign stock. There are, however, problems with purchasing ADRs. First, they are available for only the largest companies, so you'll still miss out on some of the smaller, faster-growing foreign companies. Also, due to accounting-rule differences, the financial statements of foreign companies may be somewhat more difficult to interpret. For example, U.S. companies must write off goodwill, the additional value a company has over and above its tangible assets due to its good reputation or solid clientele. That write-off reduces earnings, over a maximum of 40 years. International standards, however, have no maximum, allowing companies to take smaller write-offs over a longer period of time, thereby reducing the impact those write-offs have on earnings. The international accounting rules also typically require less disclosure. Another issue investors must deal with when purchasing ADRs is that they fluctuate in value, not only based on supply and demand, but also due to the foreign-currency fluctuations against the dollar. And even more difficult to track, investors need to understand the politics of the country where the company is located. If the country is about to go through a revolution, that won't bode well for your stock.

When dealing with ADRs, the tax issues can also become somewhat more complicated. If you buy a company that pays a dividend, foreign taxes will be deducted from that dividend and you'll have to reclaim that money on your tax form at the end of the year. While ADRs are a valid option, it's important that investors are also aware of the potential pitfalls.

Another option in adding an international flavor to your club's investment portfolio is to purchase global or international mutual funds. We'll discuss the pros and cons of that option in Chapter 13.

While investors have options in adding an international component to their portfolio, some of the options don't really achieve the goal very easily. They can purchase U.S. conglomerates that conduct a large portion of their business in other countries, but the amount of international exposure you receive from those stocks is minimal. If your club wants to tackle an ADR, they're available but slightly complicated. In Chapter 13 we'll discuss the best way for you to get that international spice into your portfolio.

When discussing diversification, one question that surfaces is: How many stocks should an investment club own? When a club first forms, it should try to build a portfolio as quickly as possible so members can see progress and stay interested. Typically, a new club will purchase eight to 10 stocks in the first year. Because some of those purchases will probably be for small amounts of stock due to the club's lack of money, during subsequent years they may want to add to the holdings they think are great investments. As the club ages, it may increase its holdings to 20 to 25 stocks. Most important is that your club doesn't purchase more stocks than your members can monitor.

Buying on Margin

At one of your meetings, John announces that he attended an investment seminar since your last meeting and learned about a great way for your club to increase its profit potential. It's called *buying on margin*.

Buying on margin: Purchasing stocks with money that the investor has borrowed from the brokerage firm.

John's right. Buying on margin can increase your club's profit potential. It can also increase your club's risk—substantially. Here's how it works.

Your members vote to purchase 100 shares of Big Mistake Corporation at $40 per share for a total cost of $4,000. The stock price increases to $45 per share and your club decides to sell the stock. You receive $4,500. Your profit is $500. Now let's look at the same transaction using margin.

Your club purchases 200 shares of Big Mistake Corporation at $40 per share for a total cost of $8,000. Your club pays $4,000 and borrows the other $4,000 from your brokerage firm by pledging the shares. When the prices of the stock goes up to $45, you sell the 200 shares and receive $9,000. You pay back the $4,000 you owe your brokerage firm, and your profit is $1,000. (For the sake of simplicity, we're ignoring any commission or interest charges in these examples.) By investing the same $4,000 and using margin, your profit jumped from $500 to $1,000! Before John gets too excited about this, the other members have to calm him down and explain the other side of the story.

First, it's important to know that under *Regulation T*, the Federal Reserve Board allows investors to borrow only 50 percent of the total value of their brokerage account from their brokerage firm.

Regulation T: Federal Reserve Board rule that limits the amount of credit a brokerage firm can give to its clients.

Following is the list of an investment club's stock holdings. The club has a $10,000 portfolio.

Big Mistake Corporation	100 shares	$40 per share	$4,000 total value
Good Purchase Corporation	100 shares	$25 per share	$2,500 total value
Strong Financials Company	175 shares	$16 per share	$2,800 total value
Cash			$ 700
	Total Portfolio Value		$10,000

If your club's account is worth $10,000, under Regulation T you can borrow a maximum of $5,000. So you borrow $4,000 and buy an extra 100 shares of Big Mistake Corporation on margin. But after you purchase those

200 shares of Big Mistake Corporation the price drops from $40 to $18 per share. In fact, the market takes a downturn and Good Purchase Corporation's stock drops from $25 per share to $20 per share, and Strong Financials Company's stock drops from $16 per share to $13 per share. Now your portfolio looks like this:

Big Mistake Corporation	200 shares	$18 per share	$3,600 total value
Good Purchase Corporation	100 shares	$20 per share	$2,000 total value
Strong Financials Company	100 shares	$13 per share	$1,300 total value
Cash			$700
	Total Portfolio Value		$7,600

Your total portfolio value is now only $7,600. But remember, you have a $4,000 loan outstanding with your brokerage firm, and Regulation T says you can only borrow 50 percent of your total portfolio value. Unfortunately, $4,000 is more than 50 percent of $7,600. Now what happens? Trouble.

Your brokerage firm has an established, preset percentage of how low your account can slip before you get a call. When your account has dropped by that amount you'll get a *margin call* from your broker.

Margin call: A call from your broker telling you to deposit cash or securities in your account so that it meets the Regulation T margin requirements.

In our example, he'll tell you that he needs to have an extra $400 worth of value in your portfolio so that the portfolio has a total value of $8,000, making your $4,000 loan 50 percent of your portfolio. You have three options:

1. Your members can ante up an additional $400 and send it to the broker.

2. You can deposit $400 worth of additional stock in your portfolio (not a real option for an investment club because you probably don't have additional shares of stock at another brokerage firm).

3. You can sell a portion of your stock holdings at its currently reduced price to reduce the amount of the loan so that it once again equals 50 percent.

None of these is a good option, but you're lucky the shortfall is only $400. If the market had really taken a nosedive, or if your portfolio and margin positions were larger, you could really get into trouble.

How quickly you have to ante up the money you owe depends on the brokerage firm you use. The exchange rules allow up to 15 days. Most traditional brokerage firms allow customers two weeks, but most of the online firms allow you only two or three days.

Buying stock on margin should not be an option for an investment club. If your club has adopted a long-term buy-and-hold investment philosophy, then buying on margin isn't an investing strategy you should use. Buying on margin lends itself to speculation, quick decisions, and, oftentimes, deep pockets. That's not what an investment club is all about.

Shorting Stock

After your club went through the fiasco of Big Mistake Corporation's stock price dropping from $40 to $18 per share, John comes up with another stellar idea that he picked up at the investment seminar he attended—*shorting stock*.

Shorting stock: Selling borrowed stock in the hope that the price will drop so you can buy it back at a lower price.

John claims that if the club had shorted Big Mistake Corporation when it was at $40 per share, you would have made a killing. Let's see if he's right.

When your club buys stock, they're taking what's called a *long position*.

Long position: Buying stock and hoping that the price will increase so you can sell it for a profit.

You buy the stock, hope for the price to go up, and eventually sell it for a profit. But when you short stock, you sell it, wait for the price to go down, then buy it back. The first step in shorting stock is to sell it. Of course, to sell it, you have to have it. But you can depend on your broker for that. He'll let you borrow the stock from the brokerage firm. So you borrow 100 shares of Big Mistake Corporation's stock and sell it for $40 per share for a total sales price of $4,000.

When Big Mistake Corporation's stock price drops to $18 per share, your club can purchase 100 shares at $18 per share for a total cost of $1,800. You give that 100 shares back to your broker to replace the shares you borrowed, and you made a profit of $2,200. You sold it for $4,000, bought it back for $1,800, and made $2,200. John's excited again! Unfortunately, it's time to calm him down one more time and explain the rest of the story. Your club borrowed and sold 100 shares of Big Mistake Corporation's stock at $40 per share, for a total sales price of $4,000. But what if Big Mistake Corporation suddenly reports that it just created a system that would make the whole Internet totally secure to use. No one would have to worry any more about secure lines, viruses, or having information accessed without permission. Investors assume this company is going to make billions of dollars from this system, so they start buying the stock. The stock's price jumps to $60 per share in one day.

But you're stuck with a short position you have to cover. At some point, you need to buy 100 shares and return those shares to your broker. If you do it now, the 100 shares will cost you $6,000. You only received $4,000 for them, so you'll have a $2,000 loss. Should you just sit on the short position and wait for the price to come down? Nice try, but no.

Once again, your broker calls. He doesn't want to get stuck with your loss so he wants some money from you to cover that potential loss. If you don't have it, he can force your club to cover its short position at a loss. You buy back the shares, replace them, and take a $2,000 loss.

In the long run, maybe you were lucky. What if Big Mistake Corporation's stock had gone up to $80 per share or $100 per share? When you short stock, your potential loss is unlimited. When you take a long position in stock, however, the stock's price can't drop any lower than zero. You can't lose more money than you put into it. Having an unlimited loss potential isn't the only problem you have when you short stock.

If you still have a short position in Big Mistake Corporation when the company decides to start paying its shareholders a dividend, your club won't get that dividend. Your club will have to pay that dividend—to the brokerage firm that lent you the shares. The original owner of those shares is still the rightful owner and should collect the dividend. But you sold the shares, so you owe the dividend.

Even worse, when your club initially sold those shares for $4,000, you didn't get the $4,000. The broker kept it. And chances are, unless you negotiated it beforehand, you won't even get the interest that $4,000 earns while you have your short position open.

Shorting stock can be extremely dangerous and not an investing strategy an investment club should use. There are other investing strategies, such as using puts and calls, that you can combine with shorting stock to reduce your risk, but that just adds one more layer of complication to investing. Instead, explain to John that your club is going to find good companies with strong fundamentals, buy those stocks, and hold them for the long term. It's worked for thousands of other investment clubs. If done properly, there's no reason it won't work for yours.

POTENTIAL PROBLEMS

At each monthly meeting, in addition to providing each member with the monthly valuation report, the treasurer will also give everyone a copy of the club's brokerage statement or, at the least, pass around the original. As we discussed earlier, reviewing the brokerage statement is simply a good way to check that the treasurer is completing transactions as the club wishes. But there is one other reason why everyone should scrutinize the brokerage statement every month.

Probably 99 percent of all stockbrokers are honest and reputable people. But there are a few who are not. Despite the fact that your club researched your broker and the brokerage firm prior to opening an account, you can never be sure. There are a couple types of problems your members should watch for that can be found on your monthly statement.

Unauthorized Trades

Stockbrokers make money by collecting commissions from their clients when they buy and sell stock. The more stock transactions the client completes, the more money the broker makes. Some stockbrokers periodically decide to make a little extra money by making *unauthorized trades* in a client's account that the client didn't request or wasn't aware of.

Unauthorized trades: Buy and sell transactions a stockbroker makes in a client's account without that client's permission or knowledge.

Unauthorized trades are easy to detect if investors review their monthly statements. Let's say that last month your members voted to buy 50 shares of Wal-Mart and to not sell any stocks. When your treasurer gets the next monthly statement, it shows that not only did your club purchase 50 shares of Wal-Mart, but it also sold 100 shares of Abbott Laboratories and bought 75 shares of the Walt Disney Company. Your stockbroker is making unauthorized trades in your account.

If that happens, the treasurer should call the broker and ask why those trades were made. If the broker doesn't reverse the trades and make your club whole again, talk to the branch manager. If you still don't get satisfaction, you have other avenues you can pursue. But first, let's look at the other problem you could encounter.

Theft

Stockbrokers run into money problems just like everyone else. But because they work around money every day, they may be tempted to solve their personal money problems through unscrupulous means. If a broker needs a quick $2,000 and sees that money in your account, he may withdraw the money and pocket it. Of course, that withdrawal will show up on your club's next brokerage statement and you'll know there's a problem. That's possible, but it's also possible that the withdrawal won't show up.

Brokers have been known to steal from their clients' accounts and then, without the brokerage firm's knowledge, confiscate the client's monthly statement and print a new statement showing the account intact. The problem for the broker, however, is that he doesn't have the ability to print an actual brokerage statement. He'll have to create one that looks as similar to the real thing as possible.

If your club suddenly receives a statement that has a different look than the statements you've received in previous months, don't call your broker. If he's stealing money from your account, he'll simply say the firm now has new statements. Instead, call the branch manager and ask if the firm is now using new statements. If not, you're conversation with the branch manager will last a little longer.

Those are the two potential problems your club could encounter with your broker. Take heart, though. Because you're an investment club, there are other problems, such as churning (a broker convincing a client to transact innumerable buy and sell orders just to increase commissions) and unsuitability (a broker selling a client an investment that's much too risky for her needs) that aren't really relevant. Your members should be making all of your own buy and sell decisions. If you don't depend on the broker to help you make those choices, he really doesn't have the opportunity to churn your account or sell you unsuitable investments.

Getting Recourse

If your club experiences a problem with unauthorized trades or theft, and the brokerage firm's branch manager won't help you, you have other options. Your best choice is *mediation*.

Mediation: A process in which a single mediator assists two parties in determining a mutually agreeable resolution to a dispute.

Through the authorities, you can have a mediator assigned to your case who will listen to both sides of the story and help you come to a mutually agreeable resolution. Mediation is a fairly quick and easy resolution to stockbroker problems.

If, for some reason, mediation doesn't work, your next step would be *arbitration*.

Arbitration: A system for resolving disputes in which the two parties submit their disagreement to an impartial panel for binding resolution.

In arbitration, a panel of arbitrators is assigned to listen to your case. Each side presents its case and the panel makes a final and binding decision. By the time you complete all the necessary steps, the process will probably take a full year. The arbitration process can also be costly because you'll probably need to hire representation. If the dispute is for $1,000, arbitration is obviously not worth it.

If, however, your club is facing a loss at the hands of your stockbroker for several thousand dollars, you might want to consider arbitration. And, in fact, because the investment club's members can all chip in and share the costs of pursuing recourse and hiring representation, it's actually less costly per person than if you were an individual victim of an unscrupulous stockbroker and had to pay the expenses yourself.

To start the mediation or arbitration process, call the National Association of Securities Dealers Dispute Resolution Office. They have several offices across the country, but to find the one nearest you, call the New

York office at 212-858-4400. If you need to find representation, you can call the Public Investors Arbitration Bar Association (PIABA) at 888-621-7484 for a referral.

Chances are your club will never encounter a problem with its broker. And if you do, you can probably get it taken care of easily and swiftly through the broker or the brokerage firm's branch manager. If they're not willing to rectify the problem, however, it's important to know your options for resolution.

You should also be aware of one problem you don't need to worry about with your brokerage firm: If it goes into bankruptcy, your account will be safe because you're covered by the *Securities Investor Protection Corporation (SIPC)*.

Securities Investor Protection Corporation {SIPC}:
A nonprofit organization established by Congress in 1970 to protect the cash and securities investors hold at their brokerage firms in the event the firm fails and is liquidated.

SIPC insures your club's brokerage account for up to $500,000, including $100,000 in cash. If your brokerage firm goes into bankruptcy your account would either be transferred to another brokerage firm or you would receive certificates for your stock holdings and a check for the cash.

Of course, your brokerage firm isn't the only entity that may cause you problems. Corporations have been known to commit illegal acts, such as lying about the company's performance and future prospects. While the SEC deals with those problems, the Dough Makers Investment Club of Kankakee, Illinois, found that investors can also become involved. They owned the stock of a company whose management got caught lying about the company's performance, and the club is now part of a class-action lawsuit. Becoming part of that lawsuit simply involved filling out a questionnaire. Whether they'll ever get any recourse remains to be seen.

As your investment club ages and builds its portfolio, you'll probably encounter most of the above investment issues, use the investing strategies, and, hopefully, never have to deal with the potential problems. If your club members understand:

✔ how dividends work,

✔ the effects a stock split has on your portfolio,

✔ the importance of diversifying your portfolio,

✔ the motive of a stockbroker who offers you an IPO,

✔ the pitfalls of buying on margin and shorting stock, and

✔ how to deal with a problem broker,

then your club is certainly informed and ready to deal with the nuances of building a stock portfolio.

To Sell or Not to Sell

One of the goals of an investment club is to build a nest egg by buying stocks and creating an investment portfolio. But that doesn't necessarily happen by a straight-line method. To build that portfolio, you'll not only have to buy stocks, but you'll also have to sell stocks and replace them with new ones. Very few investors can choose stocks that continually do well and increase in price year after year. You'll definitely end up with a few losers along the way. In fact, there's a theory called the Rule of Five that suggests that for every five stocks you own over a five-year period, one will disappoint you, three will perform as you expected, and one will demonstrate stellar performance. But how do you know if a stock really is a loser? How do you determine when to sell?

Those are questions that have been debated by investment professionals for years. There are no real answers, but there are guidelines your club can follow. Making a sell determination doesn't come from gut feeling or from a headline in the newspaper. A gut feeling or a newspaper headline may provide an indication that selling a stock could be a possibility. But deciding to sell should be based on research and knowledge, just like making the decision to buy a stock. If you don't take your time and do your research, you may jump out of a stock, then watch its price soar. There's nothing more disheartening than owning a stock for a long time, deciding it's a laggard, selling it, then the next month watch it go up six points.

Bob McClow and the MAJEC Investment Club in Phoenix, Arizona, learned that lesson with Wal-Mart Stores. Wal-Mart Stores was one of the first stocks the club bought. After they had owned it for four years, the stock was at approximately the same price they paid for it. A couple of members decided the club should sell and started convincing other members that the stock would never move. It was brought to a vote and the majority voted to sell the stock. Six months after they sold, Wal-Mart Stores stock started increasing in price. It has now doubled from where they sold it. But McClow looks at that mistake as a learning experience and says that anyone who hasn't had that happen to them hasn't done much investing. The problem may have been that the club based that sell decision on the stock's price, rather than on the fundamentals of the company.

When a member does a stock presentation, she's recommending that the club buys that stock. She's based that recommendation on hard work and research. She's reviewed the company's publications, third-party publications, and crunched some numbers. She's decided this is a good stock for the club to buy because of specific reasons. Those specific reasons are based on certain fundamentals of the company.

If those fundamentals that convinced you to buy the stock remain the same, there's no reason to sell the stock. However, a change in the fundamentals should trigger an impulse to do a little research. How do you know there's a change in the fundamentals? Hopefully, the club member who's responsible for monitoring that stock will know. That's why it's so important to have members monitor the stocks you own in your portfolio. Below are some situations that may spark a thought that selling a stock may be wise. If you find one of your stocks in these situations, it's time to do a little research.

WHEN TO CONSIDER SELLING

Deteriorating Financials

Let's say one of the reasons your club bought a stock was because the company continuously increased its revenues and net income from quarter to quarter. Then, one quarter the company issues its report and you find that revenues and net income have taken steep drops. That's a change in one of the fundamentals that spurred you to buy that stock. That calls for some research.

Read the report. A sudden drop in revenues and net income should be discussed in the CEO's letter to the shareholders. Maybe the dip is a short-term problem caused by some unforeseen situation and the company will recover next quarter. If so, there's probably no reason to sell. If the reason is that the company lost a couple of major customers, find out why. If a couple of customers left, there may be more on the way out. If the company doesn't seem to have a plan to quickly rectify the problem, you may want to sell.

Industry Laggard

We discussed that when you're researching a company whose stock you may want to buy, it's important to compare that company to other ones in the same industry. Obviously, with the stocks your club owns, that comparison was positive. Otherwise, you wouldn't have purchased the stock. But all of a sudden, the person monitoring the stock realizes that during the past year your company's stock price increased by 10 percent, but the stocks of other companies in the same industry increased their prices by 20 percent. Find out why. You may have to call the company's investor-relations department to get an answer. If the answer sounds viable and you believe the company can turn the problem around, there's probably no reason to sell.

Management Changes

Maybe one of the reasons your club purchased a stock is because you liked the company's CEO. Perhaps he was at another company that had serious financial problems and he turned the company around and made it profitable. He then went to work at the company you're considering buying and within the first year the company's profit margin improved dramatically.

But one day you're reading the *Wall Street Journal* and find that the CEO has decided to retire and the company just announced the name of the new CEO. Should you sell? Not necessarily. Check out the new person. If he was the previous CEO's right-hand man, he'll probably have the same type of management style and philosophy. If he comes from outside the company, check him out. What sort of results did he produce at his previous job? Did he fire a third of all the employees and practically run the company into bankruptcy? If so, sell. If it appears that he did a good job, hang on to the stock, keep monitoring it closely, and see how he does.

Expiring Patents

A lot of companies, such as pharmaceutical companies, depend on patents. Those patents protect their sales of certain products. What happens when several of the company's patents expire and the competition steps in? Has the company built a strong enough sales base that the competition won't hurt them? Or have they developed other products that are just beginning their patent periods and will replace the older products? If the company has six products and they're all under patents that expire this year, there's reason to be concerned.

Growing Competition

When new industries hit the marketplace, it takes time for companies to understand that industry's needs and begin to take advantage. Some companies enter the fray faster than others do and those earlier entrants have a distinct advantage. When the Internet first became popular, there were very few companies offering the services that were required to utilize what the Internet could offer. Those companies that saw the need and got in early had a window of time in which there was practically no competition. They may have done well for a time, but were they able to sustain that performance when other companies offering the same services jumped into the arena?

When competition suddenly heats up, find out how your company is reacting. Do they have a plan, or are they simply plugging along, hoping that the competition won't affect them? If the company can do well when they're the only game in town but can't figure out how to thwart new competition, you may want to sell and replace that company's stock with the stock of a more aggressive company in the same industry.

Changing Economic Factors

Companies typically have no control over economic changes that can have huge impacts on their profitability. But while they have no control, they do have the ability to manage those changes. For instance, maybe you own the stock of a company that produces a product that's predominately made out of aluminum. For some reason, the price of aluminum increases by one-third. If a company doesn't have a plan in place to manage that type of change, it can be devastating. Or maybe you own an airline stock and the price of oil increases, as it often does. Is the company managing those fuel expenses effectively so that an increase in oil prices won't wipe out their profits?

When those types of situations occur, you should call the company and find out if management hedges its product purchases so that they're setting the prices of the materials they'll need in the future. Of course, that price increase will affect them eventually, but if they're properly managing those costs the effect will be much less dramatic than if they're not. Other types of economic changes may be spikes or declines in interest rates, changes in the inflation rate, or other increases or decreases in the prices of the materials required to produce a product.

Dividend Reduction

If a company that's been paying a dividend for years suddenly decreases the amount of dividend or eliminates it completely, that's a red flag that it is having dire financial problems and profits are drying up. Companies pride themselves on paying a string of increasing annual dividends. To have to cut a dividend is not an easy decision and is typically made only when there is no other option.

If a company whose stock you own cuts its dividend, call and find out why. Chances are, you'll find the company is in serious trouble. Hopefully, the member who's monitoring that stock will have already picked up on those problems and you'll have already sold the stock prior to the dividend cut.

Portfolio Rebalancing

If your club purchased 50 shares of Cisco Systems at $64 per share in 1998 for a total investment of $3,200, by early 2000, after two two-for-one stock splits, you would have owned 200 shares. At the early 2000 price of $72 per share, your investment in Cisco Systems would have been worth $14,400. If your club's total portfolio value was $28,000, Cisco Systems would have represented more than 50 percent of your portfolio value. A portfolio with 50 percent of its value in one stock isn't very diversified.

In a situation like this, you may want to rebalance your portfolio by selling some of your Cisco Systems stock and locking in that profit, then reinvesting that money in another stock. In fact, to help ensure your portfolio is diversified, Section 10.1 of the sample bylaws in Chapter 4 stated that one company's stock can't represent more than 20 percent of your club's total portfolio value.

Cashing Out a Departing Member

At times, your investment club may choose to sell stock to cash out a departing member. That option, however, isn't necessarily always the best way to handle that situation. There are other means a club can use to pay out a member who resigns from the club. We'll discuss those options in Chapter 12.

Tender Offer

Sometimes a company decides, for various reasons, that it wants to buy some of its stock back. Or Company A will take over Company B and buy Company B's stock from the shareholders. In a *tender offer,* you'll be offered a set price from them to buy your stock by a certain date.

> **Tender offer:** A situation in which a public company offers to buy back from the shareholders its own company's shares, or the shares of another company that's being taken over, at a set price.

The price you're offered is usually slightly higher than the current market price. When given a tender offer, find out why the stock is being purchased and decide whether selling is an option that's best for the club.

The above are red flags that should alert your members that it's time to do a little extra research on a company to determine if you should sell their stock. Sometimes, however, situations develop that cause investors to panic and they immediately sell a stock without doing any research at all. Panic is an evil enemy of investors. If you panic during a catastrophe such as a fire, a major potential accident, or a sudden serious illness such as a heart attack, the chances of your survival are diminished. Experts tell us that when we're facing a catastrophe, the first rule is to remain calm.

That advice can also be followed when it comes to the stock market. If the stock market as a whole or an individual stock you own faces a catastrophe, you should remain calm, get the facts, and make an educated decision as to whether you should keep the stock or sell. Below are some of the situations that cause investors to panic.

WHEN SELLING MAY BE A MISTAKE

Market Correction

When a market correction hits, investors start to wonder what's next. The Dow Jones Industrial Average (DJIA) drops a few hundred points in the course of one trading day and investors wonder if that drop will continue the next day. It certainly will if people panic and start selling.

The investment community puts a lot of importance on the DJIA. Its daily opening and closing levels are reported on TV and radio programs and in the newspapers. Investment experts try to guess where the number will stand at year-end, by next year, and even 10 years out. Just what is this number that makes investors so nervous?

In 1882 Charles Dow and Edward Jones opened the firm of Dow, Jones & Company. In 1889, working on a hand-cranked printing press, they published the first edition of the *Wall Street Journal*. Actively writing about the stock market, they decided that there was a need for an average, or index, that could be used as a standard for following the progress of the market. Choosing 12 stocks—American Cotton Oil; American Sugar; American Tobacco; Chicago Gas; Distilling and Cattle Feeding; General Electric; Laclede Gas; National Lead; North American; Tennessee Coal & Iron; U.S. Leather; and U.S. Rubber—that they thought were good representations of the industrial stock market, they created the DJIA. That was in 1896.

Still considered the benchmark of the stock market, the DJIA currently consists of the following 30 stocks:

AT&T	Honeywell International
Alcoa	IBM
American Express	Intel
Boeing	International Paper
Caterpillar	Johnson & Johnson
Citigroup	McDonald's
Coca-Cola	Merck
Disney	Microsoft
DuPont	Minnesota Mining
Eastman Kodak	J.P. Morgan
Exxon Mobil	Philip Morris
General Electric	Procter & Gamble
General Motors	SBC Communications
Hewlett-Packard	United Technologies
Home Depot	Wal-Mart Stores

In the past, the DJIA stocks had all been ones that traded on the New York Stock Exchange. In 1999, however, the first NASDAQ stocks became part of the DJIA with the inclusion of Microsoft and Intel. Changes will continue to be made from time to time as to which companies are represented in the DJIA as Dow Jones strives to keep the index up-to-date.

Because it's called an average, most people would assume that the DJIA number is derived by adding the per share price of each of the 30 stocks and dividing by 30. Unfortunately, it's not that easy. Due to additions and deletions in the stocks that make up the average, stock splits, and other machinations of the market, the computation is a complicated weighted average.

But how it's calculated is irrelevant. The important point is that when the compilation of those 30 stocks moves up or down, investors pay attention.

Many investment professionals question the validity of this average. There are hundreds of stocks available for investors to purchase. Thirty of those stocks is a rather small number of stocks to be representative of the entire market. Therefore, many prefer to follow other averages, such as the Standard & Poor's Composite Index, which follows the stocks of 500 different companies.

While the DJIA may not be the best bellwether, it's the one that the investment community follows. When it sinks several hundred points, many investors panic and start selling out their portfolios. But that isn't necessarily the right tact to take. First, just because those 30 stocks dropped doesn't mean that the price of the stocks your club owns dropped. In fact, they may have even gone up in price. You need to consider not the market as a whole, but the individual stocks you own. Secondly, if your stocks do follow the DJIA down, instead of indicating a rush to sell, it may be an indication to buy. Historically, when the DJIA drops, it always surges back, surpassing its level prior to the drop. Your club's reaction to a correction in the DJIA should be that if the fundamentals of the companies whose stocks you own were good yesterday, and that hasn't changed, why would you sell? In fact, it may be a good time to add to some of your holdings. Instead of panicking at a correction, take advantage of it.

Bad News

Just like in our personal lives, companies sometimes have catastrophes happen to them. An airline company's plane crashes. A tornado wipes out a corporation's largest manufacturing facility. The government recalls the company's product because it's considered unsafe. When these types of problems arise, investors oftentimes panic and sell their holdings in the company. But instead of immediately selling, they should do a little research and find out how the company is handling the bad news. If they handle it well, their stock price will probably bounce back and continue its climb.

For example, when the Union Carbide plant in Bhopal, India, emitted fumes in the air and killed people, it was a terrible tragedy. While the company's stock price immediately declined, it later rebounded due to management's astute handling of the problem. The same with Johnson & Johnson, when someone placed a foreign substance in Tylenol capsules and people died. Management went to the public, admitted they had a problem, explained their plan for rectifying that problem, and took care of it. If a company has good management, they'll have a disaster plan in place and handle any catastrophes that come their way.

When catastrophe strikes one of the companies whose stock your club owns, determine how management is handling it. Are they denying the problem? Are they too busy to rectify it because they're trying to place blame elsewhere? If so, this may not be the type of company you want to own. If they don't handle the problem well, the company's stock price may continue to drop. In the worst case, the company may not even survive. But if management is admitting to the problem, has a plan of attack, and is putting that plan into action to resolve the problem, chances are that the company's stock price may drop initially, but will probably come back and continue its way upward.

Bankruptcy

Most beginning investors would think that if a company whose stock they own filed for bankruptcy, that would be a sure sign to sell. But that's not necessarily the case. Filing for bankruptcy doesn't mean a company is going out of business. Most business bankruptcies are what's called *Chapter 11*, which basically just gives the company a little breathing room.

Chapter 11: A type of bankruptcy filing in which a company is given a period of time during which it can reorganize without creditors seeking payment.

It means that their creditors must give them time to reorganize without expecting payments during that period. Many companies have gone into Chapter 11 bankruptcy, reorganized, and come back stronger than ever. If one of your companies files for bankruptcy, take the time to find out what caused the problem and whether they have a workable solution.

Price Targets

Some investors set price targets when they purchase a stock. If they buy a stock at $20 per share, they may plan to sell it when it hits $40 per share. When it hits that mark, they either sell it, or at least revisit their reasons for setting that target.

When using this strategy, it's important to remember that an investment club should have a buy-and-hold, long-term strategy. Just because a stock's price doubles doesn't mean it can't continue to go up. Let's look again at Cisco Systems. If your club purchased that stock at $28 per share in 1991 and sold it in 1992 when it hit your price target of $55, wouldn't you have been disappointed when that stock soared to $78 per share? If a soaring stock price creates a situation in which that stock represents a huge percentage of your portfolio, you may need to consider rebalancing, but selling the whole position because of a predetermined price target may be a mistake.

Conversely, some investors also set price targets on the opposite end. They may buy a stock for $25 per share and decide that if it drops 15 percent, to $21.25 per share, they'll sell. It's a viable strategy, but the real question is, why did the price drop by 15 percent? If the fundamentals are still in place and the company is still doing well, that drop may just be a vagary of the market. In Chapter 6 we discussed the whisper number that analysts use when predicting a company's earnings per share. Many times, if a company misses the analysts' number the stock's price will drop. But that was just a number the analysts predicted and it may have been overly ambitious. If the company is strong, it will overcome the drop in its stock price and rebound. You'd hate to sell at $21.25 per share, then see the stock rebound.

When a stock's price drops, it's time to check the company's fundamentals to determine if anything has changed. Call the company's investor-relations department and ask their opinion as to why the stock is depressed. Then make an educated decision whether to hold or sell. You may find that the real answer is not to sell, but to buy. If the price has dropped, but you believe the company's problem is temporary and that the stock's price will come back and continue to increase, you may want to use the strategy of *averaging down*.

Averaging down: Purchasing additional shares of a company whose stock price has decreased, subsequent to your initial purchase, to reduce the average price of your stock holdings in the company.

For instance, if your club purchased 50 shares of a stock at $25 per share and the price drops to $20 per share, you won't be at breakeven again until that price comes back up to $25. But what if, when it's at $20 per share, the club buys another 50 shares? Then, when the price comes back, you'll be at breakeven when the stock reaches $22.50 because you've reduced your average price per share to $22.50. When the stock price hits $25, you've made money.

Volatility in a stock's price can be very advantageous to investors who are willing to use the strategy of averaging down. If one of your stocks takes a dip in price but your members really think it will rebound, averaging down is a good strategy. Of course, a mistake can be costly. If the price continues to decrease, instead of losing money on 50 shares, you're now losing money on 100 shares. It's a viable strategy, but just like with any investing strategy, it's important to use it in a studied and intelligent way.

Stagnation

In this era of instant gratification and all the talk about *day traders* supposedly making big bucks, investors expect to buy a stock and a week later see that its price has moved up at least a few points.

Day traders: Investors who buy and sell stock—typically online—and close out their positions at the end of each day. Their hope is to make money on small movements in a stock's price.

If that gain doesn't show up quickly, they sell and move on to another stock. But sometimes it takes a stock time to move. Take the case of Wal-Mart Stores. Its price lagged below $20 per share from July 1996 until November 1997, then traded between $20 and $35 during the next year. If you're going to expend the time and effort required in researching a stock, and you find one that you think has great promise, at least give that stock time to perform. Always keep in mind that an investment club has a long-term investment philosophy of buy and hold. That "hold" doesn't mean for just two months!

Insider Trading

The management personnel of a public company usually own large chunks of their company's stock because part of their compensation package includes stock options.

Some of the stock, called *restricted stock*, is regulated by the SEC and the executives are restricted from selling it under certain conditions.

Restricted stock: Stock that cannot currently be sold due to SEC regulations.

Most executives, however, also own company stock that they can sell if they want.

When these management people decide to sell all or part of the stock they own in the company, they're required by the SEC to report that *insider trading* by filing an SEC Form 144.

Insider trading: When a company's management personnel buy or sell shares of their own company's stock.

Those filings are often reported in newspapers. Therefore, if the CEO of a company plans to sell 30,000 shares of his company's stock, the public will know.

When investors see that an executive has decided to sell his own company's stock, they often interpret that as a negative sign. They wonder if he knows something the rest of us don't know. That may be a possibility, but you can't be sure. Maybe the CEO's daughter is getting married and he's selling stock to pay for the wedding. Maybe he has triplets who are all starting college this year and he needs money for tuition. When you see insider trading, you can't be sure of the motive behind it.

Another problem with this strategy is that these management personnel must complete the SEC paperwork if they decide to sell their company's stock. After they complete the paperwork, however, and it's reported to the public, if they decide not to sell that stock, they don't have to. So it may be reported that a CEO is selling stock, but it never happens.

If, however, you suddenly see that five or six of the company's executives are selling big blocks of the company's stock, you might want to find out why. If that many insiders are dumping stock, it could be a sign of rough times ahead for the company.

Institutional Investors

Companies that manage huge pension funds or retirement plans invest a lot of the money they manage in stocks. When these *institutional investors* buy and sell stocks, they buy and sell blocks of at least 10,000 shares. Those trades are reported in the business section of most major newspapers.

 Institutional investors: Large investors, such as pension-plan managers, who buy and sell huge blocks of stocks at one time.

Some investors believe that if there is a lot of institutional selling in a specific stock that the managers of those institutions know something about the company that makes them want to sell. They're also concerned that these huge blocks of stock that are being sold will drive the price of the stock downward.

Just like individual investors, institutions sell stocks for a number of reasons. Maybe they need to raise cash for a retirement-fund payout, or maybe they need the cash to cover another investment that's gone bad. Just like with insider trading, you can never be sure of the motive behind the sale. Also, by the time any institutional trading is reported in the newspapers, any affect that trading would have on the stock's price has already happened. Besides, an investment club has a buy-and-hold, long-term investment philosophy. If the price of a stock dips a bit because of an institutional sale, don't worry about it. Chances are the stock will rebound and continue to increase in price.

If, however, you suddenly notice that several institutions are dumping huge blocks of the company's stock, you may want to do a little research. Many times one institution will follow another's lead without any real good reason for selling. Call the investor-relations department and find out what they have to say about the situation. You may also be able to find information in many business newspapers or on TV business news or programs.

The Fed

The *Federal Reserve* is the arm of the government whose job is to determine our country's monetary policy.

It does that by influencing the money supply and thereby affecting the cost of money.

Federal Reserve: The governmental agency that controls the country's monetary policy.

The primary enemy the Fed is fighting is inflation. When inflation heats up and wages and prices start to increase, business expansion is severely impacted. That affects everyone in the country. The Fed can fight inflation by altering the money supply with these two tools:

1. *U.S. Government Securities:* The Fed has the ability to go into the open market to buy and sell U.S. government securities. When they sell those securities, the government takes in money and reduces the amount of money in the marketplace, slowing the economy. When they buy those securities back, they put money back into the system.

2. *Federal Funds Rate:* Also called the discount rate and known to most investors simply as the interest rate, it is the rate the Federal Reserve charges banks to borrow short-term money to increase their reserves. As the Fed alters that rate, making banks' costs higher or lower, there is a comparable effect on the price companies must pay to borrow money. When the price of credit increases, companies borrow less and the economy slows. With less money at their disposal, companies can't expand and grow as quickly. When investors see companies pulling back and their growth slowing, they aren't as apt to rush to buy their stocks. With demand fading, the market turns downward.

Rumors constantly fly as to the Fed's actions. But no one ever knows for sure what the Fed will do until it does it. If your members believe the Fed is going to raise the discount rate or start selling U.S. government securities, thereby causing the stock market to take a dip, should your club consider liquidating part of your portfolio?

The answer to that question reverts directly back to the original research your members conducted before you bought those stocks. When the Fed takes action to slow the economy, it does indeed have an effect on corporate America. The market, as a whole, may settle back. That doesn't mean the companies whose stock your club owns will necessarily decrease in price.

If the fundamentals of the companies whose stocks you own are still the same and no negative situations have developed, except for the potential action you're expecting by the Fed, there's no reason to sell your stock. Besides, that Fed action affects the entire market. So if you decide to sell stocks because rates may rise, where are you going with your money? Any other stock you're considering will also be affected, so why pay commissions to sell one stock, only to buy another that will have the same situation? The only other option is letting the money sit in your brokerage cash account collecting minimal interest. You're better of with the stocks you own that you've researched and feel comfortable with.

Rumored Fed action always creates a lot of hoopla in the media. But investment clubs buy stocks for the long term. Over a 10- or 15-year holding period there will be plenty of Fed actions. Take note, then keep building your club's portfolio with good solid stocks that you can own for years to come.

* * * * *

Trying to determine when to sell a stock can be difficult. We're all human and we're all prone to jumping to conclusions, worrying at the thought of losing our money, and panicking at the slightest downturn. But, typically, most investors are more likely to sell a stock too early rather than too late.

It's important to understand that selling has its costs—and they're not minimal.

First, when your club sells a stock, it has to pay commissions to sell and commissions to reinvest that money in another stock. That could range anywhere from 1 percent to 5 percent, depending on the brokerage firm your club is using. Secondly, there is a *bid-ask spread*, which is the difference between the price at which you sell and the price at which you buy stocks.

Bid-ask spread: The difference between the price an investor will receive when selling a stock and purchasing a stock.

In the marketplace, you may sell a stock for $26.25 per share, but when you purchase it back, you may have to pay $26.50 per share because of the bid-ask spread.

In addition, if your club makes a profit on the stock it sells, the members have to pay capital-gains taxes on that profit. Of course, you'd have to pay those taxes at some future point, but the longer you can defer them, the longer you can earn money on those taxes you'd pay. When you add up all the costs of selling one stock and buying another, you're probably paying anywhere from 3 percent to 6 percent, plus taxes. The new stock has to perform substantially better than the old stock to make up that difference. In fact, according to the *American Association of Individual Investors (AAII),* investors who turn their portfolio over several times a year have to outperform the market by 10 percent or more just to stay even with an investor who adopts the buy-and-hold approach to investing.

**American Association of Individual Investors
{AAII}:** Not-for-profit corporation that offers education, information, and research to individual investors.

In a study, the AAII depicted the difference between buying and selling versus holding for the long term. They determined that if an investor purchased all the stocks that comprise the S&P 500 at the beginning of the year, then sold all those stocks at the end of the year, she would have closed out her position with a loss 20 times over the last 73 years, or 27 percent of the time. If, however, she had held those stocks for five years before selling them, she would have had a loss at the end of only seven years, or about 10 percent of the time. Increase that holding time to 10 years, and she would have had a loss only 3 percent of the time. Obviously, a buy-and-hold strategy works.

Of course, sometimes a stock simply doesn't perform as your members had anticipated. As new stocks are presented, you may find opportunities that you want to take advantage of but may not have enough funds to do so. You may decide to sell the loser, take your losses, and replace it with the stock that has promise. That happened with the Lady Traders of Osceola Investment Club. They owned Priceline.com but were losing money on it. When a member presented Lucent Technologies to the group, everyone believed the research pointed to a stock that would demonstrate good growth. The members decided to sell Priceline.com and use the proceeds to purchase Lucent. Despite the cost of selling one stock and buying another, they believed the transaction would pay off. Being the first time the club had sold a stock since their inception three years before, it was a good decision.

When contemplating selling a stock, your club should also take into consideration what will be done with the money received from the sale. Do you have another stock in mind to replace the one you're selling? You don't want to leave your money in a cash account earning just a few percent for very long. Before selling, try to have a replacement—the stock of a company that has more potential for growth than the one you're selling. For instance, the MAJEC Investment Club sold their stock in Albertson's because the company's profit margins were very thin and the members didn't think the company had much potential. A member had presented Lucent and the club thought it would be a much more attractive company for the future than Albertson's. They sold Albertson's and bought Lucent, and were happy with the outcome of that decision.

At some point, your club will decide that it's best to sell a certain stock out of your portfolio. It's inevitable. But when you do, be sure you have good reasons for selling, and that selling is definitely the right decision.

12

Dealing with Membership Changes

Your investment club has been operating for several years and, for the first time, you're losing a member. Jack has gotten a great offer from another company that's offering him more benefits and a much higher salary than his current employer. The only problem is that he has to move a thousand miles away from his home. It's a tough decision, but he decides to take the job. Of course, that means he'll have to resign from his investment club. Jack puts his resignation in writing and regretfully submits it to the club's secretary.

It's important to understand that joining an investment club is a long-term commitment. You don't join a club, then decide to resign six months later. That's why, when starting an investment club, you need to take time and care in choosing the right people and ensure that each one is committed to being a long-term member.

Of course, this is life. People get transferred to new jobs, move to other cities to fulfill obligations, and retire and move to a better climate. No matter how well you screen your members, there will be times when a member will resign. When that happens, the club has to determine the best method of paying out the resigning member. When the club secretary receives the resigning member's notice, the value of that person's capital account is fixed as of the date on the valuation statement distributed at the next monthly meeting. The remaining members have four options in determining how to cash out the resigning member.

CASHING OUT A RESIGNING MEMBER

1. Paying in Cash

Jack's investment club has a total portfolio value of $60,000. There are 12 members, but since the club uses unequal ownership, Jack has contributed enough to be a 10 percent owner. When he leaves, the club will owe him $6,000. Hopefully, no investment club would have $6,000 lying around in its cash account. The money should be invested in stocks. But stocks are liquid and can be sold.

If the remaining club members decide they want to pay Jack his portion of the club ownership in cash, they can use whatever cash is in their account, then sell enough stock from their portfolio to raise the remainder of the cash needed. If they sell stock to pay Jack out, the expenses incurred to do so would be paid by Jack—not the club. Or, as noted in the NAIC sample partnership agreement in Chapter 4, the resigning member would either pay the commissions required to sell the stock or receive only 97 percent of his capital account, whichever is less. The exact procedure is the club's choice and should be outlined in the club's partnership agreement. The point is, the only reason the stock is being sold is because of the member's resignation; therefore, that member should incur the cost.

There are a couple of reasons your club may not want to use this method. First, the point in time when the member chooses to resign may not be a good time to sell stocks. The market may be in a downturn and most of your stocks may be down in price. But these are stocks that your club has confidence in and believes will surge back. It would be a shame to sell those stocks at a loss just to pay out a departing member.

Conversely, if a stock has performed well, and the club has a good paper profit, you may not want to sell because the sale creates a taxable event for all the members of the club. Let's say the club has $700 in its cash account, so they need to raise $5,300 in cash to pay Jack. One of the club's stocks is currently trading at $54 per share and the club owns 100 shares. If they sold that stock, they'd raise $5,400, less commissions. With the cash they already have, that would be enough cash to pay Jack out.

But what if the club purchased that stock a few years ago at a price of $15 per share? That means the club has a profit of $39 per share, or a $3,900 profit for the 100 shares. That $3,900 profit would be divided up among all the members according to their percent of ownership, and they would be responsible for paying tax on that profit. They don't get the money—that goes to Jack—but the members would each have to pay tax on their pro rata share of that profit.

If the club doesn't want to have to sell stock at a loss, or create a taxable event for everyone, consider one of the other options.

2. Paying in Stock

Shares of stock are easily *transferable*.

Transferable: When the ownership of a negotiable instrument, such as shares of stock, can be changed from one person's name to another person's name without having to sell and repurchase the shares.

Therefore, instead of selling stock and giving the proceeds to Jack, the remaining club members can choose a stock in their portfolio, determine how many of the shares at the current price equate out to the amount of money needed to pay Jack, and transfer those shares to him. In fact, rather than transferring the total holdings of one stock, the members may choose to transfer partial holdings of various stocks to Jack to equate out to $6,000 (or $5,300, if they also utilize their cash). By transferring shares, there is no taxable event because no stock was sold and no profit was realized. Jack will not even have to pay tax on the transferred stock until he sells it.

Transferring shares of stock is an easy process. If the club chooses this option, the treasurer should call the club's stockbroker, explain what needs to be done, and the broker will walk the club through the transaction.

The resigning member should not be given a choice as to which stock or stocks in the club's portfolio he wants transferred to his name. Choosing which stock to transfer is the decision of the remaining members, a point that is outlined in the partnership agreement. If Jack doesn't want the stock but wants cash, he can immediately sell the stock that's transferred to him.

3. Buying the Person Out

Another option is for the remaining members to buy out Jack's position. The members could pay Jack $6,000 out of their personal funds and divide up his portion of the club's assets. If your club is using equal ownership, all of the members would have to agree to the buyout and each person would have to pay an equal amount. If the club is using unequal ownership, not all members would have to participate in the buyout. A few of the members could raise the money and buy out Jack's portion, as long as that additional stock doesn't raise any of the individual partners' capital account above 20 percent of the club's total assets.

If the club chooses this option, when the members purchase Jack's capital account, they should make their checks payable to the investment club, have the treasurer deposit those checks to the club's account at the brokerage firm, then write a check on the investment club's account payable to Jack. By following that procedure, the club has a perfect paper trail to show exactly how the transaction was completed.

4. Having a New Member Buy the Person Out

Some investment clubs have a waiting list of potential members who want to join the club when an opening occurs. If the club has a potential new member interested in joining, and the club has approved this person, that new member can simply buy out Jack's position. Of course, that means that person has to come up with $6,000. That's a pretty big chunk of change for anyone. But if the person is willing, it's a good option. Or, if your club's membership isn't filled, you may want to invite two new members to join, with each person purchasing a portion of Jack's membership.

Again, when the new person buys Jack out, the check should be made payable to the investment club, deposited to the club's account, and then a check should be written to Jack from the club's account. Having the new person write the check directly to Jack is not a good accounting procedure.

Those are the options the club has in cashing out a resigning member. The options could also be combined. Maybe you want to use the cash the club has in its brokerage account, bring in a new member for $2,000, and have some of the remaining members buy a portion of Jack's position. It doesn't make any difference how he's cashed out, as long as the assets he receives total $6,000.

If, however, you use a combination of the options, the treasurer needs to be extremely careful in calculating the remaining partners' capital accounts. If a new person puts in $2,000, three current members put in $1,000, $1,500, and $1,500 respectively, it's important that each person's capital account is correctly calculated to include their fair ownership value.

When a member resigns, it's also important to remember to remove that person's name from any club documents. Have the remaining members sign a new copy of the partnership agreement so that the resigning member's name is eliminated. If the resigning member had check-signing privileges on the club's account, that should also be changed. You don't want a nonmember still having access to the club's assets.

Never having a member resign from your club would be wonderful, but not realistic. You will eventually have people leave. Sometimes you may lose a member who has been a main cog in your investment club and no one will want to see that person leave. Other times, you may have a member leave who everyone likes, but agrees doesn't quite fit the group for one reason or another. For example, the MAJEC Investment Club had a member leave once because he preferred to invest in mutual funds and didn't think he was making the best use of his time trying to learn how to invest in stocks. That's a fit that would be uncomfortable for everyone.

At some point, you'll have to deal with cashing out a member. When that happens, offer all the options and have the remaining members choose the option that best fits your club's situation.

BRINGING IN A NEW MEMBER

When a member resigns, your club shouldn't feel compelled to immediately find another member to replace that person. Chances are that someone will eventually express an interest in your club. It's better to wait to find the right person than to rush the recruiting process and bring in someone who turns out to be a mistake. When looking for new members, find out if other members have a friend, a relative, or a coworker who may be interested.

One option investment clubs should not use in seeking out new members is to advertise because it could result in your club violating federal and state securities laws. Investment clubs are typically not subject to regulation under securities laws; however, NAIC states that "the policy statement warns that there are circumstances where offering a membership in an investment club may require registration under the Federal Securities Act." Registration is not a requirement an investment club would want to be responsible for because it's an expensive, time-consuming, and very complicated process. While the announcement that an investment club is looking for new members could be construed by the authorities as a public offering, chances are they would never bother with it. But there's no reason to take any chances. Your best bet is to find new members through word of mouth. You'll avoid any legal conflicts and you'll find potential members who already come with a recommendation from a current member.

When an investment club invites a new member to join, they should be just as careful about finding someone who will be committed to the club as they were in finding the initial members. Some clubs ask potential members to submit a résumé or complete a questionnaire. Invite potential members to attend a couple of meetings so the other members can meet the new person. This also gives the potential member an opportunity to see the club in action. If the potential member is still interested in joining after attending meetings, the club members should vote as to whether this is a person they want as a new member. In a partnership, as it states in the club's partnership agreement, it takes the unanimous consent of all the current members to admit a new member to the club. If the new person is voted in, the club needs to take care to bring that person up to the experience and comfort level of the other members.

One of the goals of an investment club is not just learning how to invest, but learning how to invest in a comfortable and nonthreatening environment. If your club has been operating for two years and you bring in a new member, imagine how nervous that person must be.

Here's a group of people who have been meeting once a month for two years. They all know each other. They have two years of investing experience behind them. They've had the advantage of hearing guest speakers at their meetings, listening to educational tapes or watching videos about investing, and sharing the knowledge the various members have brought to the meetings. They know how to research a stock and do a stock presentation.

The new member is probably new to investing—doesn't know the terminology, how to do a presentation, or how to research a stock. Worse yet, the new person probably only knows one or two people in the group.

It's important to make a new member comfortable. The best way to do that is to assign a mentor to that person. Have the mentor and the new member spend a little time together discussing how the club operates, how to research a stock, and how to put together a presentation. Before becoming a member, the person should have attended a few meetings as a guest, so he or she knows how the meetings are conducted. But chances are, the new person has a lot of questions and may be hesitant to ask those questions in a group environment. By having a mentor, the new person has someone he or she can call to ask questions in private.

The mentoring process doesn't have to last a long time. Most people assimilate into a group rather quickly. Having a mentor just gets the person over that initial nervousness of coming into a group, meeting new people, and learning the basics.

In addition to working with a mentor, the new member should also be encouraged to attend seminars, workshops, or classes that are offered in your area by NAIC or local schools.

PARTIAL WITHDRAWALS

From time to time you may have a member who runs into a money crunch and needs to make a partial withdrawal from his investment club account. While this certainly isn't an activity the club should encourage, there are situations in which it's necessary to be accommodating.

When a withdrawal is necessary, the club can choose to transfer cash from the club's account or shares of stock from the club's portfolio, or other members could pay out the withdrawal and increase their percentage ownership in the club—as long as their ownership remains below 20 percent. The partner requesting the withdrawal would pay either the amount of any commission charges incurred, or 3 percent of the withdrawal amount.

If your club has been in operation for years and you have a huge portfolio in place, withdrawals aren't really a problem. But when a club is young and their portfolio small, withdrawals should be made sparingly. Otherwise, too many withdrawals could cause the club to fall apart. Your club isn't in existence to provide members with cash—it's in existence to help them build a nest egg. And that means investing, reinvesting, and letting the money grow.

Dealing with membership changes is an ongoing activity that all clubs will experience sooner or later. As long as the club has a plan in place and follows the procedures they've laid out in their club documents, paying out a resigning member or bringing in a new member should never cause a problem.

Chapter 13

Diversifying Your Club's Options

A s we discussed in Chapter 3, except for taxes, there are no laws governing how an investment club should be structured and operated. So far, we've discussed how the typical investment club would operate. But not everything is typical in this world, and people often choose to do things out of the ordinary. That can certainly be the case when dealing with investment clubs. Below are some of the unique and different types of activities investment clubs may consider.

SHOULD YOU INCLUDE MUTUAL FUNDS?

Oftentimes, a question that arises among investment club members is whether they can invest in a *mutual fund* in addition to individual stocks.

 Mutual fund: An investment company that is formed specifically to pool investors' dollars and invest them in stocks.

One of the goals of an investment club is to learn how to invest. The members do that by researching and buying individual stocks. We've also discussed diversifying the club's portfolio—buying stocks of companies of varying sizes and in different industries. If a club truly builds a diversified portfolio, that portfolio will basically be a mutual fund. The definition of a stock mutual fund is an investment company that is formed specifically to pool investors' dollars and invest them in stocks. Sound familiar? It's your club!

Mutual funds are great investment vehicles for individual investors, but the advantages they offer may not necessarily be of benefit to an investment club. The advantages mutual funds tout are:

1. Instant Diversification

Your club portfolio is already diversified. The addition of a mutual fund to your club's portfolio, in fact, could even create havoc with your level of diversification because the fund may hold stocks in its portfolio that you already own, creating a double holding of those stocks.

2. Convenience

Most mutual funds offer a family of funds so that their investors can switch their money from one fund to another—from a technology fund to a value fund to a large-cap fund. If your portfolio is already diversified, you don't need to switch money around.

3. Professional Management

Having a professional manager make the buy and sell decisions for your club defeats the investment club goal of learning how to invest. How can you learn how to invest if someone else is doing all the research and making all the decisions? In addition, NAIC is quick to point out that most mutual funds don't beat the S&P 500 index, but many investment clubs do. Why pay for professional management when you can probably do a better job on your own?

Some of the disadvantages of investing via a mutual fund include:

1. Loss of Control

Because a professional manager is making the buy and sell decisions in a mutual fund, your members have no say in which stocks to own. If your members don't like a specific stock and the mutual-fund manager decides to buy it, your club will own it.

2. Expenses

A professional manager doesn't work for free. Every mutual fund charges various levels and types of fees. Why pay those fees when your members can build and manage their own investment portfolio?

3. Taxes

When your club sells a stock for a profit, everyone in the club has a tax liability but, because investment clubs reinvest their profits, the members won't receive any money to use to pay those taxes. But that's a minimal problem compared to the tax ramifications you can become involved in when you own a mutual fund. Not only will you have a tax liability if you sell your mutual-fund shares, but you can incur a tax liability when the mutual-fund manager sells shares of stock within the fund.

Owning mutual funds in an investment club's portfolio defeats the goal of learning how to invest and can create redundancy in your plan to diversify your portfolio. There is, however, one reason that your club may want to consider one type of mutual fund.

In Chapter 10 we discussed adding an international flavor to your portfolio. If your club invests in only U.S.-based companies, you're investing in only one-third of the world's stock market. Without utilizing international stocks, you'd miss out on two-thirds of the stocks that exist in the world. But with a stock market that does as well as ours, why bother with international stocks?

That's what investors who lived in Japan thought in 1989. At that time, Japan's economy was the second largest in the world. Why should they invest in other countries when their economy was so strong? Because eventually the downturn came, and the Nikkei index fell from 39,000 yen to 14,000 yen, leaving a lot of Japanese investors with big losses. If they had diversified their stock holdings, the investments they had in companies based in other countries would have helped support their portfolios when the Japanese market crashed.

Will our stock market crash? No one knows. It will have corrections, however, and when that happens, having a few international holdings may help to support the performance of your club's portfolio.

Your club can add a little international flavor by buying the stocks of U.S. companies that conduct a portion of their business in other countries, but that gives you minimal international exposure. For instance, if the international division of the company doubles in size, but the U.S. portion of the company doesn't do well, the return generated by the international division is canceled out.

The other option, as discussed in Chapter 10, is to purchase ADRs. Investment clubs can easily buy ADRs, but it can be tough to obtain research material on the underlying companies and even more confusing to try to decipher it. It can also be difficult to stay on top of what's happening in the country where the company is located. How would you know if they're having economic or political instability that could affect the price of your stock? While ADRs offer Americans an easy way to participate in the stocks of foreign companies, they can be difficult.

The only other way to add international stocks to your portfolio is to buy mutual funds. By using mutual funds, you eliminate the problem of trying to obtain research material on a foreign company and trying to interpret it. The mutual-fund manager will handle that for you. You can also leave the questions of economic changes, political unrest, legal and regulatory differences, and currency fluctuations to the fund's portfolio manager.

There are approximately 1,026 mutual funds that invest in companies outside the United States. They are divided between the two categories of mutual funds.

1. *Open-End Mutual Fund*

> **Open-end mutual fund:** A mutual fund that accepts new investors' deposits and redeems outstanding shares on a continuous basis.

An open-end mutual fund is one that accepts money from a multitude of investors, pools it, and invests it in stocks. Management sells as many shares of the mutual fund as investors are willing to buy and redeems the shares as investors desire. Because the amount of money the fund has to invest changes regularly, the manager is constantly buying and selling stock. Therefore, the total value of the fund fluctuates daily. Of all the mutual funds that invest in stocks of other countries, 956 are open end.

To determine the daily value of an open-end mutual fund on a per-share basis, management adds up the value of all the stocks in the portfolio, adds in any cash the fund might be holding, and divides the total by the number of mutual-fund shares outstanding. That number, called the *net asset value*, is the value of one share of the mutual fund's stock.

> **Net asset value:** The actual value of shares in a mutual fund. Calculated by dividing the current value of all stocks owned in the fund, plus any cash, by the number of shares outstanding on any given day.

The net asset value of open-end mutual funds can be found in most daily newspapers.

2. *Closed-End Mutual Fund*

Closed-end mutual fund: A mutual fund that sells a prescribed number of shares and then closes as of a specified date. Those shares then trade over a public stock exchange.

A closed-end mutual fund also accepts money from a multitude of investors, pools it, and buys a portfolio of stocks. But a closed-end fund sells only a finite number of shares. After those shares are sold, there are no more available. Those shares then trade on a public stock exchange, just like a stock, and investors can buy and sell them through their stockbrokers. The price of the mutual fund's shares fluctuates based on supply and demand. Therefore, the price you pay for a closed-end mutual fund's shares may be higher or lower than its net asset value. There are 70 closed-end mutual funds that invest in the stocks of foreign companies. Their prices are also quoted in most major newspapers.

An open-end mutual fund can be purchased directly from the mutual-fund company or directly from your stockbroker. If you choose to purchase an open-end fund through your broker, however, you will pay a fee that supposedly pays for the assistance your broker gives you in choosing which mutual fund to purchase. Since your investment club will make that decision on its own, go directly to the mutual-fund company itself to purchase your shares and avoid paying double fees. Be aware, however, that every time you purchase a mutual fund directly from the mutual-fund company, you'll receive a monthly statement from them. Your club will then receive two statements—one from the brokerage firm and one from the mutual-fund company—each month to review. Unlike an open-end mutual fund, a closed-end mutual fund must be purchased through your stockbroker because the fund trades on an exchange just like a stock.

If your club uses a mutual fund to add an international component to your portfolio, you would probably be wise to choose an open-end mutual fund over a closed-end. Your choices are greater, its price doesn't sell above or below its net asset value, and you can purchase it directly from the mutual-fund company.

When considering a mutual fund to add an international component to your club's portfolio, it's important to understand the difference between the following two categories of mutual funds that purchase non-U.S. stocks.

Global Mutual Funds

A *global mutual fund* (also called a world mutual fund) purchases the shares of companies that are located outside the United States, but also purchases the shares of U.S.-based companies.

Global mutual fund: A mutual fund that invests in the stocks and bonds of companies located outside the United States, but also includes a portion of U.S. investments.

The reason your club would even purchase a mutual fund is to have the ability to invest in foreign companies. The club can invest in the U.S. companies on its own. Therefore, the global fund would not be the one your club would want to purchase.

International Mutual Funds

An *international mutual fund* (also called a foreign mutual fund) purchases only the stocks of foreign companies. It does not include any U.S.-based companies.

International mutual fund: A mutual fund that purchases only the stocks and bonds of companies located outside the United States.

This is the type of mutual fund an investment club would want to purchase to add that international element to their portfolio.

When it comes to international mutual funds, there are lots of choices. There are general funds that invest in companies around the world, and funds that invest in companies located in certain continents, certain regions, or just one country. The narrower the area, such as the funds that invest in only one country, the higher the level of risk that fund will carry. International funds may focus on small-cap, midcap, or large-cap stocks. The various types of international funds that are available are extremely broad.

When trying to determine which fund would be best for your investment club, you should read the Morningstar reports, which can be found at most public libraries. You will probably only be able to find the Morningstar reports, however, for the open-end mutual funds, as their closed-end mutual fund reports can only be accessed from a CD-ROM the company sells, which most libraries would not carry. You can also access information from Morningstar at their web site at www.morningstar.com.

Figure 13-1 shows a sample of a Morningstar report for Fidelity International Growth and Income Mutual Fund.

Some of the information that's included in the Morningstar reports that you should consider are:

1. Past Performance

Past performance won't guarantee what the future will bring, but it can give you an idea of management's expertise. Look at the last five or 10 years to determine if performance has been positive and consistent.

2. Management

Check to see if the current portfolio manager has been in that position at least five or 10 years. If the fund has a good track record, but management has recently changed, past performance means nothing. Check out the new portfolio manager to determine how well she performed in her last position.

3. Fee Structure

Some of the fees mutual funds charge their shareholders include management fees, administrative costs, and marketing, or 12b-1, fees. The total amount of those fees divided by the net assets of the fund is called the *expense ratio*.

Expense ratio: The total amount of fees charged to investors by a mutual fund, divided by the mutual fund's net assets.

Published December 7, 1999. Reprinted by permission of Morningstar.

Fidelity International Growth & Inc

	Ticker	Load	NAV	Yield	Total Assets	Mstar Category
	FIGRX	None	$28.42	0.3%	$1,080.8 mil	Foreign Stock

Prospectus Objective: Foreign Stock

Fidelity International Growth and Income Fund seeks capital growth and current income.

The fund normally invests in foreign securities. It is typically diversified across several countries and regions. Management considers the size of the market in each country relative to the size of the international market as a whole when allocating assets. It may also invest in equity and debt securities of U.S. issuers.

	73%	69%	55%	63%	69%	71%	84%	97%	

Return Above Avg
Risk Below Avg
Rating ★★★★ Above Avg

Investment Style
Equity
Average Stock %

▼ Manager Change
▽ Partial Manager Change

Fund Performance vs. Category Average
▥ Quarterly Fund Return
+/– Category Average
— Category Baseline

Performance Quartile (within Category)

Bill Bower. Since 5-1998. MBA U. of Michigan. Bower is currently a portfolio manager with Fidelity Investments. He joined the firm in 1994 as an analyst covering the building-materials, housing, recreational-vehicles, and manufactured-housing industries. He became a portfolio manager in December 1994. In August 1996, he joined Fidelity's international group as an equity analyst where he served as sector leader of international research. Funds previously managed: Fidelity Sel Constr&Hous (12-1994 - 08-1996).

	11.79	13.88	13.00	13.87	13.09	17.57	16.53	17.95	19.55	19.70	20.91	28.42	NAV
	11.56	19.12	−3.23	8.04	−3.34	35.08	−2.87	12.23	12.69	7.12	9.98	35.92	Total Return %
	−5.05	−12.56	−0.11	−22.45	−10.96	25.02	−4.19	−25.30	−10.26	−26.23	−18.60	21.75	+/– S&P 500
	−16.71	8.58	20.22	−4.09	8.83	2.52	−10.65	1.02	6.64	5.34	−10.02	19.41	+/– MSCI EAFE
	1.86	1.36	3.10	1.31	2.31	0.46	0.00	3.63	1.62	1.89	0.46	0.00	Income Return %
	9.70	17.76	−6.33	6.73	−5.65	34.62	−2.87	8.60	11.07	5.23	9.52	35.92	Capital Return %
	78	55	4	80	43	53	70	25	43	38	67	22	Total Rtn % Rank Cat
	0.20	0.16	0.43	0.17	0.32	0.06	0.00	0.60	0.29	0.37	0.09	0.00	Income $
	0.00	0.00	0.00	0.00	0.00	0.05	0.53	0.00	0.37	0.88	0.63	0.00	Capital Gains $
	2.58	1.92	1.98	1.89	1.62	1.52	1.21	1.18	1.14	1.15	1.13	—	Expense Ratio %
	1.08	1.98	2.31	2.86	2.78	0.87	2.16	2.98	2.76	2.33	1.62	—	Income Ratio %
	112	147	102	117	76	24	173	141	95	70	143	—	Turnover Rate %
	30.9	33.0	33.8	58.7	65.2	1,068.3	1,272.6	941.6	1,080.5	1,030.3	871.0	1,080.8	Net Assets $mil

	1st Qtr	2nd Qtr	3rd Qtr	4th Qtr	Total
1995	2.84	0.76	5.43	2.72	12.23
1996	1.73	3.34	1.27	5.85	12.69
1997	0.41	9.73	2.55	−5.20	7.12
1998	12.13	1.95	−17.41	16.48	9.98
1999	3.11	5.15	9.57	—	—

Trailing	Total Return%	+/– S&P 500	+/– MSCI EAFE	%Rank All	%Rank Cat	Growth of $10,000
3 Mo	17.58	12.20	9.15	11	27	11,758
6 Mo	32.87	25.64	16.44	7	23	13,287
1 Yr	40.69	19.95	19.59	12	22	14,069
3 Yr Avg	17.35	−6.91	5.36	21	26	16,162
5 Yr Avg	15.25	−12.18	4.20	33	21	20,329
10 Yr Avg	10.94	−6.85	4.46	41	33	28,247
15 Yr Avg	—	—	—	—	—	—

Tax Analysis	Tax-Adj Ret%	%Rank Cat	%Pretax Ret	%Rank Cat
3 Yr Avg	15.90	25	91.6	40
5 Yr Avg	13.83	19	90.7	34
10 Yr Avg	9.95	28	90.9	17

Potential Capital Gain Exposure: 41% of assets

Time Period	Load-Adj Return %	Risk %Rank¹ All	Cat	Morningstar Return	Morningstar Risk	Morningstar Risk-Adj Rating
1 Yr	40.69					
3 Yr	17.35	56	12	2.44	0.60	★★★★
5 Yr	15.25	66	7	2.18	0.58	★★★★
10 Yr	10.94	72	8	1.82	0.64	★★★★

Average Historical Rating (120 months): 3.3★s

¹1=low, 100=high ² I–Bill return substituted for category avg.

Category Rating (3 Yr)

Other Measures	Standard Index S&P 500	Best Fit Index MSCI WdxUS
Alpha	−0.8	5.3
Beta	0.73	0.97
R-Squared	54	83
Standard Deviation	19.37	
Mean	17.35	
Sharpe Ratio	0.72	

Return Above Avg
Risk Below Avg

Share change since 10–98 Total Stocks: 263	Sector	Country	% Assets
⊕ BP Amoco	Energy	United Kingdom	1.96
⊕ Nokia Cl A ADR	Technology	Finland	1.66
⊖ Elf Aquitaine	Energy	France	1.51
⊖ Nestle (Reg)	Staples	Switzerland	1.31
⊕ Shell Transp & Trad (Reg)	Energy	United Kingdom	1.25
⊖ Takeda Chemical Inds	Health	Japan	1.24
⊕ Novartis (Reg)	Health	Switzerland	1.23
⊖ British Telecomm	Services	United Kingdom	1.18
⊖ Lloyds TSB Grp	Financials	United Kingdom	1.16
⊖ Mannesmann	Industrials	Germany	1.15
⊗ Telecom Italia (RNC)	Services	Italy	1.13
⊕ ING Groep	Financials	Netherlands	1.11
⊕ DDI	Health	Japan	1.09
⊕ Smithkline Beecham	Health	United Kingdom	1.09
⊗ DaimlerChrysler (Reg)	Durables	Germany	1.09
⊕ Total Fina Cl B ADR	Energy	France	1.04
⊕ Credit Suisse Grp (Reg)	Financials	Switzerland	1.02
⊖ Glaxo Wellcome	Health	United Kingdom	1.02
⊖ Vivendi	Utilities	France	0.99
⊖ Telefonica	Services	Spain	0.96

Current Investment Style

Style		Stock Port Avg	Rel MSCI EAFE Current	Rel EAFE Hist	Rel Cat
Value Blend Growth	Price/Earnings Ratio	35.2	1.03	0.90	1.08
	Price/Cash Flow	17.9	1.12	0.87	1.06
	Price/Book Ratio	6.1	1.28	0.88	1.22
	3 Yr Earnings Growth	—	—	—	—
	Med Mkt Cap $mil	22,351		0.8	0.5	1.31

Country Exposure 04-30-99	% assets
United Kingdom	24
Japan	18
France	10
Switzerland	7
Netherlands	6

Hedging History: Never

Special Securities % assets 04-30-99	
Restricted/Illiquid Secs	1
Emerging–Markets Secs	4
Options/Futures/Warrants	Yes

Composition % assets 04-30-99			
Cash	0.5	Bonds	0.2
Stocks	98.1	Other	1.1

Regional Exposure 04-30-99	% assets
Europe	65
Japan	18
Latin America	0
Pacific Rim	0
Other	4

Sector Weightings	% of Stocks	Rel Cat	5-Year High	Low
Utilities	3.5	1.2	10	0
Energy	7.5	1.7	11	1
Financials	24.4	1.2	46	5
Industrials	8.9	0.6	40	9
Durables	6.3	0.8	32	6
Staples	5.5	1.0	9	1
Services	21.0	1.0	22	2
Retail	5.4	1.1	15	3
Health	9.6	1.4	10	1
Technology	7.9	0.7	24	2

Fidelity International Growth and Income has flourished in its new form, but it's far from unique.

This fund has put up a good showing so far in 1999. For the year to date through July 29, it ranks in the foreign-stock category's top half—a distinction it shares with all of Fidelity's other foreign offerings.

Performance isn't all these funds have in common. When manager Bill Bower took charge of this fund in May 1998, he recast its portfolio in a style similar to its siblings'. The fund did away with a requirement to hold a quarter of its assets in bonds, and Bower filled the portfolio with the top picks of Fidelity's analysts. He also adopted a growth-at-a-reasonable price discipline, not unlike the one used by Fidelity Overseas and International Value manager Rick Mace.

As a result, it's become difficult to distinguish between this fund and Fidelity's other foreign-stock offerings. For example, all

the funds count such multinationals as Telefonica, Novartis, Elf Aquitaine, and Nestle among their top holdings. And although Bower says this fund will try to distinguish itself by dabbling in mid- and small-cap stocks, International Value has already been doing that in an effort to distinguish itself from Overseas. Indeed, this fund and International Value have both benefited from their exposure to Japanese small- and mid-cap stocks in 1999.

That's not to say that the fund isn't worth owning. It's likely to be more consistent in its new form than it has been in years past. Bower doesn't have the freedom to make sizable country bets like his predecessor did, and will be forced to compete on stock-picking alone. So far in his short tenure, he has shown himself to be up to the task by picking such diverse winners as Nokia, BP Amoco, and Softbank. Still, because the fund isn't required to own bonds anymore, those in search of income will be disappointed here.

Address:	82 Devonshire Street Boston, MA 02109 800–544–8888
Web Address:	www.fidelity.com
Inception:	12-31-86
Advisor:	Fidelity Management & Research
Subadvisor:	FMR (U.K)/FMR (Far East)/Fidelity Intl Investment
NTF Plans:	Fidelity, Fidelity Inst., Muriel Siebert, Waterhouse

Minimum Purchase:	$2500	Add: $250	IRA: $500
Min Auto Inv Plan:	$2500	Add: $100	
Sales Fees:	No-load		
Management Fee:	0.45%+0.52% max./0.27% min.(G)		
Actual Fees:	Mgt: 0.74%	Dist: —	
Expense Projections:	3Yr: $372*	5Yr: $644*	10Yr: $1420*
Avg Brok Commission:	—	Income Distrib: Annually	

NTF Plans: — | Total Cost (relative to category): —

©1999 Morningstar, Inc. 312–696–6000. All rights reserved. The information contained herein is not represented or warranted to be accurate, correct, complete or timely. Past performance is no guarantee of future performance. Visit our investment web site at www.morningstar.com.

M⊙RNINGSTAR Mutual Funds

Figure 13-1: Morningstar Report
Source: Morningstar, Inc.

According to Investment Company Institute in Washington, D.C., the average annual expense ratio for international and global stock mutual funds is 1.52 percent. Be sure the fund you choose is in line with the average. Also, look at the fund's *turnover ratio*, which tells you how many times management buys and sells stocks during the year. The higher the turnover, the higher the fees will be.

Turnover ratio: Relates to how many times the portfolio manager of a mutual fund buys and sells stocks during the year.

Other fees a mutual fund may charge are front-end and back-end loads. A *front-end load* is charged when you purchase your shares. It's incorporated right into the price.

Front-end load: A sales charge that is incorporated into the price of a mutual fund's shares.

That means if you invest $1,000 in a mutual fund that has a front-end load, fees will be taken out of the $1,000 before it's invested. If the fund has a 4 percent load, you'll really be investing $960 rather than $1,000.

A *back-end load* is charged when you sell your shares.

Back-end load: A fee a mutual fund charges to investors who sell their shares within a few years after purchasing them.

That charge is highest if you sell your shares within the first year of ownership. The charge then typically decreases each year until, by the fifth or sixth year, there's no charge at all to sell your shares.

4. Risk Level

The Morningstar reports offer risk-level measurements so you can determine how much risk a specific fund offers relative to other funds in the same category.

5. Minimum Investment

How much money will your club need to open this account? If your club has $1,000 to invest in an international fund but the minimum investment is $2,000, it won't work.

When an investment club purchases a mutual fund, it should employ the same ground rules as when it purchases a stock. Assign a member to monitor the investment by reading the mutual fund's shareholder reports, referring back to the Morningstar listings, which are updated every six months, and watching for information regarding that fund in the media.

If your club decides to use mutual funds to add foreign stocks to your portfolio, be sure to apply the same investment philosophy to a mutual fund as a stock—it's a long term, buy-and-hold investment. If an investment club wants to include an international component in their portfolio, open-end mutual funds are probably the best way to accomplish that.

SHOULD YOU INCLUDE PREFERRED STOCKS?

All of the stocks we've been discussing so far have been *common stocks*.

Common stock: The type of stock a company issues that gives the investor the right to receive dividends and vote on company issues.

There is, however, another type of stock called *preferred stock*.

Preferred stock: The type of stock a company issues that gives investors preference when it comes to the payment of dividends and the liquidation of the company's assets.

But just because its name says it's preferred, it may not be the right preference for an investment club.

A preferred stock represents ownership in a company, the same as a common stock does. The primary difference between the two lies in the dividend. The word "preferred" means that those stockholders get preferred treatment when it comes to the company paying dividends.

Each quarter a company's board of directors decides how much the dividend will be on the company's common stock based on how well they performed during that quarter. If they want, they can change the amount every quarter. They can even eliminate it if they want. The dividend paid on preferred stock, however, is set when the stock is initially issued. That dividend remains the same from quarter to quarter and doesn't fluctuate based on the company's performance. In fact, if the company has financial difficulties, the dividend on the common stock will be eliminated before the dividend on the preferred stock can be altered. Also, if a company files bankruptcy and ends up being liquidated, the preferred shareholders' claims against the company's assets will be satisfied before the claims of the common stockholders. For the privilege of having this preferential treatment, the investors who own a company's preferred stock do not have voting rights.

Many companies go one step further and issue *cumulative preferred stock,* which means that if the company does have to stop paying dividends to both the common and preferred stockholders, the dividends that should have been paid on the cumulative preferred stock accumulate.

Cumulative preferred stock: A type of preferred stock a company issues in which any dividends that are not paid to investors must be accumulated and paid prior to common stockholders receiving their dividend payments.

When the company once again begins paying dividends, all the missed dividend payments on the cumulative preferred stock have to be repaid before they can start paying a dividend on the common stock.

Having a guaranteed dividend is a nice perk. The problem, however, is that the price of a preferred stock remains fairly stagnant. You may buy a common stock and, if the company performs well, the price of that stock can increase substantially, giving you a nice gain. The company's preferred stock price, however, moves very little because it isn't tied to the company's performance. Instead, it's the level of interest rates that drives the price of the preferred stock.

For instance, let's say your club buys a preferred stock at $24 per share. That stock pays a quarterly dividend of $.60, which is $2.40 per share per year. That's a 10 percent return. Later, interest rates decline in the general market. When other companies issue their preferred stocks, they'll probably pay a lower rate of interest because current rates are lower. If a new preferred stock pays only 8 percent, which preferred stock would you buy: the one that still pays 10 percent or the new one that pays 8 percent? Everyone will want the 10 percent preferred stock.

But the market has a way of making everything even out. If the current rate on new preferred stocks is 8 percent, that 10 percent stock will also become 8 percent. That happens through price movement. The price of that stock will move up to $30 per share, so the $2.40 dividend equals 8 percent (8 percent times 30 equals $2.40). When interest rates decline, the price of the preferred stock increases.

If interest rates go up, just the opposite happens. If rates are 12 percent, that preferred stock's price will go down to $20 per share (12 percent times $20 equals $2.40). Therefore, as interest rates increase and decrease, the price of the preferred stock will move in the opposite direction.

Preferred stocks are often purchased and held in the investment portfolios of large corporations and institutions. That's due not only to the fact that those dividends are fairly large and secure, but also because there are provisions in the tax laws that allow the dividends corporations and institutions receive from preferred stock to be largely tax exempt. Individual investors, however, don't have that tax-exempt status when it comes to dividends from preferred stock.

In an investment club, you're trying to build a nest egg by buying growth stocks that increase in price as the company increases its revenues and profits. That's why your members research companies and look for those with good fundamentals. Buying a preferred stock in which the price fluctuates primarily with interest rates denies your club the opportunity to make money through capital appreciation. Why invest in a preferred stock that gives you only one opportunity to make money when you can invest in a common stock that gives you the opportunity to make money through both dividends and capital appreciation? Therefore, if a member suggests your club buys a preferred stock, politely point out that you'd be reducing your profit potential. You have a goal of building a nest egg. You may as well take every opportunity you have to make that egg as big as you can.

INVESTING IN YOUR MORALS AND ETHICS

In 1970 our country celebrated Earth Day for the first time. The purpose was to bring attention to the importance of taking care of our planet—not polluting our waters, not destroying our forests, and not wiping out certain types of species. From that celebration came the concept of *socially responsible investing*.

Socially responsible investing: An investing
strategy in which investors purchase only the stocks
of companies that adhere to the investor's ethical and
moral beliefs.

Socially responsible investing is the investment strategy of matching our investments to our moral and ethical beliefs. If the members of your investment club agree on the importance of certain issues, your club may want to consider adding this investment concept to your portfolio.

The first step in socially responsible investing is to determine the criteria by which your club's members want to invest. Maybe your members believe that tobacco is not a product that should be sold because of the health problems it causes. Therefore, your club would not invest in tobacco companies or other companies related to the tobacco industry. Or maybe your members believe that paper-producing companies don't do enough to restock the land with new trees as they harvest timber. Your club would not buy the stocks of paper-producing companies.

The industry a company represents isn't the only measure for determining your criteria. A company may be in an industry your members approve of, but the company has been repeatedly fined for polluting the air. Or maybe the company produces its products in a sweatshop in an underdeveloped nation. Or maybe your members are all loyal union members and a certain company is known as a union buster.

In addition to boycotting companies that don't match your members' moral and ethical beliefs, you may choose to support companies that do match your criteria. For instance, you may want to consider companies that win awards for the extremely high level of benefits they offer their employees, or companies that are in industries such as recycling, or companies that are known to donate large amounts of money to worthwhile charities. The options your members have in determining a socially responsible criteria are endless. How you create that criteria is up to you, but it's probably important that whatever guidelines you choose to follow, you have unanimous consent. If some members want to boycott alcohol companies and others don't, you'll have problems.

After your members have developed the guidelines they want to follow for their socially responsible investments, they should follow the same rules that they'd follow in making any other investment. Just because a company fits your moral and ethical beliefs doesn't necessarily mean it's a good investment.

You still have to do your homework. Find good companies with good products. Research those companies by reading company literature and third-party reports. Study the company's financial statements and crunch the numbers. Determine whether this is a company that has good fundamentals. If not, it could be the most ethically and morally proper company in this country, but you'll lose money on its stock.

A company may treat its employees with the utmost respect, never pollute, and produce a product that helps keep the earth clean, but if it's losing money and has no plan to turn the company's performance around, you don't want to buy it.

Socially responsible investing doesn't change the basic premises of finding a good company to invest in. It simply adds one more element to your investment criteria. And at the same time that you're building that profitable investment portfolio, maybe your club can also be making this world a better place!

SHOULD YOU INCLUDE CHILDREN AND TEENS?

Speaking of making the world a better place, wouldn't it be nice if everyone knew how to invest their money and was able to save and invest during their whole life so they'd have a substantial nest egg when they retired? The younger we are when we start investing, the easier it will be to build a portfolio that will be significant enough to carry us through our retirement years. The chart in Figure 13-2 was developed by NAIC and depicts how easy it would be for a child who is 12 years old today to build a portfolio valued at well over a million dollars by age 65. The chart assumes a 9 percent annual compound rate of return and begins with the child investing just $10 per month at 12 and increasing that amount over the years.

By investing just $92,280 over 53 years, this 12-year-old could have a nest egg worth $1,339,443. With just a minimal amount of money, the power of time and compounding can help build a retirement fund that will take care of him for the rest of his life.

The key is to get our children started and interested in investing. The schools, unfortunately, teach our children the skills they need to go into the world, succeed in their chosen careers, and make money, but they don't really teach them what to do with that money after they earn it. For the most part, that responsibility lies with the parents.

Some schools, however, have started adding classes on investing to their curriculums. The Securities Industry Foundation for Economic Education offers schools a program called the Stock Market Game, in which each student

Your Age	Amounted Invested Over a Year	Year-End Total Value	Your Monthly Invested Amount	Stages of Lifetime Investing
12	$120	$131	$10 each month	*begin to invest
13	$240	$404	$20 each month	
14	$240	$702	$20 each month	
15	$360	$1,158	$30 each month	*High School investing years
16	$360	$1,654	$30 each month	
17	$480	$2,326	$40 each month	
18	$480	$3,059	$40 each month	
19	$1,000	$4,424	$83 each month	
20	$1,000	$5,913	$83 each month	*starting a new job or college
21	$1,000	$7,535	$83 each month	
22	$1,000	$9,303	$83 each month	
23	$2,000	$12,320	$166 each month	
24	$2,000	$15,608	$166 each month	
25	$2,000	$19,194	$166 each month	*working in your career - investing for retirement
26	$2,000	$23,101	$166 each month	
27	$2,000	$27,360	$166 each month	

Figure 13-2: Compounding Chart *(continued)*

28	$2,000	$32,003	$166 each month	
29	$2,000	$37,063	$166 each month	
30	$2,000	$42,578	$166 each month	
. . .	. . .	. . .	. . .	
35	$2,000	$78,559	$166 each month	*the "home_stretch"
40	$2,000	$133,919	$166 each month	
45	$2,000	$219,098	$166 each month	
50	$2,000	$350,156	$166 each month	
55	$2,000	$551,805	$166 each month	
60	$2,000	$862,067	$166 each month	
65	$2,000	$1,339,443	$166 each month	
			Total Dollars Invested $92,280	
Total Value at age 65			**$1,339,443**	

Figure 13-2: Compounding Chart
Source: National Association of Investors Corporation (NAIC)
www.better-investing.org

is given a hypothetical $100,000 to purchase stocks and build a portfolio over a 10-week period. Teams of students then compete against teams from other schools. The program is designed for students who are at least in the sixth grade.

If your children's school doesn't offer any classes on stock-market investing, it may be a good idea to get your child involved in an investment club. Being a member of an investment club is a great learning experience for children. Not only does it teach them the basics of investing their money, but it also teaches them math, reading, economics, teamwork, and decision making.

Of course, if you belong to an investment club of adults, you probably can't expect the other members to include your 14-year-old in the club. Instead, you might want to start a family investment club in which parents and their children are all members. Maybe the child's cousins and their parents, or neighbors who have children, want to participate. A group of parents and their children would be a great way to teach your children, spend time with your children, and start building that college fund. Or, if parents are stretched to their limit on time, this activity may be one that the child's grandparents would enjoy. A retiree may jump at the chance to have a new activity and at the same time spend time with a grandchild.

If you get your children involved in an investment club, be sure to give them responsibility. Set an amount they must contribute each month, even if it's only $5 or $10. Allow older children to choose a stock, research it, and do a stock presentation. Or you could assign one parent and one child to work together on a stock presentation. Help the child choose companies he is familiar with, can relate to, and will enjoy reading about. Allow the child to help monitor a stock the club has purchased and show him how to read stock tables. If you don't allow the children the opportunity to participate, they'll quickly lose interest.

Because it's illegal for minors to own securities, the parent or guardian will need to act as custodian for the child and manage the account until the child turns 18 or 21, whatever is considered the legal age of majority in your state. You'll need to establish a brokerage account in the child's name with you as custodian through the Uniform Gifts to Minors Act (UGMA) or the Uniform Transfers to Minors Act (UTMA), whichever one is recognized in your state. The child's Social Security number would be used on the account for tax-reporting purposes. The assets in the account are the property of the child and cannot be used by the custodian.

When the child reaches the legal age of majority, the account would be turned over to him by reregistering the account in his name alone. When it comes to voting on matters within the investment club, you can allow the child to vote; however, the custodian really carries the voting power.

NAIC even offers a special youth membership. The child enjoys all the same benefits adults receive through membership, plus a newsletter entitled *Young Money Matters,* which contains articles, games, news, suggested web sites, and more, all geared to children.

Below is a list of other tools and web sites you can research if you're looking for more ways to teach children of all ages about money and investing.

Stein Roe Mutual Funds
Young Investor Fund
800-338-2550
www.steinroe.com

Offers a mutual fund that is geared specifically toward children. The fund invests in growth-oriented companies. As a shareholder of the mutual fund, the child will receive an owner's manual, an activity guide, and a newsletter entitled *Dollar Digest*.

Liberty Financial Companies
800-403-KIDS
www.younginvestor.com

Offers a free booklet entitled *Young Investor Parent's Guide,* and a free copy of their Young Investor PC Game.

Young Americans Bank
303-321-BANK

Offers bank-by-mail accounts in which children receive special worksheets with their quarterly statements to help them learn how to balance their accounts.

Web Sites:
National Center for Financial Education: www.ncfe.org
Investing For Kids: tqd.advanced.org/3096
Securities Industry Association Stock Market Game: www.smg2000.org

Utilizing the preceding options may help increase your children's interest in money and investing. Once they're interested, an investment club is the perfect next step. Including children in your investment club will obviously create a little more work for the adult members. But teaching them the basics of investing will help them build not only a stock portfolio, but also a level of knowledge that will be invaluable throughout their lives.

* * * * *

Those are just some of the different ideas and concepts your investment club can consider adopting. As your club continues to operate and the years pass, there may be other unique ideas that develop that your club may want to consider. As long as those new ideas don't inhibit your achieving the three goals of an investment club—(1) building a nest egg, (2) learning how to invest, and (3) having fun and meeting new people—you may want to consider trying some of them out. Change is inevitable in this world. As long as your club follows the basic premises of investment club operations and achieves the proper goals, it doesn't hurt to be a little flexible.

Chapter 14

Meeting in Cyberspace

With the Internet growing in popularity, it was only a matter of time before it created a unique twist to investment clubs. In Chapter 3, one of the decisions investment club members had to make was where they wanted to hold their meetings—in restaurants, at members' homes, at the library, or in other public buildings. Some clubs are now opting to hold their meetings in cyberspace by communicating via the Internet rather than physically getting together in one room. They're starting *online investment clubs*.

Online investment clubs: Investment clubs whose members conduct all their club business via e-mail and chat rooms, with the members never physically meeting face to face.

While going online certainly gives an investment club a whole new perspective, it's still possible to achieve the three goals. You learn to invest because you still have to research stocks and prepare stock presentations. You're definitely building that nest egg, and you're meeting new people, although you may never meet them face to face. Because these are long-distance relationships, you probably won't be able to have a holiday party or a summer picnic, but you'll still have plenty of contact with the others and get to know them pretty well.

GOOD CANDIDATES

An online investment club can work for anyone, but they're particularly convenient for:

✔ *People Who Frequently Relocate:* Many people are in jobs with companies that transfer them from one city or state to another every couple of years. It would be difficult to establish yourself in an investment club if you knew you'd probably be moving away in the next 18 months. That was the case with Shannon Sennabaum. Her husband is in the military and they have the potential of moving at any time. By being the member of an online investment club, she can move without losing the investment of time and effort that she's put into her club. All she needs is her computer.

✔ *People Working Odd-Hour Jobs:* An online investment club is also great for people who work odd hours and wouldn't be able to make it to traditional investment club meetings during the day or early evening. Many people work swing shifts or are on call and never really know for sure when they'll be home and when they'll be working. That type of schedule makes it difficult to plan and difficult to commit to attending meetings every third Wednesday at 7 P.M.

✔ *The Disabled and Handicapped:* Some people may have the time, but not the ability, to attend an investment club meeting they have to travel to because of a disability. If someone can't drive or can't easily travel from one place to another, an online investment club is perfect. Or, if someone has a handicap, this may be the perfect solution. The Cross Country Investment Club once had a member who was partially deaf. Sitting in a meeting with several people would have been difficult for her because she would always be concerned that she'd miss something that was being said. By joining an online investment club, she didn't have to worry about that.

✔ *The Isolated:* Some people are geographically isolated. Maybe you live in a rural area, far from a major city. You're too far from the city to travel there for meetings, but there aren't enough people living within a reasonable vicinity who are interested in starting a club. Without the online option, you'd probably never have the opportunity to join an investment club.

✔ *Americans Abroad:* Many Americans live in Europe, Asia, Africa, and everywhere else around the world. Starting a traditional investment club would be very difficult for them. If there aren't other Americans in their area, starting an investment club with citizens of another country could be difficult due to language problems, currency differences, and the members' ability to research stocks of another country. But an American living abroad could easily join an online investment club and attend the meetings as easily as someone living in St. Anne, Illinois, or Los Angeles, California. Geography becomes irrelevant with an online club.

✔ **Extended Families:** Many investment clubs are comprised strictly of one family's members—brothers, sisters, cousins, aunts, and uncles. But families today don't all stay in the same area. They live around the world. The option of an online investment club is perfect.

If an online club fits your lifestyle better than a traditional club, you may be able to go online and find one. But be careful. Paul Thomasson found the beginning of his investment club when he was surfing the Web looking for new sites that would help him learn about investing. He found a message on a message board from someone who was trying to start a new club. He replied to the message, as did 10 other people, and the club was on its way. Or so they thought.

"It turned out that the person who posted the message wanted to be a tyrant," says Thomasson. "He wanted complete control. He wanted to choose the officers and have everyone send him the money. He basically wanted to set up a mutual fund and have us invest with him."

After arguing through e-mail with him for more than a month, everyone who had replied to his initial e-mail request finally gave up and left. But they kept in touch with each other and managed to start the Coast to Coast Online Investment Club. Two years later they have 14 members and a portfolio worth $17,000.

FINDING MEMBERS

When starting an online investment club, you could find members the same way any club would. You may know two or three people who are interested and those people may know two or three people who are interested. Or, you may post an online message that people can respond to. That's how Shannon Sennabaum found the Cross Country Investment Club. She subscribed to an e-mail list that NAIC sponsored and found someone who wanted to start a club.

Another option is to attend investment classes, workshops, and conferences. The other attendees are obviously interested in investing and may be open to an investment club. With the option of using an online club, it doesn't make any difference if you live in Seattle, Washington, and you attend an investment conference in Boston, Massachusetts, and meet people from New Orleans, Louisiana, who are interested.

No matter how you find members, it's important to get to know the people before you start contributing money. But members of online clubs insist that they know their fellow members just as well as members of a traditional club know each other. In fact, because online club members are constantly in contact, they may know each other better. Chances are you'll get to know the other members fairly quickly when you begin structuring the club and going through the process of writing your partnership agreement and bylaws.

STRUCTURING YOUR CLUB

Your club members will still have the same five decisions to make when structuring your club: creating a name, electing officers, determining meeting times (if you plan to have regular meetings), making assignments for presentations, and determining your investment philosophy. An online club and its members can also join NAIC.

The money issues will also need to be determined. What brokerage firm will you hire? How much money will each person contribute each month? Will you use equal or unequal ownership? Will each person contribute an initial kicker to get the club going?

It's important that your online club creates a partnership agreement and bylaws. For the most part, those documents will be the same as discussed before, but with a few alterations. You'll want to add a statement that any new member must have Internet access and must have a certain level of expertise with computers. You'll want to include that your club will meet electronically rather than face to face. You'll need to include information as to how contributions are made and stock presentations are accomplished. You may want to discuss the responsibilities of the individual members which, while basically the same, may be accomplished through different methods in an online club.

If you have members who live abroad, you may want to stipulate in your partnership agreement or bylaws that all monthly contributions must be made in U.S. currency. You may also want to spell out how much of a time commitment will be expected of members to check e-mail, send e-mail, participate in chats, and complete other duties that may be unique to online clubs. As you write your partnership agreement and bylaws, you may find other stipulations you need to include and will have to alter the documents to reflect the procedures your members expect to follow.

CONDUCTING MONTHLY MEETINGS

After your club is structured and all the documents are in place, it's time to start conducting business. But if the members aren't all in one room, how can you do a stock presentation? How can you conduct business? Different clubs use different methods. You can follow other clubs' lead or you may find your own unique way to handle your meetings.

Some clubs set up a chat room where members meet at a specific time each month. The Coast to Coast Online Investment Club conducts their meeting the fourth Tuesday of each month via a chat room they've set up through Internet Relay Chat. They've arranged it so the members can come into the chat room and converse with each other. Nonmembers are able to come into the chat room, but they can only view the meeting—they can't participate.

By the time the members come to the meeting, the presentation is basically done. Here's how: Each month, three or four members are assigned the task of finding a stock to present. They determine which industry they want to consider, then choose a few companies. They research the companies, then the three people determine which company they will present to the group. Prior to the meeting, the presentation information is e-mailed to the other members who are responsible for reviewing it prior to the meeting. At the meeting, the members discuss the presentation and vote as to whether they want to buy the stock.

In addition to the presentation and voting, during this meeting the members who are monitoring stocks the club owns would discuss any information they've acquired about those companies during the month.

While some online clubs schedule a chat meeting at a regular time each month, other online clubs choose to never really even have a meeting where everyone comes together at one time. Again, the member who's responsible for that month's presentation would do the research and e-mail the information to the other members. Those members can ask questions and discuss the presentation with each other throughout the whole month via e-mail. By a certain date, each member must forward his or her vote to the secretary.

The secretary tallies the votes, informs the treasurer of the vote, and, if required, the treasurer makes the purchase.

That's basically the format that Cross Country Investment Club uses. They designate what responsibilities need to be completed during each week of the month. They have their members sign up to do presentations three or four months in advance, then one presentation is completed each month. During the first week of the month, the presenter completes the presentation and e-mails it to each member. During the second week of the month, members discuss the presentation via e-mail. During the third week of each month, members can challenge the presenter and ask her questions. The final week of each month is designated "business week," and that's when everyone votes.

At 2 P.M. (Eastern standard time) on the Sunday of business week the members do have a chat. The chat, however, is voluntary and the agenda is usually limited to one or two general topics, but if members want to talk about other issues, it's allowed. At every chat, however, a moderator is assigned and is responsible for ensuring that the chat remains focused and on target.

The Cross Country Investment Club uses a list server for their e-mail, where a member can send an e-mail to the list server and the list server forwards it on to all the other members. The list server also provides the club with a site where they can archive their e-mails and presentations. When the members vote on issues, however, they don't do so through the list server. Instead, the members prefer to have secret voting; therefore, each member e-mails his vote directly to the secretary. The club's Sunday afternoon chats are done through Yahoo Club Chat. Yahoo offers clubs free, private chat rooms to use and each member is given the password required to enter. To set up the chat room, the founding member of the club must join Yahoo, create the club, and then invite the other members to join. Another chat software program that is available to investment club members is AOL Instant Messenger.

COLLECTING THE CONTRIBUTIONS

Obviously, members can't bring their checks to an online meeting. Instead, contributions must either be mailed or transferred by wire to the treasurer by a certain date. The Cross Country Investment Club requires members to send three months' worth of contributions to the treasurer four times a year. All the club members have access to the online brokerage account so they can ensure that contributions are being deposited, trades are being made, and no unauthorized withdrawals are being taken out. By a certain date every month the treasurer e-mails to each member the valuation statement listing the club's portfolio and each person's capital account.

There are other safeguards clubs can take. They can utilize the bonding service discussed earlier that's offered by NAIC. Also, clubs can designate one member to audit the books on an annual basis, or designate an assistant treasurer whose job is to check that the treasurer is completing her job correctly. The Cross Country Investment Club even has the assistant treasurer maintain a full set of up-to-date discs and documents in case the treasurer's home would be burglarized or burned and the club would lose all its information. While all these safeguards are good options for any club, they seem to be used more often in online clubs.

DEALING WITH MEMBERSHIP CHANGES

If a member leaves an online investment club, the remaining members have the same options of cashing that person out as a traditional club would. When bringing in a new member, the procedures would also be basically the same. Assigning a mentor to a new member would be important so that the new person has someone he or she can contact to discuss procedures and responsibilities.

In a traditional investment club, most new members come to a club via a friend who is already in the club and invites them to join. It's no different in an online club. Or, some clubs create their own web site for anyone to view. Online investment club web sites may include the club's stock presentations, bios of members, the club's partnership agreement and bylaws, and other club information. The web site should include an e-mail address an interested person could write to for more information.

You might want to develop an application and have potential members complete it and e-mail it back to the club secretary. That's what the Coast to Coast Online Investment Club does. They've created their own web site where people who are interested can review information about the club, then request an application. Some of the information they request in their application includes:

✔ Name, address, phone and fax numbers, and e-mail address.

✔ Occupation, age, and hobbies.

✔ Have you reviewed the material on the club's web site?

✔ Can you spend two hours or more per week doing assigned work, research, and stock studies?

✔ Our meetings are held on the fourth Tuesday of each month at 8 P.M. EST. Would you be able to attend these meetings on a regular basis?

✔ Are you able to invest $20 per month, minimum, plus pay our one-time, nonrefundable, start-up fee of $25 to help pay for organizational expenses?

✔ What is your computer access and proficiencies with software, web browsing, and research on the web?

✔ Can you accept e-mail attachments?

✔ What is your investing expertise (novice, intermediate, expert)?

✔ Do you currently invest in individual stocks or mutual funds?

✔ Do you have expertise in a specific area of investing?

✔ Are you now or have you ever been a member of an investment club?

✔ If so, how long were you a member, and were you an officer?

✔ Write an essay explaining your approach to investing, why you want to be a member of our club, your expectations of the club, and what you hope to learn and achieve.

While it certainly seems like a lot of work to complete the Coast to Coast Online Investment Club's application, you can be sure that someone who does complete it is serious and really wants to become a member. Others who have a passing interest and probably wouldn't be committed members to the club anyway probably would be scared off by the amount of work it takes just to apply. That's one way to ensure you're getting members who will be responsible and will pitch in and work.

After a potential member completes an application, have this person attend a few monthly meetings, just as you would if you were operating a traditional club. Because this person isn't a member yet, he wouldn't contribute any money or be allowed to vote, but he certainly could contribute knowledge and a little bit of work. Giving that person a few small assignments will help the current club members determine whether this person will be a dedicated member who's willing to take on responsibility. After two or three meetings, the current members can vote as to whether they want this person to join their club.

CONTINUING EDUCATION

Just because a club is online shouldn't stop it from devoting itself to continuing education. A member can be assigned to research an aspect of investing and e-mail a short write-up to the other members. A chat can be conducted with a guest speaker. Members can agree on a book or magazine that they can all read, then discuss it online. If a member finds a web site that is particularly educational, she can e-mail the address to the other members. Or, during a chat, if a topic is brought up that most members don't understand, a short tutorial can take place right then.

Structuring and operating an investment club online may be a departure from the ordinary, but it works. Of course, there are advantages and disadvantages that are specific to being online.

DISADVANTAGES

- ✔ *Unresponsive Members:* Because members converse electronically, quick responses are essential. If a member e-mails a question about a stock presentation to the person who prepared it, he needs an answer fairly quickly. If members don't check their e-mail for days, that could hinder the transfer of information and frustrate those who are trying to make decisions as to whether they want to purchase a stock that was presented.

- ✔ *Internet Reliability:* The Internet is not always reliable. Members may be in the middle of a meeting when they suddenly hear, "Goodbye!" They then have to scramble to get back to the meeting. Or, they may have trouble logging on at a specific time and end up missing a portion of the meeting.

- ✔ *Social Aspects:* Because of geography, members will probably never have the opportunity to get together for social functions, which adds to the members' ability to get to know each other better and become a cohesive group. However, despite the lack of face-to-face social activities, members of online clubs contend that because they have so much more contact with each other than members of traditional clubs, they really get to know each other better.

- ✔ *Time and Effort:* Shannon Sennabaum of the Cross Country Investment Club believes that the time and effort that must be devoted to an online club can be a disadvantage for some. The perpetual nature of the club can cause many members to burn out quickly. In a traditional club, you go to a meeting, go home, and you may not see or talk to the other members until the next monthly meeting. In an online club, however, the meetings basically go on 24 hours a day right in your own home. Shannon was president of her club for a year. It wasn't odd for her to turn on her computer and find 10 e-mails to answer. If she went away for a week, she felt lost when she came back. At the end of her one-year term, she was exhausted from constantly trying to steer the club in the right direction.

While an online club has more flexibility and can move more quickly because members are in constant contact, that fast pace can be too much for some. Typically, the members who resigned from the Cross Country Investment Club did so because they couldn't keep up with the constant information flow and the amount of time required of them.

ADVANTAGES

✔ *Geographic Diversity:* With an online club you can have members who live everywhere. That may offer your club knowledge of a broader base of industries. Someone who lives in Detroit, Michigan, may be more aware of the nuances of the auto industry, whereas someone who lives in San Jose, California, may have more information about the high-tech industry because most of the players are right outside her door.

✔ *Flexibility of Time:* Because an online club is always at your fingertips, members have a lot of flexibility of time. If you can't sleep at 2 A.M., and you have information you want to share with the other club members, you can do so right then. If one person works days and wants to review stock presentations at night, no problem. If another member works nights and wants to review stock presentations during the day, no problem. Each can contribute his share of work to the club on his own time schedule. Also, no time is wasted driving to and from meetings. For most people, it's just a few short steps to their computer to attend a monthly meeting.

✔ *Diversity of Backgrounds:* An online club may have more diversity of backgrounds. A regular investment club may have three people who work together at one company, four who work at another company, and a few more who work at other places. But the members of an online investment club will probably each have very different jobs with very different companies. Each person brings a wealth of information about a certain aspect of the industry in which he works.

Being a member of an online or a traditional investment club primarily involves all the same procedures and responsibilities, and both can achieve all the same results. If you'd like the ability to contribute work to the club on a flexible schedule and never have to leave the comfort of your own home to attend a meeting, an online club might be perfect for you. If you like to sit in the same room with the member presenting a stock and ask questions of her directly and get an immediate answer, it might be best that you stick with a traditional club.

Which type of club you choose isn't important. What's important is that you choose to join a club and start achieving the goals that are so crucial in ensuring that your financial future is secure.

Chapter 15

Using Your Investment Club Knowledge to Go It Alone

Investing on your own can be a frightening prospect when you don't know the investing terminology, don't know how stocks work, and don't know how to research a company. There's no way you'd even know where to begin on your own. But after a few years of being a member of an investment club, you'll have gained not only knowledge, but also confidence. You'll understand the inner workings of the stock market. You'll know how to obtain the materials you need to research a stock and how to utilize those materials. You'll know how to deal with a stockbroker and how to ensure that your investments are properly diversified.

Because of the knowledge and confidence gained from being the member of an investment club, nine out of 10 investment club members choose to start building a personal portfolio outside of their investment club after only five years of membership. While they certainly don't want to give up their membership in their club, they do want to enhance the investments they've made through the club and start building a portfolio on their own. Terri Hult of the Dough Makers Investment Club says that the members of her club have discussed the fact that without the experience of being a member of an investment club, many of them would not have invested in stocks and started a personal portfolio on their own. But now, almost all of the 15 members have begun investing on their own, and many are even building portfolios that are doing better than the investment club's!

Obviously, however, people have only so much money. It's important to note that prior to starting an investment portfolio of your own, and even prior to investing via an investment club, you should first be sure that you're contributing to any company-sponsored retirement plans your employer may offer. Many times, these plans match the contributions that you make to the fund. If you invest a dollar, the company may add $.50 to that. That's free money! You don't want to miss out on that.

Also, the company-sponsored retirement plans that are available to you may be investing your money prior to the IRS getting hold of it. If you're able to invest pretax dollars, you should definitely take advantage of that, too. Why pay taxes to the government when you could be investing that money for your future instead? After ensuring that you're utilizing any company-sponsored plans to your advantage and investing via your investment club, if you still have money that you can set aside for your future you may want to start investing outside your club. If you decide to start building that personal portfolio, there are a few issues you need to take into consideration.

INVESTMENT PHILOSOPHY AND STRATEGY

Whether investing through an investment club or on your own, you need to develop an investment philosophy and create an investment strategy you can follow. Your investment club has determined an investment philosophy and strategies that it follows, so let's look at that philosophy and those strategies to see if they work individually.

Buy and Hold

We've already discussed that market timing doesn't work. Buying a good stock and holding it for a long period of time tends to give investors better results than buying a stock, selling it after a few months, and buying another. Because of the expenses involved in buying and selling, you're much better off selling a stock only when it's absolutely necessary. Whether investing via an investment club or on your own, staying in for the long haul is the key to growth.

Buy Growth Stocks

If your club adopted NAIC recommendations for investing, you're trying to double your money every five years. To accomplish that, you need to buy growth stocks—stocks that are increasing their earnings by almost 15 percent per year. When investing individually, you certainly can't go wrong with a strategy like that.

Diversify Your Portfolio

Whether you're buying stocks through an investment club or on your own, diversification will help to reduce the amount of risk your portfolio carries.

Why not take advantage of any strategy that can help to reduce risk? In fact, in your personal portfolio your diversification will be even more pronounced because, as we'll discuss under asset allocation, you'll want to include another type of investment in your portfolio in addition to stocks.

Reinvest Earnings

The power of compounding helps increase the size of an investment portfolio. There's no reason that an individual or an investment club should withdraw earnings or dividends. Making withdrawals decreases the size of your portfolio and only hurts you and your financial future.

The investment philosophy and strategies you developed for your investment club through those NAIC recommendations seem to fit the investing you're planning to do individually, and should serve you well in building your personal portfolio.

ASSET ALLOCATION

Asset allocation is an issue that's never really addressed in an investment club because they typically invest only in stocks.

Asset allocation: An investment portfolio's division among various classes of investments.

When investing individually, however, there is another type of investment you'll want to include in your portfolio. That security is *bonds*.

Bond: A security that a company or government issues in order to raise money. The investor is paid a specified rate of interest for a specific number of years until the security matures and the principal is repaid.

If an investment club invested in bonds, it would defeat one of the goals of an investment club—learning to invest. That's because there's really nothing to learn by buying bonds. You give your broker a few pieces of information and the broker finds a bond that fits your criteria. But when you start investing individually, you'll probably want to include a few bonds in your personal portfolio to help reduce your overall risk level.

What Is a Bond?

When you invest in a bond, you're basically making a loan to a corporation. For example, let's say you buy a $10,000, five-year bond that pays 6 percent. You give the corporation $10,000. Every quarter or six months, the corporation pays you any interest that is due for that time period. Then, at the end of five years, the corporation pays you your $10,000 back. That's called a *corporate bond*.

Corporate bond: A negotiable security a corporation sells to raise money through debt. The interest earned on a corporate bond is taxable.

There are also *municipal bonds*, which are issued by municipalities such as states, counties, or cities.

Municipal bonds: Bonds that are sold by states, cities, and municipalities. The interest earned on a municipal bond is tax-free.

The two types of bonds work exactly the same except that a corporate bond pays investors a slightly higher rate of interest. But the interest you earn on a corporate bond is taxable. The interest you earn on a municipal bond is tax-free. Taking into consideration the interest rate you'd receive on a corporate bond and the taxes you'd have to pay on the interest you receive if you're in the very highest federal tax bracket, you'd be better off buying the municipal bond. If you're not in the highest federal income tax bracket, you'd be better off purchasing the corporate bond. Therefore, which type of bond you purchase is determined by your tax bracket.

Just like any type of investment, however, bonds also carry risk.

Credit Risk: Credit risk is the risk that the company or municipality that issued the bond will default.

Credit risk: The risk to investors that the corporation or municipality that issued bonds will default and the investors will not be repaid the money they invested.

If you lend them money by purchasing their bond and then they go into bankruptcy and have no funds available to pay their bondholders, you'll lose your money. You can, however, control the level of credit risk you assume when buying bonds by checking the bond's rating.

Value Line and Standard & Poor's are two companies that rate bonds based on the issuing company's ability to repay the bond. The best and safest rating is triple A, then double A, then single A. The next rating is triple B and so on. When you get to the C-rated bonds, those are junk bonds that carry an extreme amount of risk. If you always purchase double or triple A-rated bonds, you're reducing your exposure to credit risk because you can be fairly certain that the bond issuer will have the wherewithal to pay you back.

Interest-Rate Risk: If you hold a bond to maturity, interest-rate risk is not a concern because, if you've bought a double- or triple A-rated bond, you'll receive your total principal amount when the bond matures.

Interest-rate risk: The risk to investors that the bond they purchased will decrease in value due to an increase in interest rates.

You can, however, sell bonds prior to their maturity date. If you do, you need to understand how interest-rate risk affects the value of bonds. When interest rates move, they affect bonds the exact same way as they affect preferred stock, as we discussed in Chapter 13.

Let's say you buy a $10,000 bond that has a five-year holding period and pays you a 6 percent interest rate, which is $600 per year. During that holding period, the value of that bond can increase and decrease based on the current interest rate. If interest rates increase to 7 percent and companies are selling new bonds that pay that rate, no one will want to buy your bond because it pays only 6 percent. But if you decrease the price of your bond to $8,571, then the $600 interest payment the bond pays equals a 7 percent interest rate. Therefore, if you want to sell that bond prior to maturity and interest rates have increased from 6 percent to 7 percent, you'll lose $1,429.

Conversely, if interest rates move from 6 percent to 5 percent after you purchased the bond, everyone will want your bond because it pays a higher rate than what is being offered in the marketplace on new bonds. Therefore, you'll be able to sell your $10,000 for $12,000 because the interest payment of $600 would equal a 5 percent return on a $12,000 bond. If you sold your bond now, you'd make a $2,000 profit.

The value of a bond moves in the opposite direction of interest rates—interest rates go up, the value of the bond goes down, and vice versa. But, if you've purchased a good bond that has a safe rating, and you hold that bond to maturity, you'll get your money back at the end of the specified period of time. By holding a bond to maturity, you eliminate interest-rate risk.

Call Risk: Some bonds are callable, meaning that if a municipality issues a 10-year bond, but they decide to call it back in seven years, they will pay you out and you'll have to find another investment for your money.

Call risk: The risk that a bond will be paid off prior to its maturity date.

The risk is that you thought you had your money invested so that you'd receive a certain rate of return for 10 years, but after seven years you suddenly have to look for another investment and try to replace the rate you were receiving on the bond that was called. Not all callable bonds, however, are called. You may own a callable bond until its maturity. Typically, the call feature relates primarily to municipal bonds.

The reason bonds are called is because interest rates change. If a municipality issues a bond that pays 10 percent and seven years later interest rates have slipped to 7 percent, they can call the 10 percent bonds and issue new bonds at 7 percent, saving them money in interest.

Inflation Risk: As we discussed earlier, the value of a bond increases and decreases as interest rates move up and down. But interest rates are driven higher and lower by inflation.

Inflation risk: The risk that the inflation rate will rise, forcing interest rates up and the value of your bond down. If the inflation rate is higher than the interest rate you're receiving, you'll also be losing purchasing power.

If you own a bond that pays 6 percent and the inflation rate moves up to 10 percent, you're really losing 4 percent on your investment. But you can't really sell the bond and replace it because you'd take a loss on the sale of the bond. That's because if the inflation rate has risen, so have interest rates, which force the value of your bond down. If you hold the bond to maturity, you'll still receive your full principal, but during the time you hold it, you'll be losing ground to the high inflation rate.

Despite the risks associated with bonds, they're still considered less risky than stocks. That's because you can eliminate interest-rate risk by holding a bond to maturity. You can control credit risk by buying bonds with triple- or double-A ratings. Call risk is really just an inconvenience, and inflation risk can be minimized by using the strategy of *laddering*.

Laddering: Strategy of purchasing bonds so that one bond matures each year.

Laddering means that when you purchase individual bonds, you wouldn't buy bonds that all have the same maturity date. Instead, you'd buy one bond that matures in four years, one that matures in five years, and one that matures in six years. That way, you'll never have the problem of holding all your money in one bond that has decreased in value and pays an interest rate that is lower than the inflation rate.

Another reason bonds are considered less risky than stocks is that if a company has financial difficulties, the interest that company pays on its bonds takes precedence over the dividends it pays on its common stock. Therefore, the income investors receive on bonds is safer is than the income they'd received on the same company's stock.

While bonds offer less risk than stocks, it's important to note that they also offer a lower potential rate of return. A stock's price can increase substantially, whereas a bond's value is not nearly as volatile. Therefore, your potential of making money is much higher with a stock than a bond.

Because bonds carry less risk than stocks, rather than having your portfolio consist of all stocks, you'll probably want to reduce the risk level of your personal portfolio by adding a few bonds.

To purchase a bond, you'll need to give your stockbroker four pieces of information.

1. How much money do you want to lend, or invest—$5,000, $10,000, $30,000, or some other amount?

2. For how long do you want to lend the money? Maturities range from one to thirty years.

3. What rating do you want? (You should purchase triple- or double-A-rated bonds.)

4. Do you want a corporate or municipal bond? If you're in the highest tax bracket, you're probably better off choosing municipal. If not, corporate may be best for you.

Life-Cycle Investing

The strategy of *life-cycle investing* is a rule of thumb that you can use to help determine the proper asset allocation for your personal portfolio.

Life-cycle investing: An asset allocation strategy that matches investors' investments to their current needs based on their age and risk tolerance.

In life-cycle investing, you divide your life into three stages.

1. Accumulation Stage: This stage ranges from age 20 to 45.

Accumulation stage: Stage of life-cycle investing when an investor is age 20 to 45, is accumulating the bulk of his assets, and has a long-term horizon and a high-risk tolerance.

During this period of your life, you're getting your first job and beginning to accumulate your assets—a car, a house, your furniture. You have a long time until you're ready to retire, so you can adopt a fairly aggressive investing strategy. If you make a mistake and lose money, you have plenty of time to earn that money back. Therefore, the largest portion of your portfolio would be in stocks, which carry more risk, but also offer more potential for higher returns.

You would probably put about 80 percent of your money in stocks. Those stocks would be divided between those of smaller, fast-growing companies and larger, more well-established companies. The remainder of your money would be in bonds. Because you're probably not in the highest tax bracket during the majority of this period of your life, you'd want to use corporate bonds.

2. Transition Stage: This stage stretches from age 46 to 60.

Transition stage: Stage of life-cycle investing when an investor is age 45 to 60, is at the peak of his earning ability, and has diminished risk tolerance.

During this time, you're probably at your peak earning ability due to the raises and promotions you've received over the years. You probably also have lower expenses because your house may be paid off, or your children may be finished with college. Your time horizon—the amount of time you have until you retire—however, is shorter, so you'll want to assume a little less risk than you did during the accumulation stage.

You'd probably want to have about 65 percent of your money in stocks. That portion of your portfolio would be weighted more heavily with the stocks of large, well-established companies, and you'd have fewer small, fast-growing companies. The other 35 percent of your money would be in bonds. Since you're in your peak earning years, you may be in the top tax bracket. If so, you'd want to switch to municipal bonds.

3. Retirement Stage: This stage spans from age 61 and older.

Retirement stage: Stage of life-cycle investing when an investor is age 61 and older, is ready to stop working, and has a very low risk tolerance.

It used to be that financial experts told investors to put all their money in bonds as soon as they reached retirement age. You could then live off the interest, use some of the principal, and not run out of money during the few remaining years of your life. But due to the great strides that have been made in medicine and Americans' willingness to live a healthier lifestyle, that advice has changed. Life expectancy tables tell us that after we retire, we still have another 25 to 30 years left to live. If we put all our money in bonds, there's a good chance we could outlive our money. Of course, we need to be careful. If we make a mistake and lose money during the retirement stage, we have no way to earn it back.

While you should invest about 30 percent of your money in stocks during this stage, you should choose conservative stocks that pay good dividends. The remainder of your money would be invested in bonds. Since you'll probably be in a lower tax bracket during this stage of your life, you'd want to choose corporate bonds.

It's important to remember that when it comes to asset allocation, the strategy of life-cycle investing is simply a rule of thumb. It's a starting point that you can use to help determine what your asset allocation should be based on your age and risk level, but it must be adjusted to fit your needs. For example, if you're 35 years old and life-cycle investing tells you that you should have 80 percent of your money in stocks, but you get upset and nervous every time the market moves down, then that's the wrong asset allocation for you. The most important aspect of asset allocation is that you're comfortable with your investment portfolio.

MUTUAL FUNDS VERSUS INDIVIDUAL STOCKS AND BONDS

Except for international stocks, mutual funds don't work very well for an investment club because they defeat the goal of learning how to invest. The advantages of instant diversification and having a professional manager are irrelevant because your club is building a diversified portfolio and your members are managing the investments themselves. But in your personal portfolio, mutual funds may be the perfect investment for you. The primary reasons are the amount of money you'll be investing and the instant diversification a mutual fund can offer.

Because you have several members in your investment club all pooling their money, you'll probably have $500 or more to invest each month. But the chances of your coming up with $500 or more to invest on your own each month probably aren't very realistic. If you have $50 or even $100 each month to invest, it'll be difficult to purchase individual stocks and bonds. By the time you pay commissions, you won't have much money left to invest. And if you can only afford to buy a few shares each month, it'll take you a long time to build a portfolio that's truly diversified. Therefore, when starting your own personal portfolio, you'll probably want to use mutual funds. After you've built a sizable portfolio through mutual funds, and you want to switch to individual stocks and bonds, you can certainly do so.

When you research stocks, there are certain aspects of a company you need to research—earnings growth, competition, market share, and more. When you research a mutual fund, however, you'll be focusing on the mutual fund's past performance and its management team rather than on the performance of the underlying stocks and bonds the fund owns.

When considering a mutual fund, call the company and ask for a copy of its *prospectus*.

Prospectus: The document published by a mutual-fund company that includes information about the fund's investment philosophy and strategy, fee structure, past performance, management, and other information.

This document will provide you with the information you need to know before investing your money in a mutual fund. In addition, there are third-party reports you can review that rate mutual funds. Below are several reference publications that can be found at most public libraries that you can use to research a mutual fund.

✔ CDA Weisenberger: This company is a mutual-fund rating service that publishes the monthly *Mutual Fund Report,* the monthly *Mutual Fund Update,* and the annual *Mutual Fund Yearbook.*

✔ Value Line: This company publishes the *Value Line Mutual Fund Investment Survey.*

✔ Morningstar: This company publishes *Morningstar Mutual Funds,* and a newsletter entitled *Morningstar Investor.*

All of these publications can be extremely helpful to you in finding a mutual fund that fits your needs.

There are six aspects of a mutual fund you should research:

1. Past Performance

If a mutual fund achieved a 25 percent return for its investors last year, that doesn't mean investors will receive a 25 percent return this year. Look at the past returns the fund has achieved over the past 10 years. Have they been consistent or volatile? You want a fund that has a proven track record of achieving consistent returns for its shareholders.

2. Management

One of the biggest selling points of a mutual fund is that it offers professional management. But professional management doesn't always mean good management. If you're depending on that manager to invest your money in stocks and bonds, you want to be sure she's competent. Look at her track record. Has she performed well despite what the stock market as a whole has done? Has her performance been in the top third of her peer group? If the manager is new to the fund you're considering, check her track record at the previous fund she managed. If she did a horrible job there, she probably won't do any better at this new fund.

3. Fee Structure

A mutual fund offers professional management, but it doesn't offer it for free. The fee you're charged for that service is called the fund's expense ratio. Each fund determines its own expense ratio. Be sure the fees charged by the fund you're considering are in line with those charged by other comparable mutual funds.

4. Risk Level

If you're near retirement age, you don't want a mutual fund that carries a lot of risk. Both Value Line and Morningstar include a risk measurement in their mutual-fund reports so you can determine the risk level of a fund and be sure it fits your needs.

5. Minimum Investment

If you're ready to start building your personal portfolio outside of your investment club and you have $500 to start with, you need to find a mutual fund that has a minimum investment of $500. Also, if you plan to add $50 per month to the fund, be sure the fund you're considering will accept that amount each month.

The minimum investment that many funds advertise, however, may be negotiable. If you're willing to participate in the fund's automatic monthly investing program, in which the fund's management automatically draws a set amount of money from your bank account each month and invests it into the fund, they may waive the minimum initial investment requirement. In exchange for an automatic investment of $25 or $50 per month, you may be able to get into the fund for much less than the advertised minimum. For a list of mutual funds that you can buy into for small monthly deposits, visit the Mutual Fund Education Alliance web site at www.mfea.com. Click on the caption, "Funds for Fifty Dollars."

6. Additional Services

Some mutual funds offer their shareholders an investment newsletter that's included with each monthly statement. Some funds will offer to automatically deduct money from your bank account each month to invest in the mutual fund, saving you from having to write checks and transfer money from account to account. And most mutual funds offer their shareholders a family of funds so that you can switch from one type of fund to another at no cost as your needs change. Below is a list of some of the different types of funds that may be available.

Growth Fund: A growth fund invests in growth stocks, which we've discussed earlier as being the type of stocks that investment clubs should purchase.

Growth fund: A mutual fund that focuses on purchasing only growth stocks.

Because growth stocks demonstrate above-normal growth and capital appreciation, they're great investments for a person who is in the accumulation or early transition stages of their life-cycle investing strategy.

Aggressive Growth Fund: An aggressive growth fund takes on a large amount of risk in an effort to garner capital appreciation.

Aggressive growth fund: A mutual fund that focuses on achieving capital appreciation and, therefore, carries a high level of risk.

The manager of this type of mutual fund would invest in stocks of companies that pay little or no dividends, but have a high potential for capital appreciation. Much of the money would be in stocks of very small companies, which increases the risk level of the mutual fund. Some managers may even trade stock options or stock-index futures. This type of mutual fund is very risky and would, at best, be included as a very small percentage of your total portfolio during the accumulation stage of life-cycle investing.

Income Fund: An income fund is one that focuses on producing income, rather than capital appreciation.

Income fund: A mutual fund that focuses on producing income.

Therefore, this type of fund would invest in bonds and dividend-paying stocks. An income fund would carry less risk than a growth fund and may be a fund you'd want to use in the latter part of the transition stage or in the retirement stage.

Balanced Fund: This type of fund combines the capital appreciation of a growth fund and the income of an income fund by purchasing growth stocks, dividend-paying stocks, and bonds.

Balanced fund: A mutual fund that focuses on garnering both capital appreciation and income.

Of course, every manager has his own idea of how those investments should be combined. Some may weight the portfolio toward growth stocks, giving the fund a higher level of risk, while other managers may do just the opposite. Depending on the risk level of the specific fund, a balanced fund could be used during all three stages of your life-cycle investing strategy.

International Stock and Bond Fund: In Chapter 13 we discussed using this type of mutual fund in an investment club to give your portfolio a little international flavor. When investing on your own, you still might want to focus on international funds rather than American Depositary Receipts (ADRs) to add that international portion to your portfolio.

Index Fund: An index fund invests only in the stocks that comprise a specific index.

Index fund: A mutual fund that mimics the holdings of a specific index.

For instance, the S&P 500 index has 500 stocks in it. An S&P 500 index mutual fund would purchase only those 500 stocks and nothing else. Therefore, management doesn't really have to manage an index fund because there are no buy and sell decisions to make. Because there is less buying and selling in an index fund, there are fewer commissions generated, so the fees charged to shareholders are lower than other categories of funds.

Bond Fund: A bond fund buys only bonds, with a focus on generating income.

Bond fund: A mutual fund that focuses on producing income by purchasing only bonds.

Before you purchase a bond fund, however, it's important to determine what type of bonds the manager is purchasing. If he's building a portfolio of double- or triple-A bonds, you can use this fund during your retirement stage. But if he's buying junk bonds, you may never want to use this fund in any stage.

While there are other categories of mutual funds, those listed above are the most widely recognized and the most prevalent. Before buying any type of mutual fund, call the company and get the fund's prospectus. Read through it and determine whether this is a fund that truly fits your needs. Make a quick trip to the library and read what Morningstar, Value Line, and CDA Weisenberger think about it.

When investing outside of your investment club, you'll probably have to start with mutual funds because you're dealing with a smaller amount of money. But once you've built a portfolio of at least $20,000 or $30,000, you can always switch to investing in individual stocks. Keep in mind, however, that you're one person. You'll have to do all your own research, which involves more work than it does in an investment club, where 10 or 20 people are sharing the responsibility of finding and researching stocks.

REAL ESTATE INVESTMENT TRUSTS

When you're investing on your own, there's one other type of investment that may interest you. Even though it's a stock and not a bond, it has many of the attributes of a bond. Its price fluctuates with interest rates, and it's an income-producing investment in that it pays a fairly high dividend. It's a *real estate investment trust,* or *REIT* (pronounced reet) for short.

Real estate investment trust {REIT}: A company organized to pool investors' funds for the purchase or financing of real estate.

Just like a mutual fund, a REIT accepts money from thousands of investors and pools that money to make investments. Therefore, a REIT gives investors instant diversification because when an investor purchases one, she immediately owns a piece of all the REIT's assets. A REIT, like a mutual fund, also has professional managers who handle the day-to-day operations. A REIT, however, invests only in the real estate industry by purchasing real estate or offering real estate financing to others. At the beginning of 2000 there were 199 publicly traded REITs in existence in the United States that had a total market capitalization of $122.58 billion. There are three types of REITs.

1. Equity REIT

An equity REIT uses the money it collects from investors to buy large pieces of real estate—shopping centers, apartment complexes, hotels, office buildings, and more. An equity REIT earns income through the operation and the eventual sale of the real estate it purchases. There are 165 publicly traded equity REITs that have a total market capitalization of $117.9 billion.

2. Mortgage REIT

A mortgage REIT uses the money it collects from investors to make mortgage loans to others to finance the purchase of real estate. It earns its income from the finance charges and the interest it collects on the mortgage loans it makes. There are 24 publicly traded mortgage REITs that have a total market capitalization of $2.02 billion.

3. Hybrid REIT

A hybrid REIT is one that uses some of the money collected from investors to buy real estate, and some of the money to make mortgage loans. There are 10 publicly traded hybrid REITs that have a total market capitalization of $2.66 billion.

One of the major benefits of a REIT is that it offers investors a fairly high rate of return. We discussed earlier how the board of directors of public companies can determine each quarter how much they want to pay their shareholders in dividends. That's not the case with REITs. By law, a REIT is required to pay out at least 95 percent of its income to its shareholders each year. In addition, when a corporation pays a dividend, that money has already been taxed at the corporate level prior to being distributed to the company's shareholders as dividends. When the shareholder receives the dividend, he also has to pay tax on it. That money is taxed twice. But a REIT pays no income tax so there is no taxation at the corporate level. The shareholder pays tax on the money when he receives it as a dividend. The money is taxed only once, leaving more money for the REIT to distribute to its shareholders.

The primary issues investors should be concerned about when purchasing a REIT are to make sure the underlying properties or mortgages of the REIT are sound and that management is competent. If the properties are in a bad neighborhood and are deteriorating, or the mortgage loans they're making are questionable credits, that's not a good investment. That's also not good management.

Before purchasing a REIT, check out management's past performance and experience level. Look at the underlying properties the REIT owns or the properties against which they are making mortgages. Make sure the dividend payments have been consistent and are in line with other similar REITs. Just like with any stock, you can call the company and ask them to send you their annual report and other documents so you can research the company.

If you're investing on your own and want to dabble in the real estate industry, want good diversification within that industry, and are looking for a high rate of return, you may want to add a REIT or two to your portfolio. When investing via your investment club, however, you probably wouldn't want to consider a REIT because an investment club's focus is to buy growth stocks.

For more information on REITs, you can visit the National Association of Real Estate Investment Trusts' web site at www.nareit.com, or you can call them at 800-3NAREIT.

Investing on your own can be a somewhat different experience than investing via an investment club. For instance, you'll include some investments in your personal portfolio that you wouldn't include in your investment club portfolio. Also, when investing on your own you won't have the advantage of having other peoples' expertise on whether a stock is a good buy. Conversely, Howard Clarke of the Central Maine Investors of Augusta points out that when you're investing on your own, you also have the ability to make your own decisions without worrying about having 15 people vote on whether they want to buy the stock you're considering. He quickly corrects that statement, however, by adding that he does discuss the stocks he's considering with his wife, and she certainly gets to vote!

Being an active member of an investment club gives you choices that you probably never felt you had available to you before. You've gained the knowledge and the confidence you need to build a portfolio of mutual funds or individual stocks and bonds. Without having been a member of your investment club, you may never have gotten to this point.

Chapter

16

Continuing Education

W hether you want to be a gourmet cook, an expert woodworker, an accomplished musician, or a knowledgeable investor, learning your craft is a lifetime experience. By keeping the learning process alive, you'll ensure that your investment club members will remain interested and that your club won't become stagnant.

We've discussed having your vice president of education obtain audio- or videotapes to play for the members at meetings or having a speaker come in and talk to your club. We've even discussed having individual members research specific areas of investing and present their research at the regular monthly meetings. But sometimes it's nice to get out and go visiting. Below are other activities an investment club can engage in that can accomplish two investment club goals at once: learning about investing and having fun.

ATTENDING THE ANNUAL MEETING

If you've invested in a company that's located close to where your investment club is located, consider going to the company's annual meeting. Each year when you receive the company's annual report, you'll also receive a proxy statement and proxy card, which is a ballot for voting. The proxy is your invitation to attend the annual meeting and will explain what issues will be brought to a vote at the meeting. Some of the issues included may be the election of the board of directors, the issuance of new stock, a corporate reorganization, and other matters the company must deal with that require a shareholder vote.

Whether you go to the annual meeting or not, when the treasurer receives a company's proxy and proxy card, she should bring them to the investment club's next meeting and explain the issues being voted on. The membership as a whole should have the opportunity to know what the issues are and decide how the club will vote. After the proxy is voted, it should be returned in the envelope supplied by the company. (If your club's stock is in street name, the proxy materials will be sent to you via your brokerage firm.) Even if you plan to attend the annual meeting, it's best to send your proxy card in beforehand so the company can tally up as many votes as possible prior to the meeting. As shareholders, it's important that you always vote your proxy, just like as American citizens, it's important that you always vote in elections. It's your chance to have your voice heard.

By attending the annual meeting, you'll have an opportunity to actually see the people who are running this company. Depending on the company whose stock your club owns, some annual meetings draw a small attendance and are very legalistic and mundane. On the other end of the spectrum are companies that add a lot of glitz and hoopla to their meeting. Most companies conduct an annual meeting that is somewhere in between.

Typically, a couple of key management people will speak at the annual meeting. Speakers may include the president or chief executive officer discussing general information about how the company performed during the past year and what management has planned for the next year and beyond. Or the chief financial officer may present an overview of the key financial statistics that depict how the company has fared. The person in charge of marketing may discuss new marketing plans, and oftentimes management will use the annual meeting as an opportunity to showcase a new product or a new television or radio ad they've created that hasn't started running yet.

At the end of the prepared speeches, management usually opens the floor for questions. Shareholders can stand and ask questions about the company and their investment directly to management personnel. Not only will you get your questions answered, but you'll also get the opportunity to see how management handles this portion of the annual meeting. Do they openly address the questions—even the tough ones—or do they avoid questions by changing the subject? Do they act more like responsible management leaders, or politicians trying to hide what they've done? You can get a good feel as to the management of a company just by watching and hearing their responses to shareholder questions.

If you have a question you'd like to have answered, go ahead and ask. But remember, there are only certain questions management is allowed to answer. If your question involves a topic that's common knowledge or an issue that's previously been announced by the company, it's fair game. But there are other questions management won't be allowed to answer. If they're embroiled in a lawsuit that hasn't been resolved, they may not be able to divulge exactly what the current situation is. If they're in the middle of union talks, they may not be able to discuss some of the issues being negotiated. If you ask if they're considering any mergers soon, even if they're currently in the middle of merger talks with another company, they won't be able to admit it. They won't be allowed to divulge any nonpublic, confidential information, which is called *inside information*.

Inside information: Information a company has not yet made public.

It's illegal for a company to divulge inside information to a group of people prior to announcing that information to the general public. In fact, if a management person gave you a piece of inside information and you purchased or sold the company's stock based on that information, you've just committed an illegal act.

Management also won't make predictions for you, so don't bother to ask what earnings will be next year or where the company's stock price will be in the next six months. They don't know and they're not going to guess because they could open themselves up to all kinds of problems.

Several years ago a technology company made an earnings projection for their next fiscal year. When they didn't meet that projection, the company was sued. The case was dismissed as frivolous, but the plaintiff amended the complaint and refiled it. Once again, it was dismissed. But the plaintiff didn't give up. In a second appeal, it was once again dismissed as frivolous—the third time the courts dismissed it. While the company basically won, it took them a year and a half to fight this lawsuit. That fight cost the company approximately $800,000 in legal fees.

But the cost wasn't the only problem. Because the company didn't know what the outcome of the lawsuit would be, they couldn't really discuss the future direction of the company with the investing public. During the year and a half the company was fighting the suit, the company's stock price went down. In addition, the insurance company that insured the company's officers and directors cancelled the company's insurance policies. Without insurance coverage, the company couldn't attract new board members. Despite the fact that the company never did anything wrong, it almost failed. With horror stories like that, no company management is willing to issue projections in an annual report or at an annual meeting.

While you won't get projections, annual meetings can be a wealth of information for shareholders. It's probably your only opportunity to see management in action, which gives you one more piece of information about the company whose stock you own. The more you know about the company, the better and more informed decisions your club can make as to whether this is a stock you want to continue to own.

VISITING AN EXCHANGE

Stock exchanges are the heart of our financial markets. Without them, we wouldn't be able to invest in the companies that provide us with the products and services we require to survive. It's easy to call a broker, place a buy order, then get your confirmation in the mail. You purchased stock and you now own part of corporate America, but how did it happen? If, after you place a buy order, you envision your stockbroker or his representative walking into another person's office, asking to purchase shares for you, then exchanging shares for money, do you have a surprise coming!

Visiting a stock exchange is a great excitement not only for a new investor, but for any investor. Standing in the visitor's gallery, you can't help but stare in disbelief and feel your pulse race just a bit. If you've never seen it, it's worth the time and effort to get to the exchange nearest to you and spend an hour or two!

Who would expect respectable sellers of the stocks of corporate America to be screaming at each other, making hand gestures to each other, and pushing each other around? Who would expect the floor of a stock exchange, that is a monument to capital formation, to be littered with paper? The first time you see a stock exchange in action, you'll decide it's mayhem and total disorganization. But in reality it's very organized—every person has a job and does it—and trades actually get transacted in a timely manner.

Whether individually or as a group, your investment club members should try to visit an exchange. It will give you a new respect for the process that takes place after your club gives that buy or sell order to your stockbroker. The biggest exchange in the United States is the New York Stock Exchange, but there are other smaller exchanges across the country where you can visit and see how it all works. Of course, we talked earlier about the NASDAQ, which is an over-the-counter market. Because it is simply a network of phone lines and computer connections, the NASDAQ obviously can't be visited.

VISITING THE FEDERAL RESERVE BANK OF NEW YORK

If you make it to New York City to visit the New York Stock Exchange, you might also want to stop at the Federal Reserve Bank and take their free one-hour tour. If you plan to do that, however, be sure to arrange it at least one month in advance. If you have a large group, you'll need to make your arrangements three months in advance. There are only six tours per day, with just 30 people per tour.

While the tour doesn't necessarily encompass the topic of investing, it will offer insights that will help you understand how our banking system works and how our monetary policy is set. You'll learn about the central banking functions that the Federal Reserve System performs. You'll see the bank's vault of international monetary gold that's housed five stories below street level in the bedrock of Manhattan Island. You'll also experience FedWorks, an interactive multimedia exhibit center where you can participate in monetary policymaking simulations and learn about the Fed's role in the economy. If you have at least 15 people in your group, you can also schedule a one-hour lecture about the Federal Reserve system.

To arrange a tour and lecture, call the Federal Reserve's Public Information department at 212-720-6130 or write to the Federal Reserve Bank of New York, Public Information Division, 33 Liberty Street, New York, NY 10045, or e-mail your request to FRBNYTOURS@ny.frb.org.

VISITING YOUR STOCKBROKER

You've never been in a stockbroker's office before? If you're using a brick-and-mortar brokerage firm, ask your treasurer to arrange a field trip for your members to visit your broker's office. The field trip would certainly have to be arranged through your broker, and for a specific time after the market has closed for the day. The hours when the markets are open are your broker's busiest time—not a time for visitors.

Unless you've invited your broker to one of your meetings, probably the treasurer and possibly one other member are the only ones in your club to have met her so far. This is not only the opportunity to meet her, but also the chance to learn how she places trades for you, checks prices, handles checks, and obtains information and recommendations for your club.

The Wall Street Watchers Investment Club once conducted their monthly meeting at their broker's office. One of the members prearranged with the broker to have an online investing class. When the members arrived at Charles Schwab, the conference room was set up with a computer terminal. The members got a hands-on class in online investing. After the class, the broker offered to let them to stay in the conference room and conduct their business meeting.

While a broker's office may not be nearly as exciting as a stock exchange, this could be your members' opportunity to ask detailed questions as to how the brokerage business works. The more you know about the inner workings of the markets, the better informed you'll be about investing.

VISITING A COMPANY

If you've purchased the stock of a company that's located not too far from your area, or if you're considering buying that company's stock, maybe your club could take a tour of the company. Some manufacturing companies offer the public tours. Most of these tours are informative and give you a chance to see the manufacturing process at work.

If the company you're considering doesn't offer public tours, call the company, explain the situation, and ask if they could arrange a tour for your group. Some companies will turn you down flat with lots of excuses, but other companies may be open to the idea. If they're willing, your members will probably have to adhere to the company's schedule, but grabbing that opportunity may give you just the insight you need to decide whether to purchase its stock. Again, the more information you have about the companies you purchase, the better and more sound your investment decisions will be.

VISITING THE COMPANY'S PRODUCTS

Has your club invested, or is it considering investing, in a company that includes a chain of restaurants, shopping centers, or amusement parks? If a company whose stock your club has bought is in a business where the public can shop, eat, or be entertained, why not take a group visit? If you haven't bought the stock yet, the outing may make you change your mind. Or maybe it will make you realize that a stock you purchased was an even better buy than you thought!

VISITING THE CLASSROOM

Whether you want a class that lasts a few hours or a whole semester, there are plenty of opportunities for classroom instruction that your members can enroll in as a group. NAIC, local colleges, and even private adult-education facilities offer classes on investing. If you prefer a conference-type of atmosphere, NAIC offers its National Congress & Expo every year in addition to plenty of regional investor fairs. Other organizations often advertise investment conferences in newspapers across the country.

There are also opportunities to attend free investment seminars sponsored by brokerage firms. These seminars can be informative, but it's important to remember that the brokerage firm is hosting a free seminar because they view it as sales opportunity. Attend the seminars, take away as much information as you can, but don't be talked into making any investments—either individually or as a club. When dealing with someone who has a financial product to sell, be careful.

VISITING THE LIBRARY

When doing research for a stock presentation, you may call the company to obtain materials, download information from the Internet, or make a trip to the library. Just walking through the library on your own and browsing through the business section doesn't really give you a feel for all the resources that are available.

Have the vice president of education arrange a group tour of the business section of your local library. Have the librarian point out all the resources that are available, explain what information each of the individual resources contains, and show you how to use them. Have her recommend any investing books she thinks might be beneficial for investors at your level of expertise. Ask questions. If you tried to obtain a piece of information on a company you presented to the club three months ago, but couldn't find what you needed, ask the librarian if it can be found in the library. Ask for ideas on resources to use in trying to find good stocks to present to the club.

Librarians, like libraries, are a wealth of information. Pick their brains to come up with new and unique ideas for locating new companies, finding research on those companies, and obtaining the information you need to prepare a sensational stock presentation.

VISITING ANOTHER CLUB

If you're familiar with another investment club in your area, ask if your members could sit in on one of their monthly meetings. There are probably aspects of operating an investment club that everyone handles differently. Maybe your members will pick up some pointers, learn a new and easier way to handle some chores, or find that your club is handling certain aspects of its operation better than others.

Find out how they make assignments, ensure attendance, construct a valuation statement, conduct a presentation, monitor stocks, or decide when to sell a stock. Your club may adopt some of their procedures, or the visit may simply cement the fact in your minds that you're operating your club in the best manner possible. At worst case, you'll meet a few new people, develop some contacts for the future, and maybe make a new friend or two.

* * * * *

The preceding are all activities that will keep your members interested, keep them learning, and ensure they're having fun at the same time.

Chapter 17

Making Your Investment Club Fun

One of the goals of an investment club is to have fun. An investment club that doesn't fulfill this goal will become boring, stagnant, and uninteresting. Members will slowly wander away and the club will eventually die a slow death. Most people enjoy learning a new skill, but all work and no play . . . well, you know the rest.

Below are some activities your members can plan to keep your club entertaining, interesting, and socially alive.

INVESTMENT COMPETITIONS

An investment competition can be a lot of fun, but it can also help members learn more about investing. At the beginning of the year, give each member $50,000 of imaginary money to use to build an investment portfolio. Each member can invest the money as she sees fit. If she wants to invest it all in one stock, that's fine. If she wants to invest in 10 different stocks, that's fine, too. It's up to the individual.

At the January meeting, have the members turn in a written list of their purchases to the club's secretary. The list should include the name of the stock, the stock symbol, the number of shares purchased, the current price per share as of a specific, preset date, and the total investment in each stock. The stocks each member purchases should have a total value of $50,000. (Don't worry about commission charges—when you invest imaginary money, there are none!) During the year, the members aren't allowed to make any changes to their imaginary portfolios.

At the end of the year, the secretary records the current price per share as of a specific, preset date for the stocks in each member's portfolio and calculates the total value of each portfolio. Whoever had the most profitable portfolio wins the competition. Members can either throw in a couple of dollars each year to buy a prize for the winner, or they can buy a trophy that floats from winner to winner each year.

Another option would be to create an imaginary portfolio as a group, and then compete against other investment clubs in your area. When you award prizes at the end of the year, you could have a big party with the members from all the participating clubs—another opportunity to meet more people!

QUIZZES

The Dough Makers of Kankakee, Illinois, sometimes combine fun with education. Two of their members created a little written quiz on stock terms. On one side of the page they listed 20 terms, such as growth stock, stock split, stock dividend, earnings per share, and bear market. On the other side of the page they listed the definitions, but in a mixed-up order. The members had to match the correct term with the correct definition. It was an exercise all the members could participate in, have fun with, and learn about investing at the same time.

GUESSING THE DOW

Every year on the television show *Wall Street Week with Louis Rukeyser,* the host asks his regular panelists to submit an estimate as to what levels the Dow Jones Industrial Average will hit during the next 12 months. They provide him with their estimates of the high close for the year, the low close for the year, and the final close at the end of the year. Twelve months later Rukeyser pulls out these estimates and announces who came closest to being correct.

As we've already discussed, no one knows what the Dow will do tomorrow, let alone a year from now. And, more importantly, if you're a long-term, buy-and-hold investor, such as investment clubs are, you really don't care. So the Dow goes up and it goes down this year. You're buying stocks that you're holding for years to come, so let the Dow bounce around all it wants.

The point of guessing the various levels the Dow will hit is that it just adds one more element of competition that keeps your investment club interesting and fun. In 1999 the members of the MAJEC Investment Club each contributed $1 to a prize fund, then held a competition to guess when the Dow would pass the 10,000 mark. In 2000 they held a competition for members to guess when their club's $190,000 portfolio value would surpass the $200,000 mark. The members all chose and submitted a specific month and what they thought would be the exact value of the treasurer's valuation statement the month the portfolio value moved above $200,000 for the first time.

If your portfolio value isn't at a milestone, you could have everyone guess what the total value of the club's portfolio will be at the end of the year. That could be a tough guess, especially if your club uses unequal ownership. No one knows if next month members will contribute $30 each or $60 each. But everyone is at the same disadvantage, and it's just a game.

AWARDING HARD WORK

All members of an investment club have certain responsibilities they have to be committed to fulfilling. But all organizations from time to time have a member who stands out because she's done just a little extra work. Maybe she's brought in more new members than anyone else. Maybe it's your club's first year of operation and one member put an extremely inordinate amount of work into getting the group together, preparing the legal documents, and making sure the club got up and running. When someone stands out, reward that person for her hard work. That reward could be a small gift, a cake decorated with the member's name for everyone to enjoy after a meeting, or simply a nice announcement thanking the person for the time and effort expended.

This type of award may be a one-time event, or your club may be able to identify a different member each year who has done outstanding work. But keep this award special—if no one stood out from anyone else, don't give out an award that year. Be sure to keep the award meaningful.

HELPING OTHER CLUBS

After your club has been operating for a few years, you may want to help others get over that initial hurdle of structuring their clubs. Your members could become mentors to other clubs, or speakers who are willing to attend the meetings of other clubs and do a presentation on some aspect of investing. As the club receives requests for assistance, members could take turns in handling those requests.

Not only does this type of activity offer a great help to new clubs that are just starting out, but it also helps your members. Talking about the goals of an investment club, the principles used, and the steps involved in operating an investment club helps to reinforce those concepts in your members' minds. The more your members talk about the right way to operate an investment club, the more apt your club will be to operate properly.

VOLUNTEERING

While this is an investment club you're running, you don't have to spend every minute you're together talking about stocks. Maybe your club would like to make an investment in its community. This is a dedicated, ambitious group of people. These are the types of people who get things done. And there are always things around the community that need to be done.

Call a local charity that your members all support and volunteer a day. Go as a group and work together to help others in your community. The charity will appreciate it, but your members will also benefit by working together, getting to know each other in a different light, and becoming closer friends. Being closer friends can only help to make your investment club run more smoothly.

Another option for volunteering would be to have your members offer their time to the local NAIC chapter. The NAIC chapters are always looking for people to handle various types of responsibilities.

MEETING INVESTORS ACROSS THE WORLD

If your members are so inclined, NAIC can assist your club in finding an investment club in Europe or in the Pacific Rim with whom your club could become pen pals. Wouldn't it be fun to meet investment club members from a foreign country and find out how they operate their club, what stocks they buy, and how their club is different from yours?

You could discuss at your meetings what you'd like to ask your foreign counterparts, then let the various members take turns in writing the letters. Your members could learn a lot not only about investment clubs in other countries, but also about life. And who knows? If you get to know them well enough, that next field trip may be to France!

PARTY! PARTY!

Most investment clubs have a few parties during the year. They may invite only the investment club members or they may include the members' spouses and/or dates. Most clubs arrange to have a summer picnic, go bowling, or have a holiday party with a grab bag or ornament exchange. The Central Maine Investors of Augusta took their holiday party one step further by having all their members bring nonperishable food items to the party that the club could contribute to a local charity. The Dough Makers of Kankakee, Illinois, once had an outing on a member's pontoon boat, where they had a picnic.

One club even reserved a private room at a restaurant and hired a professional group to come in and sponsor a mystery-murder dinner. The members and their spouses and dates gathered clues during the cocktail hour and during dinner, then over dessert each person tried to guess who the real murderer was. The evening had absolutely nothing to do with investing. It had to do with having fun, getting to know each other better, and creating a more cohesive group that worked together well.

* * * * *

The above are just a few ideas investment clubs can use to keep their members interested and having fun. Your club can probably come up with a hundred more ideas. Whether you have a party, sponsor a competition, or volunteer your members' time for a day, it's important to include outside activities that will keep your members excited about being a part of this group.

There are a lot of advantages to being a member of an investment club. You'll build a nest egg that will help to carry you through your retirement so that when you leave the work force you don't have to leave behind your standard of living. You'll learn how to invest your money and make wise decisions on your own, rather than having to depend on someone else. You'll make new friends and have a good time. But most importantly, you'll feel good about yourself because of the steps you've taken to make yourself a responsible, self-sufficient, independent person. May your investment club give you a lifetime of experiences and wealth!

Looking at the Overall Picture

Investing in the stock market is the best choice you can make when building a nest egg for your future. Historically, stocks have offered long-term investors regular gains that far exceed the returns of other types of financial instruments. And, in addition to being a good investment, stocks offer investors the opportunity to actually invest in American capitalism. Without the stock market and investors like yourself, corporate America would never have been able to obtain the funds required to grow and prosper over the last century and create all the wonderful products and services that all of us enjoy today.

Investing in the stock market via an investment club adds to that experience. Through an investment club, you'll learn how to find good companies to invest in, how to create a truly diversified portfolio, and how to have patience and persistence in letting the market work for you. That's knowledge that will last you a lifetime and will help you ensure that your financial future is secure.

If, however, members of an investment club don't focus on meeting the three goals of an investment club, they're probably doomed to failure. Each member must be committed to:

1. Building a nest egg
2. Learning how to invest
3. Having fun and meeting new people

Some of the keys to achieving those goals include:

✔ Inviting only dedicated, committed people to join the club.

✔ Adopting a long-term, buy-and-hold investment philosophy.

✔ Focusing on purchasing growth stocks that will be worth more five years from now than what they're worth today.

✔ Creating a partnership agreement and club bylaws that fit your investment club's special needs.

✔ Following the procedures outlined in your club's legal documents in a consistent manner.

✔ Finding and working with a brokerage firm and a stockbroker who best fit your club's situation.

✔ Making buy and sell decisions based only on solid research.

✔ Diversifying your portfolio along industry lines and company size.

✔ Keeping your investment club meetings businesslike by following an agenda.

✔ Maintaining proper records to keep members informed of the club's and their personal club ownership status.

✔ Ensuring that a continuing-education program is in place.

✔ Reinvesting profits and dividends.

✔ Adding social outings to your club's activities.

By following a few rules, your club will be a success. But what is success? Many believe that the only measure of success is return on investment. That attitude created quite a stir over a fairly insignificant event.

Several years ago, one of the most famous investment clubs in this country, the Beardstown Ladies Investment Club of Beardstown, Illinois, was asked by someone from the media to calculate a rate of return on their portfolio. Trying to calculate a rate of return for a club that's been operating for several years can be extremely complicated. With members contributing additional money at every meeting, those contributions being of varying amounts each month, possible withdrawals being taken out of the club's account, profits and losses being taken on stocks, and dividends being collected, the calculation becomes cumbersome. But the members of the Beardstown Ladies Investment Club wanted to be accommodating, so they calculated their club's rate of return.

Unfortunately, they miscalculated the number and it was published. When the error was discovered, the media went crazy. Articles claiming the club purposely misrepresented their results appeared in publications across the country. The story was broadcast on radio and television news programs. The Beardstown Ladies Investment Club was publicly attacked.

Those members of the media who were so quick to attack, however, forgot to focus on two issues. First, the members of the Beardstown Ladies Investment Club made an error in a calculation—that's all. They weren't trying to defraud anyone. They weren't trying to pass themselves off as anything they weren't. They simply made a mistake. Of the people who attacked them, I wonder how many have never made a mistake.

The second issue is that an investment club's return shouldn't only be measured in terms of a percentage or even a number. An investment club's return to its members is much more than that. The members' real returns are:

✔ An understanding of how stocks, the best investment vehicle available, work

✔ The achievement of a comfort level in dealing with investing in stocks

✔ A stock portfolio that they've built themselves through hard work and diligence

✔ The new friends they've found and the relationships they've built that will last a lifetime

When the media attacked the members of the Beardstown Ladies Investment Club, they totally ignored the positive results that came from this group going public with their club's story. The savings rate in this country is not one that we can be proud of. But maybe part of the problem is that we were never taught in our school years how to invest our money properly. We suddenly found ourselves in the workplace with jobs and an income, but what were we supposed to do with that income? We pay our bills and, if we have anything left over, maybe we put it in a certificate of deposit or a bank account. Many of us have been too afraid to venture much farther than the simplest forms of investments. The stock market, especially, has always sounded so complicated, with its own language and set of rules.

Then we all met the women of the Beardstown Ladies Investment Club and realized that maybe investing wasn't so complicated after all. If a group of women their age could start learning how to invest and start building a portfolio, then maybe the rest of us could, too. The Beardstown Ladies

Investment Club gave many of us the confidence we needed to take that first step.

Who cares if their return on investment was 24 percent, 12 percent, or 6 percent? If we measure their success only on return on investment, we're missing the big picture. Their real success is that they're investing in the stock market and, because of them, a lot of other people also began investing. Rather than attacking the members of the Beardstown Ladies Investment Club, we should be thanking them.

Building a nest egg, learning how to invest our money, and having fun doing it are the real returns any dedicated investment club member should expect to reap. If those are the types of returns you'd like to achieve, it's time for you to start the process of creating your own investment club. Your financial future will be the better for it.

Glossary

10-K and 10-Q: Annual and quarterly financial reports a public company is required to file with the Securities and Exchange Commission.

Accumulation stage: Stage of life-cycle investing when an investor is age 20 to 45, is accumulating the bulk of his assets, and has a long-term horizon and a high risk tolerance.

Advance-decline theory: Theory used in technical analysis to determine the general trend of the stock market by comparing stocks that are increasing in price to those that are decreasing in price.

Aggressive growth fund: A mutual fund that focuses on achieving capital appreciation and, therefore, carries a high level of risk.

American Association of Individual Investors {AAII}: Not-for-profit corporation that offers education, information, and research to individual investors.

American Depositary Receipts (ADRs): Certificates sold over U.S. stock exchanges that represent shares of foreign companies.

Analyst: An employee of a brokerage firm who tracks the performance of public companies and issues reports as to whether those companies' stocks should be bought or sold. The firm makes those reports available to its customers at no cost.

Annual and quarterly reports: Publications written by public companies to communicate to the investment community the company's operations for the past year or quarter.

Annual meeting: A once-a-year meeting of a public company's shareholders, at which management presents an overview of the company's past year and discusses future plans.

Arbitration: A system for resolving disputes in which the two parties submit their disagreement to an impartial panel for binding resolution.

Asset allocation: An investment portfolio's division among various classes of investments.

Auditor's opinion: Outside accountants' opinion as to whether the statements present fairly the financial position of the company and if the results of operations are in conformity with generally accepted accounting principles.

Averaging down: Purchasing additional shares of a company whose stock price has decreased, subsequent to your initial purchase, to reduce the average price of your stock holdings in the company.

Back-end load: A fee a mutual fund charges to investors who sell their shares within a few years after purchasing them.

Balance sheet: A financial statement that looks at a company's financial status at a specific point in time, usually the last day of a quarter or fiscal year.

Balanced fund: A mutual fund that focuses on garnering both capital appreciation and income.

Bear market: A market in which stock prices are declining or are already very low.

Bid-ask spread: The difference between the price an investor will receive when selling a stock and purchasing a stock.

Bond: A security that a company or government issues in order to raise money. The investor is paid a specified rate of interest for a specific number of years until the security matures and the principal is repaid.

Bond fund: A mutual fund that focuses on producing income by purchasing only bonds.

Bull market: A market in which stock prices are increasing or are already very high.

Buying on margin: Purchasing stocks with money the investor has borrowed from the brokerage firm.

Call risk: The risk that a bond will be paid off prior to its maturity date.

Capital account: The value of each investment club member's ownership in the club.

Capital gains: The profits realized from the sale of stocks.

Cash-option program: Program offered by companies in which shareholders participating in the DRP can mail in regular cash contributions for the company to purchase additional shares of the company's stock for the investor.

Chapter 11: A type of bankruptcy filing in which a company is given a period of time during which it can reorganize without creditors seeking payment.

Charge-offs: Loans that the bank has funded but now deems to be uncollectible.

Closed-end mutual fund: A mutual fund that sells a prescribed number of shares and then closes as of a specified date. Those shares then trade over a public stock exchange.

Club's bylaws: The document that lays out the specific operations of the club, such as dates and times of meetings, officer duties, etc.

Commissions: The fees a brokerage firm charges investors to purchase or sell shares of stock. The amount charged varies widely between full-service, discount, and deep-discount brokerage firms.

Common stock: The type of stock a company issues that gives the investor the right to receive dividends and vote on company issues.

Compounding: The growth of your initial investment as it earns dividends, plus additional dividends on the money previously earned.

Consensus number: The number that a group of analysts agrees to as their projection for a specific public company's earnings per share for a specific period of time.

Contributions: The money that each member deposits into the club's pool of money each month to invest in stocks.

Corporate bond: A negotiable security a corporation sells to raise money through debt. The interest earned on a corporate bond is taxable.

Credit risk: The risk to investors that the corporation or municipality that issued bonds will default and the investors will not be repaid the money they invested.

Cumulative preferred stock: A type of preferred stock a company issues in which any dividends that are not paid to investors must be accumulated and paid prior to common stockholders receiving their dividend payments.

Current ratio: A ratio that determines how many times a company's current liabilities could be paid with its current assets.

Day traders: Investors who buy and sell stock—typically online—and close out their positions at the end of each day. Their hope is to make money on small movements in a stock's price.

Debt-to-equity ratio: A ratio that measures leverage by comparing a company's total debt to its shareholders' equity.

Declaration date: The day a public company announces the amount of its dividend for that quarter.

Deep-discount brokerage firm: A brokerage firm that offers no additional services other than completing buy and sell transactions, which clients may have to do via computer or Touch-Tone phone. Commission charges are rock bottom.

Direct stock plan: Plan offered by companies in which investors can purchase their initial shares of stock directly from the company.

Discount brokerage firm: A brokerage firm that offers fewer services, but charges a lower level of commissions than a full-service brokerage firm.

Diversification: Investing in stocks of various types of companies, including those in different industries and of different sizes.

Diversify: Invest in stocks of companies that are in different industries and that are of various sizes, rather than investing only in the same industry and same-size companies.

Dividend: The portion of a company's profits that the board of directors decides to pay to the company's shareholders.

Dividend reinvestment plan {DRP}: A plan in which the company offers the investor the option of having the dividend used to purchase additional shares of the company's stock, rather than receiving the dividend in cash.

Dividend yield: This number is the percentage return that the company's dividend represents relative to its current price.

Dollar cost averaging: Investing a specific amount of money at regular intervals. By using this strategy, the investor buys more shares when prices are low and fewer shares when prices are high.

Double password access: Having two passwords to access an online brokerage account. One password allows the user to view the account; the second password allows the user to complete transactions.

Dow Jones Industrial Average {DJIA}: A mathematical calculation of the current price of 30 publicly traded stocks, which is used as an indicator for the whole U.S. stock market.

Earnings per share {EPS}: A measure of how much money a company made during a specified period of time on a per-share basis.

Elliott Wave Theory: A theory that projects future trends in the DJIA by counting and measuring price changes.

Employer Identification Number: A nine-digit identification number issued by the IRS to corporations, partnerships, or estates for tax filing and reporting purposes.

Equal ownership: A method of determining the amount of money each investment club partner will contribute to the club each month. While this method of each member contributing the same amount is easy to track, it can cause difficulties in adding new members to the club in the future.

Ex-dividend date: The first day on which someone purchasing a company's stock would not receive the most recently announced dividend.

Expense ratio: The total amount of fees charged to investors by a mutual fund, divided by the mutual fund's net assets.

Exploratory meeting: The first meeting of potential investment club members, where the specifics of club membership are discussed.

Federal Reserve: The governmental agency that controls the country's monetary policy.

Footnotes: The section of the annual report that supports and explains the information found in the financial statements.

Front-end load: A sales charge that is incorporated into the price of a mutual fund's shares.

Full-service brokerage firm: A brokerage firm that not only fills buy and sell orders, but also gives advice and stock recommendations. Because of the additional services, it charges a higher level of commissions.

Fundamental analysis: Predicting the future movements of a stock based on an analysis of the company's financial statements, past performance, and current strategies.

Global mutual fund: A mutual fund that invests in the stocks and bonds of companies located outside the United States, but also includes a portion of U.S. investments.

Good-'til-cancelled order: An order to buy or sell stock that has a specific price tied to it. The order remains with the broker in the open market until it is either filled or cancelled.

Growth fund: A mutual fund that focuses on purchasing only growth stocks.

Growth stock: The stock of a company whose growth is faster than that of its competitors.

Income fund: A mutual fund that focuses on producing income.

Income statement: A financial statement that uses income, expenses, and profit to describe how well the company performed during a specific period of time, usually one year or three months.

Index fund: A mutual fund that mimics the holdings of a specific index.

Inflation risk: The risk that the inflation rate will rise, forcing interest rates up and the value of your bond down. If the inflation rate is higher than the interest rate you're receiving, you'll also be losing purchasing power.

Initial kicker: An amount of money that each member contributes to the club before it starts operating to create a cash account large enough to start buying stocks.

Initial public offering (IPO): The process through which a company legally creates stock and sells that registered stock to the public for the first time.

Inside information: Information a company has not yet made public.

Insider trading: When a company's management personnel buy or sell shares of their own company's stock.

Institutional investors: Large investors, such as pension-plan managers, who buy and sell huge blocks of stock at one time.

Interest-rate risk: The risk to investors that the bond they purchased will decrease in value due to a rise in interest rates.

International mutual fund: A mutual fund that purchases only the stocks and bonds of companies located outside the United States.

Investment banker: A brokerage firm that helps companies bring their stock to the public.

Investor relations: A group of employees of a public company whose function is to act as a liaison between the company and the investment community, including shareholders, brokers, and analysts. Shareholders can call the investor-relations department of any public company to request company materials or to ask questions about the company.

Kondratiev Wave Theory: Theory that the economies of the Western world are subject to 54- to 60-year economic cycles that can be used to predict stock-market movements.

Laddering: Strategy of purchasing bonds so that one bond matures each year.

Large-cap stocks: Stocks of companies whose total number of outstanding shares multiplied by the company's current stock price equals more than $5 billion.

Life-cycle investing: An asset allocation strategy that matches investors' investments to their current needs based on their age and risk tolerance.

Long position: Buying stock and hoping that the price will increase so you can sell it for a profit.

Long-term gains and losses: Profits and losses incurred from selling an asset that was held more than one year.

Margin call: A call from your broker telling you to deposit cash or securities in your account so that it meets the Regulation T margin requirements.

Market capitalization: A valuation placed on a company that's calculated by multiplying its number of shares outstanding by its current stock price.

Market timing: Making buy and sell decisions based on trying to determine when a stock's price is at its lowest and highest points.

Mediation: A process in which a single mediator assists two parties in determining a mutually agreeable resolution to a dispute.

Microcap stocks: Stocks of extremely small companies. The stock's price is typically around $5 per share or less.

Midcap stocks: Stocks of companies whose total number of outstanding shares multiplied by the company's current stock price equals between $1 billion and $5 billion.

Monitor a stock: Actively following a company's performance and stock price after the company's stock has been added to the club's portfolio.

Municipal bond: Bonds that are sold by states, cities, and municipalities. The interest earned on a municipal bond is tax-free.

Mutual fund: An investment company that is formed specifically to pool investors' dollars and invest them in stocks.

National Association of Investment Clubs {NAIC}: A not-for-profit organization formed for the purpose of providing new investors with an investment education and increasing the level of public participation in the stock market.

National Association of Securities Dealers {NASD}: The organization that enforces the rules of fair practice relative to the brokerage industry.

National Association of Securities Dealers Automated Quotations (NASDAQ): A computerized stock-trading system that provides up-to-date information on stocks traded in the over-the-counter market.

Net asset value: The actual value of shares in a mutual fund. Calculated by dividing the current value of all stocks owned in the fund, plus any cash, by the number of shares outstanding on any given day.

New York Stock Exchange {NYSE}: Also called the Big Board, millions of shares of stock trade on this public exchange daily.

Odd lot: A stock transaction that involves fewer than 100 shares, which is called a round lot. The commission cost per share that many brokerage firms charge is often higher for an odd lot than for a round lot.

Online investment clubs: Investment clubs whose members conduct all their club business via e-mail and chat rooms, with the members never physically meeting face to face.

Open-end mutual fund: A mutual fund that accepts new investors' deposits and redeems outstanding shares on a continuous basis.

Ownership units: Contribution increments of $10 that allow club members to maintain varying capital accounts.

Paper loss: An investor's unrealized difference between the purchase price and the decreased price of a company's stock.

Paper profit: An investor's unrealized difference between the purchase price and the increased price of a company's stock.

Partnership agreement: This is the document that lays out the general operations of the club, such as the purpose and the management of the club.

Payment date: The day a public company actually pays its quarterly dividend.

Preferred stock: The type of stock a company issues that gives investors preference when it comes to the payment of dividends and the liquidation of the company's assets.

Price/earnings ratio: A ratio that depicts how many times a company's annual earnings per share a stock is selling for in the marketplace.

Program trading curbs: Restrictions placed on stock transactions by the Securities and Exchange Commission (SEC) when the market reaches a specific milestone. Used to reduce market volatility.

Prospectus: The document published by a mutual-fund company that includes information about the fund's investment philosophy and strategy, fee structure, past performance, management, and other information.

Proxy: An invitation to a company's shareholders to attend the annual meeting. It explains what issues will be brought to a shareholder vote.

Proxy voting: Having another member of the club vote for you at the monthly meeting if you are absent, or forwarding your vote to the secretary prior to the meeting.

Pump and dump: A scam in which a con artist pumps up the price of a micro-cap stock by recommending it to investors, then dumps his own shares when the price increases, leaving the investors with fairly worthless stock.

Real estate investment trust (REIT): A company organized to pool investors' funds for the purchase or financing of real estate.

Record date: The day on which the company closes its books for the quarter. Any investor recorded as a shareholder on that day will receive that quarter's dividend.

Regulation T: Federal Reserve Board rule that limits the amount of credit a brokerage firm can give to its clients.

Restricted stock: Stock that cannot currently be sold due to SEC regulations.

Retirement stage: Stage of life-cycle investing when an investor is age 61 and older, is ready to stop working, and has a very low risk tolerance.

Return on equity: A ratio that shows what percentage return a company is realizing on its net worth.

Reverse stock split: A decrease in the number of shares issued by a company without any change in its financial position. Used as a ploy to increase the company's stock price.

Secondary public offering: A company's issuance of stock subsequent to its initial public offering.

Securities and Exchange Commission {SEC}: Created by the Securities Exchange Act of 1934, it is the federal agency that protects the public against fraud and ensures full disclosure of information on securities.

Securities Investor Protection Corporation {SIPC}: A nonprofit organization established by Congress in 1970 to protect the cash and securities investors hold at their brokerage firms in the event the firm fails and is liquidated.

Short-term gains and losses: Profits and losses incurred from selling an asset that was held one year or less.

Shorting stock: Selling borrowed stock in the hope that the price will drop so you can buy it back at a lower price.

Small-cap stocks: Stocks of companies whose total number of outstanding shares multiplied by the company's current stock price equals $1 billion or less.

Socially responsible investing: An investing strategy in which investors purchase only the stocks of companies that adhere to the investors' ethical and moral beliefs.

Standard & Poor's 500 Composite Index {S&P 500}: An index that tracks the movement of the stocks of the 500 largest U.S. public companies. Considered to be a broad gauge of stock-market movement.

Standard & Poor's (S&P) and Value Line reports: S&P and Value Line are companies that track the performance of various public companies and issue periodic reports. These reports are useful tools in researching stocks.

Statement of changes in financial position: Also called a cash-flow statement, it explains the difference in the amount of cash and cash equivalents the company had at the beginning and end of the year.

Stock presentation: A short overview—15 to 20 minutes—as to why the presenter believes a specific company's stock would be a good one for the group to purchase.

Stock split: An increase in the number of shares issued by a company without any change in its financial position. A two-for-one stock split doubles the number of shares outstanding and cuts the price per share in half.

Stock symbols: Shortened designations (usually one to four letters) that represent a public company.

Street name: A brokerage account in which the brokerage firm, not the investor, is listed as the owner of the securities.

Subscription period: The period of time when the brokerage firms sell the initial shares of a company's stock to investors prior to it trading on a public exchange.

T+3: Stands for trade plus three days, which refers to a law enacted on June 7, 1995, that reduced the settlement time for buying and selling securities from five to three days.

Technical analysis: Identifying trends and predicting a stock's price movement through the study of its volume and price in the marketplace.

Tender offer: A situation in which a public company offers to buy back from the shareholders its own company's shares, or the shares of another company that's being taken over, at a set price.

Ticker: A continuous reporting of stock transactions as they occur—with a slight delay. Found on certain television stations and in brokerage-firm offices.

Transfer agent: A company that provides the service of handling the details of shareholder accounts, such as mailing dividends, proxies, and other company documents, for a public company.

Transferable: When the ownership of a negotiable instrument, such as shares of stock, can be changed from one person's name to another person's name without having to sell and repurchase the shares.

Transition stage: Stage of life-cycle investing when an investor is age 45 to 60, is at the peak of his earning ability, and has diminished risk tolerance.

Turnover ratio: Relates to how many times the portfolio manager of a mutual fund buys and sells stocks during the year.

Unauthorized trades: Buy and sell transactions a stockbroker makes in a client's account without that client's permission or knowledge.

Unequal ownership: A method of determining the amount of money each investment club partner will contribute to the club each month. While this method of each member contributing varying amounts makes tracking individual ownership more complicated, it simplifies adding new members to the club in the future.

Valuation statement: The document prepared monthly by the treasurer that depicts the investment club's entire portfolio and the breakdown of individual member's capital accounts.

Whisper number: The earnings-per-share number an analyst really wants a company to report, despite the analyst's prediction of a lower number.

Withdrawal: When a partner removes funds from her capital account due to resignation from the investment club. Partial withdrawals can also be made by partners who remain in the club, if approved by the other investment club members.

Working capital: Ratio that depicts a company's available liquidity.

Year-end recap: A year-end statement that brokerage firms send to customers that recaps the activity of the account during the year, including the total amount of interest and dividend payments—information your club will need for tax purposes.

Index